Fundraising

Fundraising

Hands-on Tactics
for Nonprofit Groups

L. Peter Edles

McGraw-Hill, Inc.
New York   St. Louis   San Francisco   Auckland   Bogotá
Caracas   Lisbon   London   Madrid   Mexico   Milan
Montreal   New Delhi   Paris   San Juan   São Paulo
Singapore   Sydney   Tokyo   Toronto

Library of Congress Cataloging-in-Publication Data

Edles, L. Peter.
    Fundraising : hands-on tactics for nonprofit groups / L. Peter
Edles.
        p.   cm.
    Includes bibliographical references and index.
    ISBN 0-07-018927-7 :   —ISBN 0-07-018928-5 (pbk.) :
    1. Fund raising.   2. Corporations, Nonprofit—Finance.   I. Title.
HG177.E34   1993
658.15'224—dc20   92-24786
                                                            CIP

1 2 3 4 5 6 7 8 9 0   DOH/DOH   9 8 7 6 5 4 3 2

ISBN 0-07-018927-7 {HC}
ISBN 0-07-018928-5 {PBK}

The sponsoring editor for this book was David Conti, and the production supervisor was Pamela A. Pelton. It was set in Baskerville by North Market Street Graphics.

Printed and bound by R. R. Donnelley & Sons Company.

Trademarks
Commtact/ELS and Commtact are trademarks of Campagne Associates, Ltd.
Express Publisher is a trademark of Power Up Software, Inc.
Freelance is a trademark of Lotus Development Corporation
Harvard Graphics is a trademark of Software Publishing Corporation
Pagemaker and Persuasion are trademarks of Aldus Corporation
The Raiser's Edge is a trademark of Blackbaud MicroSystems, Inc.
Ventura Publisher is a trademark of Ventura Software, Inc.

This publication is designed to provide accurate and authoritative information in regard to the subject matter covered. It is sold with the understanding that the publisher is not engaged in rendering legal, accounting, or other professional service. If legal advice or other expert assistance is required, the services of a competent professional person should be sought.
—From a declaration of principles jointly adopted by a committee of the American Bar Association and a committee of publishers

Contents

Acknowledgments

First, to Sharon, my wife, who, with her quiet strength and resolution, always seems to say more than words can express.

Also, my thanks for their wisdom and support, some as campaigners, others not so, to Laurie and Virginia Billstone, Clyde J. Eaton, Marion Grier, Thomas Jensen, David A. Johnson, Ben and Harriet Kaufman, Dr. Ray Sansing, Steven Rindsberg, Hal Roth, J. Patrick Ryan, Milton Hood Ward, the early 80's gang of highly talented characters at MSJ, and to the little clay frog who egged me on month after month from his perch in front of my computer screen, the gift of a special friend.

Introduction

Nonprofit organization fundraising is an immense, diversified, sophisticated, and "bullish" business. Although certainly not recession-proof, it is an enterprise that has continued to grow in great leaps throughout the last three decades despite economic swings or the Dow Jones average.

The magnitude of philanthropic support in the United States is enormous. In 1991, total charitable gift income was estimated at $124.77 billion. Because of the caring and generosity of millions of our citizens, philanthropy is a major part of our nation's way of life.

There are no magical secrets, potions, incantations, or wands to wave that guarantee goal-reaching drives. Successful fundraising efforts use carefully learned and tested procedures that really work. Based on decades of experience, these campaigns employ sound organizational, management, sales, and marketing principles. Adhering to a proven format is the only way that nonprofit groups raise billions of dollars yearly.

I'm going to take you step-by-step through the logic and practical application of organizing, developing, and conducting membership and constituent fundraising drives. Employed by consultants and other top professionals, the techniques you will learn guide major religious, educational, health, human services, cultural, and other philanthropic groups throughout the nation.

Having stood the test of time, these strategies will function to your advantage— *but only if you follow them closely.* Don't be like the new cook who studies a classic recipe, decides to tamper with it, and ruins the entrée. Only an experienced cook knows how to add different spices and ingredients to a classic bouillabaisse and brew up an even better fish stew.

Forget lofty philosophies or a treatise on social science that leaves you wondering exactly how to start a campaign, no less how to end one. This book is for activists: administrators, fundraising professionals, volunteer board members, businesspeople, homemakers, educators, and artists, who take time out of demanding schedules to serve the nonprofit sector. To make the "give and take" that exists among instructors, solicitors, and prospects come alive, you will sit in on many dialogues emulating actual fundraising situations: training meetings, a face-to-face big-gift solicitation, a special event where potential donors are solicited as a group, canvassers convincing a couple to lend their support, and a phone squad in action.

An obvious way to produce maximum profits is to lessen expenses. (There are numerous cost-cutting suggestions throughout the book.) The more you know about campaigning, the less you will spend, but without sacrificing investments that are necessary. For instance, while making you privy to the way professionals go about doing things, this text cannot replace experienced consultants who furnish personal guidance to nonprofit organizations needing their services. However, the information in this book will allow you to take on many assignments "in-house" instead of paying for outside assistance. If you currently retain a consultant, the knowledge you gain by reading this book will enhance your relationship with that person or company. You will far more easily understand the rationales for advice given and be considerably more effective in putting plans into operation. Those factors lessen costs and raise net income.

Not every approach described may suit your organization's present fundraising plans. For example, some groups only concentrate on seeking large gifts. To them, planning and running a phonathon, door-to-door canvass, or mail appeal is unnecessary. But it pays to become familiar with the entire text, since it uncovers methods likely to be valuable in the future.

It's amazing how in tune with the twentieth century the Greek philosopher Aristotle was when he declared:

> To give away money is an easy matter and in any man's power. But to decide to whom to give it, and how large, and when, and for what purpose and how, is neither in every man's power nor an easy matter . . .

Competition for the philanthropic dollar is fierce. The largest and most prestigious national, regional, and local religious, health, educational, social welfare, and cultural organizations enjoy a dedicated constituency that ranks them at the top of donors' priorities. Like a "mom-and-pop" business, small, lesser-known groups, especially those with limited appeal, encounter hard going when trying to compete. So do established nonprofits who have always counted on receiving total annual funding from umbrella groups such as United Way and Jewish Federations. Because budget crunches have hit their benefactors, leaders of many beneficiary nonprofits must suddenly grapple with raising portions of their yearly budgets on their own or face cutbacks at a time when their services are needed the most. If your organization falls into these categories, don't despair: grass-roots efforts get adequately funded all the time. Concentrate on developing a loyal band of financial supporters, play out your campaigns like the big guys, and you have every chance of winning.

There is no instant gratification in the business of fundraising. The large philanthropic gifts you'll be seeking will be gotten only after long periods of crafting plans, then carrying them out; no effective shortcuts exist.

I can sum up why campaigns are successful in a few brief statements:

- The organizations that sponsor them have projects so engaging that it captures the emotions and imaginations of potential supporters.

- The best available leaders are recruited for the drive.

- Campaign volunteers are highly motivated and trained in solicitation.

- Potential donors are available, indoctrinated, and want to participate in the drive.

These principles are not my inventions. Each was used by Benjamin Franklin over two centuries ago when he campaigned for a small charitable institution that grew to be the University of Pennsylvania. How to help your organization better enact these beliefs, as valid in today's high-tech world as during Franklin's time, is the intention of this book.

If you want to raise funds, beat a drum or sing a song! Don't run around telling everyone how poor and broke you are and how they have to save you. That "Buddy, can you spare a dime?" routine will get you exactly what you ask for.

Whatever your level of experience, as you work your way through the complexities of campaigning, be proud, tenacious, and develop tunnel vision on behalf of your cause. If you're an achiever in other facets of life, you'll win awards as a fundraiser. And, no matter what happens, keep your sense of humor along with your sense of purpose.

I wish you great success.

L. Peter Edles

About the Author

L. Peter Edles is an independent consultant with more than 25 years of experience in the fundraising field. He has worked with every kind of nonprofit organization—including colleges and universities, religious, social service, and cultural and arts groups. His experience covers designing and directing both large and small campaigns across the nation. Mr. Edles also has significant experience in media production, photography, and the creation of communications packages.

PART 1

What You Should Know—Up Front

1

Fundamental Premises, Ideas, and Other Eye Openers

The Magnitude of Fundraising in America

The philanthropic marketplace in the United States is colossal. In 1990 there were over 450,000 nonprofit organizations (other than religious congregations) in this country entitled by the Internal Revenue Service (IRS) to solicit tax-exempt funds. According to Independent Sector, in 1986 religious groups raising money—not required to file with the IRS—approximated 294,000, a grand total of 744,000 organizations conducting annual or capital campaigns.

In 1992, *Giving USA*, a yearly publication of the American Association of Fund-Raising Counsel (AAFRC) Trust for Philanthropy, reported the following estimates for 1991:

- Americans donated a record breaking $124.77 billion to charitable organizations even in the most difficult of economic times, an increase of 6.21 percent over the previous year. However, this rise, unlike better years, outpaced inflation by only 1.41 percent.

- To give you an idea of the trend, in 1961, total giving was $11.56 billion; 1971, $23.46 billion; 1981, $55.58 billion.

Which group of donors would you expect to give the most money to charitable organizations? The fundraising newcomer usually responds: corporations, foundations, individuals. Let's look at the AAFRC Trust's figures for the same year.

- Contributions by individuals represented 82.7 percent of giving, or $103.13 billion, a rise of 6.76 percent over 1990.

3

It may come as a surprise, but by far the largest number of gift dollars has always been contributed by private individuals. *This is an indispensable factor in orchestrating successful fundraising drives and will be mentioned often in this book.*

- Bequests, gifts left by will, accounted for 6.2 percent of total giving, amounting to $7.78 billion, an increase of 1.85 percent. As in the past, most of these donations went to colleges and universities.

- Showing an increase of 7.33 percent, foundations handed over $7.76 billion to nonprofit groups, or 6.2 percent of total 1990 giving.

- Even with a recession on the way, a drop in profits, the impact of mergers, acquisitions, and a more conservative approach to giving, corporations donated $6.10 billion, up 1.67 percent, accounting for 4.9 percent of total contributions.

Next is a listing of organizations that benefited from these donations. Religious groups, because of large memberships and intense donor loyalty, always lead the way.

Billions	%	Organizations
67.59	54.2	Religious
13.28	10.6	Education
9.68	7.8	Health
10.61	8.5	Human Services
8.81	7.1	Arts, Culture, Humanities
4.93	4.0	Public/Society Benefit
2.54	2.0	Environmental/Wildlife
2.59	2.1	International Affairs
4.74	3.8	Undesignated

Putting Aside the Great Misconceptions

Fundraising Is Begging. Wrong!

A man I had been working with on a local theater project many years ago turned out to be head of a major fundraising consulting firm. When the undertaking was completed, he invited me to join his company. "Me?" I remember asking incredulously. "You want me to go around begging people for money? It would be too embarrassing," I told him.

The fundraising executive laughed and said, "If you knew anything about the campaigning we do, you'd know it had nothing to do with begging." I soon learned that he was right. I was confusing one type of fundraising—giving a hand to the poor and needy—with the greater part of contemporary funding programs whose aims have a completely different focus.

That was about 20 years ago. Recently I met with a client in a large sales office where it was impossible to have a private conversation. My client and I had been talking about approaches to different prospects when a salesman said to his secretary, "I'll be back in about 20 minutes. Then I can continue listening to Peter tell Ralph how to beg for money."

"But fundraising isn't a matter of begging," I told the salesman.

"Well," he said, "I was a volunteer worker and all I did was beg."

"Were you successful?"

"No, not very," he answered sadly. "And I thought I was a good salesman."

If, like the salesman, you approach fundraising with the attitude of a beggar, you too will fail.

This was my initial confusion. Begging, with its roots in ancient history, is associated with seeking money for people who are destitute, starving, downtrodden. Doubtless, these people deserve support. Today they receive it mainly from government sources (this is not the time to discuss to what extent) and comparatively few nonprofit agencies.

What I came to realize long ago is that by far the greatest portion of present organizational fundraising campaigns operate on a wholly different motivational level. Campaigns to fund an environmental program, a religious, cultural, or artistic center, to expand a medical facility, or to build a new home for the aged are examples of philanthropic efforts *to improve an already decent quality of life.* Promoting better lifestyles requires continual volunteer and donor loyalty and commitment.

Underdogs are popular in sports but not in fundraising. People want to be part of a winning organization; they are drawn to success. Tell volunteers and potential donors that your organization is a pitiful case, about to fall apart, and they will stay around just long enough to say how sorry they are . . . and good-bye. Another group down the block is doing just fine and needs their support.

Recognize that people join your organization, serve on your board and committees, give you more than a passing interest and a handout, only if they believe that your group will elevate the quality of life in their hometowns, regions, country, or the world community. So your attitude, the approach that you bring to all campaign activities, from formulating plans to asking for a gift, is critical. There is nothing wrong with telling someone you need help. Why would you be asking for money if you didn't? But ask for that help in a way that makes people proud to be part of your team and want to support your projects regularly:

"We're going to build this important new community facility, and we intend to reach our goal. When built, thousands of people will be involved in the programs offered. We want you to become part of this project and are giving you and all our citizens the opportunity to do so."

What a vast difference exists between that mindset and crying the blues: "We're trying to raise enough money to build a new facility. If you don't help us scrimp by, our project will fail and we'll be out of business forever."

If Your Cause Is Worthy, You Automatically Receive Many Substantial Contributions. Wrong Again!

If that delusion were true you wouldn't be reading this book. In campaigning, the dictionary definition of philanthropy—giving for the sake of giving—is telling us what *should be,* not what *is.* So, whatever your purpose or project, donations have to be solicited in a prescribed way. Don't count on passing the hat to solve any significant fundraising need. Except for running a crisis appeal, you won't get an outpouring of magnanimous, unsolicited donations just because your cause is justified and you've told your potential donors so. Unsolicited contributions come forward because of emergency situations: a fire burns down a church; we are shocked by coverage of starving and sickly children; an earthquake or hurricane destroys a city. People naturally want to help and will immediately react philanthropically to fellow citizens whose lives are or have been threatened. The way most organization campaigners get significant donations is to offer a worthwhile project for funding, find prospective donors who might be persuaded to support the project, and enlist highly motivated volunteer solicitors to present the product. In business terminology, they develop a marketable product, find a marketplace for the product, and recruit the best sales staff possible.

Huge Gifts Can Be Gotten from Potential Donors by Writing Letters. Again Wrong!

It's irresistible: "I have this fantastic project that I will describe in a fundraising letter and send it to . . ."

Everyone tries it: PHDs, MBAs, MDs, and truck drivers, among others.

Resist writing to affluent prospects and asking them to contribute enormous sums of money to your projects. They won't! *The power of the written word is all but meaningless when seeking large gifts.*

A friend decided to write a funding letter to a well-known philanthropist. It was a well-crafted piece, and both the project and need were sound. The writer was sure of a positive response to his $100,000 request. All he received in return was a boilerplate response signed by one of the philanthropist's staff members saying sorry and good luck. That's a common response. There are several reasons why large gift solicitation letters are ineffective, and each will be explained in future chapters. For now, save your writing skills for proposals to foundations, and as a solicitation method for seeking *small* gifts near the end of a campaign.

Our Community Is Different. Wrong!

Have you seen the map someone drew as a New Yorker's view of the United States? New York City is bounded on the East by the Atlantic and on the West by Los Angeles. Nothing lies in between. My fundraiser's conceptual map shows the total outline of the United States in black and the interior in white. That's because fundraising techniques put into action in Oregon should be no different from those used in Florida. All organizations running traditional campaigns should use the same methods. Too often, the location, size of a group, or relative affluence of an area are excuses for campaigns that are not going well. When troubleshooting these drives, it's most always found that the fundraising fundamentals were not followed. In truth, the community is not different at all.

Fundraising Campaigns Always Skim Too Much Money Off the Top for Salaries, Fees, and Other Expenses. Wrong Again!

I have no intention of protecting unethical fundraisers any more than I would stand up for other con artists. Unquestionably, there are people who take advantage of other people under the guise of philanthropy. But, if you study independently audited accounts of reputable nonprofit groups, you'll find costs to be comparatively low. As well, nonprofits are highly regulated by the IRS who regularly monitor compliance. There are also state laws regulating charitable solicitations.

If gifts came to you unsolicited, and you were staffed solely with volunteers, then running campaigns would cost hardly anything. Since this isn't ordinarily possible, campaigning, like any other business, requires money to make money: staff salaries, office and mailing expenses, special events, and printing, for example.

Those who attempt to keep watch over fundraising practices, such as the Council of Better Business Bureaus and the National Charities Information Bureau, recommend standards for nonprofit organizations. Among others, the Council says the total of fundraising and administrative costs should not exceed 50 percent of total income, the Information Bureau 40 percent. More about this shortly in "The Cost of Doing Business."

Most important is what *your* organization spends to conduct a campaign. The more knowledgeable and efficient you are, the less money needed for fundraising expenses. And it's extremely important that your members, constituents, and other prospects know you're abiding by the regulations and can account for income and expenditures.

If Each of Our Members Makes a Similar Donation, the Goal Will Be Reached. Again Wrong!

A wonderful theory that rarely works in practice. A group has 1000 members. Each member agrees to donate $100. Presto, $100,000 dollars is raised. Typically, most members won't come up with exactly $100. Another large contingent would like to, but cannot afford that amount of money. The remaining group gives nothing. You will soon see that winning campaigns use formulas that are more realistic.

Six Requirements Your Drive Can't Do Without

To conduct goal-reaching funding efforts, six major requirements must be fulfilled. Whatever time and effort it takes, each must be fully developed; there are no short-cuts or options.

1. *The goals of your organization must be compelling to ensure intense donor commitment.*[1]   Potential contributors must believe in and have a highly positive response to the reason(s) you are in business.

2. *Your organization's growth patterns must be easily perceived.*   You have to prove a winning track record. In a first-time appeal by a newly formed group, the background of key leaders must reflect a record of experience and expertise in the area(s) for which the drive is held.

3. *Your organization or its key leaders must be strongly visible to the people whose support you expect.*   You must be well known by volunteers and prospects.

4. *Your chief executive and volunteer leadership must be highly competent, totally committed, and be proven, excellent fundraisers.*   ("Chief executive" is the common term for professional administrators such as presidents of institutions and executive directors. Volunteer leadership are people who have responsibility for governing an entire campaign or a particular phase of a drive.)

5. *Your campaign's needs must be specific, attractive, people-oriented, and have a sense of urgency.*   Explain exactly what project is to be funded, why it is compelling, who the appeal benefits, and why it must be underwritten at once.

6. *The results of your campaign must be measurable.*   Tell your prospective donors exactly what will be done with contributions, and provide time frames for actions and achievements.

Does your forthcoming drive meet these guidelines? If it doesn't, do whatever is necessary to correct the weaknesses before starting out. Otherwise, the results will be disastrous.

A couple of illustrations:

I once consulted with a small think-tank foundation. It wanted to organize a big gift campaign to support and expand its research, and to hire several staff people. The founder and leader was a brilliant scholar, but remarkably shy and unassuming. He formed the foundation to investigate the comparative strength and changing role of world powers, their relationship to the United States, and this country's future as a leader in international affairs. The organization had two board members, the professor and his wife.

---

[1]For the sake of brevity, the word organization(s) will often represent all nonprofit categories: institutions, such as colleges or hospitals; organizations, such as health, cultural, and sports; and agencies, such as those dealing with social service and welfare.

From time to time this man went on the lecture circuit where he met affluent supporters of his theories. Since these people were obviously good fundraising prospects, it was the professor's fashion, following these sessions, to try his hand at solicitation.

"Harry," he told a member of his audience after one lecture, "I'm grateful for the compliments. But to further my studies I need funding from people like yourself."

"Professor," said the potential giver, "I'm interested in your theories. They should be taken seriously. However, your foundation has only been around a short time and is almost unknown. But for an expert in ancient history, you seem to have a grip on what's going on in international politics. Before I heard about this latest lecture, I was wondering what happened to you. The last time you spoke, I asked you to keep me up to date on your activities. When I didn't hear from you, I thought that your foundation went out of business."

"Oh, no," the professor responded. "We've been on hold. I've been busy teaching and researching. Look, I'll get some materials to you. My wife and I have to do everything ourselves. Sorry to bother you about money."

"You're hardly bothering me," said the prospect, "and don't ever be ashamed to ask for a donation. What is it that you want the money for?"

"Well, generally for what we discussed tonight," answered the professor. "We haven't defined each requirement yet."

"I see," the prospect responded. "Well, when you get a funding plan together let's talk again."

Since this conversation was typical of the professor's fundraising efforts, this was not the time to for him to begin a formal drive. There were too many rule violations. Let's look at the foundation's relationship to our six requirements:

1. *Compelling goals.* No problems there. The prospect was a believer.

2. *A successful organizational track record or an individual's broad experience and expertise.* The first clue to Harry's reluctance to make a gift had to do with the newness of the think-tank: ". . . your foundation has only been around a short time and is almost unknown." The second hint was when Harry said that the professor was involved in research outside his field of proven expertise—ancient history. Not that he didn't respect him, but the prospect was not entirely sold on the professor's ability to handle the complicated subject for which he was seeking funding.

3. *The organization must be strongly visible.* Harry continued by saying that he lacked up-to-date information about the foundation. There had not been any communications from the professor for a long time, and he thought the foundation might have gone out of business.

4. *Leadership must be highly competent, totally committed, dynamic, and be proven, excellent fundraisers.* There was no question that the professor was competent and committed. But he was undynamic, and not keen on soliciting. Spotting this weakness, the prospect urged him not to apologize for his fundraising efforts.

5. *Campaign needs must be concise, attractive, and timely.* Harry was told there were no defined plans and no rush to get a drive started. He responded as

prospects usually do under the circumstances—tell me when you have a workable campaign strategy and we will talk some more.

6. *Results must be measurable.*   Since there was no concrete plan, there could be no statement of what the think-tank would specifically accomplish when funded.

Unfortunately, the foundation never overcame its fundraising weaknesses and eventually had to shut down because it ran out of operating funds.

A small, midwestern college, in business almost 60 years, was barely holding its own financially. The faculty was able and the campus attractive. The institution had plenty of competition. Nearby, a large university offered an enormous curriculum. Two additional colleges were in the vicinity. The school wanted to begin a capital campaign to build new facilities, but there wasn't enough donor support.

To that setting came a talented fireball of a new president, not at all intimidated by fundraising chores. She defined the major problems:

- Too few courses in which large segments of the community could participate
- Lack of community recognition
- Many uninspired trustees
- An ineffectual fundraising program

In a short time, dramatic and lasting academic changes took place. Included was a weekend degree-granting program for adults, a downtown campus program for evening students, and continuing education courses in personal self-development for adults.

The president aggressively marketed her college's new academic flexibility to individual, corporate, and foundation community leaders, capturing their confidence, admiration, and respect. As these influential, affluent men and women became aligned with the college, new trustees were recruited to help draft policies and get involved in the fundraising program. They in turn enlisted friends and colleagues to become campaign workers.

Before the new president's arrival, the yearly fundraising program suffered because it consisted of a series of minicampaigns: a yearly drive for alumni, a separate drive for corporations, another for "friends," and yet another for parents. A new plan brought these disparate efforts together as the Annual Fund Campaign.

In two years, innovations and changes began to pay dividends. After the third year, the institution's enrollment hit an all-time high; the annual fundraising program was record-setting; the budget finally balanced. Success breeds success. In a few more years the college held its capital campaign and the goal was reached. Here's how these changes related to our six requirements:

1. *Compelling goals.*   Academic changes added a new dimension to the college's mission: providing a top-level, liberal arts education for both traditional and adult students.

2. *Growth patterns must be easily perceived.*   For decades the college was known as an academically sound institution with high standards, but was also considered somewhat stuffy and old fashioned. Because of the new programs, increased enrollment, and fiscal stability, the college was viewed as an up-to-date institution serving many segments of the community.

3. *Strong visibility.*   With its new services, and because of the marketing ability of the president and board, the college found recognition as an institution with a contemporary outlook.

4. *The chief executive and volunteer leadership must be highly competent, totally committed, and be proven, excellent fundraisers.*   The talent, energy, tenacity, and gift-getting ability of the president greatly inspired the success of the fundraising program. With essentially the same qualities, new trustees and other volunteer leaders identified and solicited prospects and inspired them to do likewise.

5. *Campaign needs must be exacting, attractive, and timely.*   The annual fund campaign became a major beneficiary of academic changes. To support new programs, the yearly drives drew specific and engaging items from the budget that required immediate funding.

6. *Results must be measurable.*   Increased enrollment meant increased revenues. Expanded services created a broader constituent base. Funding allowed new and improved facilities and equipment over a two year period.

Be dogmatic when it comes to these six principles. Devote all the time and energy necessary to create the best campaign image for your organization before starting any funding effort.

Expect the Most Money from the Least People

Often astounding to newcomers, the formulas that follow find experienced fundraisers nodding their heads knowingly. In traditional, goal-reaching campaigns:

1. Ten percent of the goal comes from a *single* gift.

2. Approximately 80 to 90 percent of incoming funds are donated by 10 to 20 percent of the membership or constituency.

The few fund the needs of many. Why does most of a campaign's income come from a comparatively few donors?

- Philanthropy is gift giving. It's not legislated as taxes are. People are free to choose whether they want to contribute funds, to whom they make a gift, its amount, in what manner, and for what reasons.

- Most people cannot afford to donate large gifts.

- Not everybody is philanthropically inclined. Consider state lotteries. If each time everyone who bought a lottery ticket gave a small portion of that money to say, cancer or heart disease research, the benefits would be awesome.

- Many people cannot afford to make any contributions, no matter how highly motivated they may be. As a nineteenth century English writer stated, ". . . one of the bitter curses of poverty [is that] it leaves no right to be generous."

- As mentioned earlier, gift averaging doesn't work. Five hundred members or constituents of an organization will not each make a $200 contribution to reach a $100,000 goal.

Using the percentages you just learned, let's see how we might get that $100,000:

1. Ten percent of the goal to come from a single gift. Expect, then, at least one $10,000 gift.

2. Eighty to 90 percent of the goal donated by 10 to 20 percent of the members. Among the 500 prospects, first we'd have to find people who would donate far more than $200. They will number about 50 to 100 persons and be expected to contribute $80,000 to $90,000 of the $100,000.

So, to reach your goals, you must rely on sizable donations called "Major Gifts." *These contributions play the most critical role in achieving successful campaign results—despite the amount to be raised.* Whether one considers a major gift as a million or a hundred dollars is immaterial; it all depends on the goal. Without major givers, a campaign begins with two strikes against it! Finding these prospects and persuading them to fund you generously is the keystone of campaigning.

The Best and Worst Ways to Ask for Funds

Fundraisers most often solicit gifts by:

1. Approaching prospects individually
2. Soliciting potential contributors as a group
3. Calling prospects on the telephone
4. Sending them letters

Let's start with the *least* potent way to ask for a contribution and end with the *most* productive method.

One day Lisa is sitting at home, the mail arrives, and she opens a letter from her college alumni association. She is asked to participate in the forthcoming scholarship fund drive by donating $150. Lisa thinks about the request, decides the old alma mater ought to be supported, and sends a check for $15.

Larry, another grad, gets a phone call. It's Sam calling from the same college. "Our scholarship fund program is in high gear," he says. "Will you consider a gift of $150?" Larry and Sam talk about the program at length, tell a few stories, have a few laughs, and Larry promises to send a check for $65.

In another city, an institution's alumni club is holding a dinner for the scholarship fund. Twenty graduates attend. As part of the evening's fundraising program they are asked to make a minimum donation of $150. Most of the gifts are in the hundred dollar range.

Sara is reading the newspaper when her doorbell rings. It's Marcia from the alumni fundraising committee. Sara and Marcia trade old school tales that lead to the scholarship fund story. Sara doesn't feel supportive at first, but it's Marcia after all, and she seems wildly excited about the project. Marcia's a good campaigner (as were the others) and she walks away with what she asked for, a check for $150.

Assuming the same income, philanthropic budget, interest level, and all else equal, *solicitation on a person-to-person basis is the most effective way to raise funds. Major gifts must always be solicited one-on-one. People give money to people, not to causes. Donors give money for a cause, but it's the dynamics of face-to-face interrelationships that inspires ideal giving.*

A close parallel to this technique, although not as popular, is asking prospects in a group to make their gifts publicly. Many organizations feel that this method is too high pressure, perhaps downright insulting. Still, when used properly, it need not intimidate anyone, and will bring about results extremely close to those of the person-to-person approach.

Reserve phoning as an option for soliciting small gift prospects. Except in the most extreme circumstances, never solicit major givers by phone.

Small gift phone soliciting is best when:

- Prospects far outnumber workers.

- Constituents are scattered about the country, often true of college alumni, for example.

- There is a time problem and a campaign must be closed out.

With all the progress direct mail campaigns have made, writing a letter to a small gift prospect is the least forcible way to solicit because it's the most impersonal; a good solicitation by telephone should be vastly superior to a good solicitation by mail. (How and when to put these solicitation methods into operation is discussed in Parts 3 and 4.)

For most organizations, advertising is useless as a practical solicitation alternative. Use it to gain increased visibility and to tell a large audience about a forthcoming small-gifts drive.

Telethons, unless you're in public broadcasting or working with big names or national organizations, are not only expensive to produce but require expertise and specialized staff to conduct. (Understand that major gift, person-to-person solicitation of individual, corporate, and foundation prospects mostly takes place off the air.)

What Type of Gifts Should You Go After?

Unrestricted—Let's say I make a contribution of $1000 to your museum campaign. You can use this gift for anything you prefer: the operating budget, a new exhibition of paintings made by a cat's paw, a children's sculpting class that your organization sponsors. There are no strings attached; I have made an unrestricted gift to your museum. This form of making contributions is the mainstay of annual giving programs.

Restricted—Another time I give the museum $1000 to fund an archeological expedition. My gift is designated solely for that adventure. I don't want it used for operating expenses or anything else; it is a restricted gift to fund a particular project. Restricted or designated giving is the backbone of capital—bricks and mortar—campaigns.

Matching Grant—Continuing to feel magnanimous, I tell you that I will donate $100,000 only if other friends of the museum first come forth with contributions totaling a like amount. My matching grant motivates other donors to make their gifts.

Corporate Matching Grant—One of my corporation's policies is that if an employee of mine makes a donation to a nonprofit group, I will match the amount with corporate funds. Let's say my manager gives the museum $200. The company contributes the same amount and the group receives $400. Among corporations that give grants, each may have a different policy. Some might match contributions on a two-to-one basis, while others have ceilings on the amounts they contribute.

Contributions to Share Plans, Clubs, and Associations—Mostly associated with acquiring donations below the major gift level, these ideas allow solicitors to ask for precise amounts of money instead of unspecified contributions, the worst possible way to request a gift. For example, you devise a share plan based on $10 per share. Potential donors are asked to contribute money for *x* amount of shares. Or you form a Century Club and ask prospects to contribute $100 to become members. Perhaps you inaugurate a President's Council to stimulate gifts of $2000.

Bequests, Annuities, and Trust Funds—The last two items are part of planned or deferred giving programs mostly used by higher education institutions and certain other large nonprofit organizations. These year-round programs are highly specialized, require special staff, and are not within the scope of this book. (*See* Recommended Reading.)

Annual Versus Capital Campaigns

Annual campaigns are ongoing, yearly appeals. These drives raise funds to keep the doors open—to support an organization's operating budget and special projects.

Since donors are asked to make a gift each year for similar reasons, annual drives can quickly lose sparkle and are often difficult to sustain.

On the other hand, capital campaigns have a mystique because they pay for land acquisitions, new or improved buildings, or both. Often startup costs for these new facilities are included. But seldom do capital drives fund such things as ongoing staff salaries, maintenance costs, and programs. Capital campaigns create lots of excitement among supporters because facilities such as expanded campuses, research labs, hospitals, gymnasiums, and cultural centers are tangible and highly visible.

Other distinguishing characteristics of capital campaigns are:

- *Higher goals.* Since the cost of building and equipping new facilities usually requires massive funding, capital campaign goals are set far higher than those of yearly appeals.

- *Far larger gifts.* Because of higher goals, gift requests on all levels must be greater than for annual appeals.

- *Less rigid time frames.* Because of higher goals and greater community participation, it takes longer to raise money.

- *Pledges instead of cash donations.* To receive adequate contributions, prospects are asked to pledge a certain amount of money to be paid over a specified period, usually three or five years. A $50,000 gift, for example, could be paid at the rate of $10,000 per year for five years.

- *The chance for donors to choose to fund particular portions of a new facility and to receive public recognition for their contributions.* This is a chief reason why capital campaigns have such strong appeal to prospects and why these people can be motivated to make exceptional contributions.

This last technique, called "Named Gifts," needs exploration. Here are two ways to approach Mr. Jones for a gift:

1. "I would like you to consider a gift of $3 million to help children who have serious developmental problems."
2. "I would like you to consider creating a new facility for the hospital, the Jones Diagnostic Center for Children. We expect that to build, staff, and start up this facility will cost $3 million."

The second approach has far more appeal to Mr. Jones and will more likely motivate his gift because the emphasis is on the Jones Diagnostic Center. Of course the prospect has heard you say that it costs $3 million. Yes, Jones has a high level of interest in children, but a prime incentive is that the center will be named after him. The new facility will benefit thousands of youngsters, be a source of great pride for Jones and his family, give them (deserved) recognition, and even a degree of immortality. The Jones Diagnostic Center for developmentally handicapped children will always be associated with the Jones' family.

Never underestimate the extraordinary power of naming an entire structure or a portion of it after a contributor. Donor response to this procedure has *always* been overwhelmingly positive. If I haven't convinced you, walk the corridors of colleges, hospitals, symphony halls, community centers, churches, and synagogues. You'll find large and small donor recognition plaques placed on many facilities, some extremely costly and some inexpensive. You will discover individual and family names and corporate and foundation titles. Named gifts are a wonderful way to say thank you to contributors from a grateful organization.

Of course, like anything else, this form of giving can be taken to the extreme. Naming a gym or a senior citizens center is routine. But the "Alpha Family Water Fountain" plaque pegged to the shiny, stainless steel frame at the far end of the tennis court may be a bit much. I've seen a named gift plaque on the restroom door of a prestigious law school.

Draw the line where you must!

As already mentioned, soliciting contributions for explicit reasons is far more appealing than requesting donations for operating funds. To make your annual drives more appealing, combine unrestricted giving programs with facility and equipment offerings that can be named. This is illustrated in the next chapter when you look at a college's "Summary of Needs."

The Cost of Doing Business

Every credible organization wants fundraising expenses to be minimal so that as much money as possible is directed to the projects for which it was raised. Costs, often expressed as a percentage of gift income, depend on the mission of an organization, its constituency and staffing, the type of campaign it runs, and its goal. Let's look at higher education. For annual drives, college and university fundraising expenses average about 17 percent. Capital campaigns, depending on their goals, average between 1 and 12 percent. As the goals increase, expenses decrease since it takes almost the same effort to raise one million or multimillions, as illustrated below.

Typical higher education capital campaigns		
Goal	% Expenses	$ Expenses
$ 1 million	10–12	100K–120K
$10 million	5–7	500K–700K
$50 million	2 (max.)	1 million

Now let's examine the costs of some well-known national organization annual campaigns. In November 1991 the *NonProfit Times,* a tabloid whose readership consists mainly of fundraising professionals, published a study of what it found to be the top 100 charities other than religious congregations or educational institutions. Total income (public, government, investment, earned, and other) and expenses were noted with other pertinent information for the year 1990. Selected examples showing a broad range of fundraising and administrative expenditures follow.

Organization	Total income (millions)	Fundraising expenses (% of total income)	Administrative expenses (% of total income)
Catholic Charities	$1,538.59	2.09	9.6
American Red Cross	$1,465.56	2.41	4.72
Boy Scouts of America	$430.00	6.34	13.02
United Jewish Appeal	$426.58	4.73	0.64
American Cancer Society	$365.50	16.12	7.04
National Wildlife Federation	$88.67	14.91	5.58
Mothers Against Drunk Driving	$49.33	21.93	5.01
National Urban League	$25.99	2.81	16.60
World Concern	$11.92	8.98	2.60

To understand why one of the above organizations spends more than another requires complete studies of the groups in question. If you feel comfortable with the Council of Better Business Bureaus recommendation that total fundraising and administrative costs not exceed 50 percent of total income, campaign or the National Charities Information Bureau's figure of 40 percent for both expenses, the above figures are in line.

There is little sense in holding down (realistic) costs if you fall far short of the goal because you scrimped on expenses that would have improved your fundraising program.

Let's say that an organization is hoping to raise a half-million dollars. Instead of projecting 17 percent ($85,000) for expenses, the executive director estimates costs at 10 percent or $50,000 because he slashed the budget by reducing staff, publications, and printing costs. The $50,000 is spent, but owing to the cuts, the campaign only raises $400,000. By reducing the budget, income disbursed for programs and services also is reduced. If the organization had spent $85,000 instead of $50,000, and the goal was reached, it could have disbursed an additional $65,000, as indicated below:

Projected income	Actual income	Cost	Disbursable funds
$500,000	$500,000	$85,000 (17%)	$415,000
$500,000	$400,000	$50,000 (10%)	$350,000
			$65,000

Only experience suggests wise spending, but be realistic. Sound organizations tolerate neither too many expenditures, nor too few.

What Makes Donors Tick?

Donors, on all giving levels, respond because other people benefit from their contributions. They see charitable giving as a way to participate in enriching the human condition, locally, nationally, globally. The level of response depends upon the intensity of interest in a project plus other equally relevant factors. One thing is certain: *high-level emotional involvement with and commitment to an organization amplifies a potential donor's willingness to give and directly influences the amount to be contributed.* Get people emotionally involved with your cause and they will give you exceptional donations within their means. Churches and synagogues know that. Major health, educational, cultural, and social service organizations realize its power. When $345 million was contributed to restore the Statue of Liberty and create the Ellis Island Museum of Immigration, the backbone of individual giving was hardly intellectual. If you want fundamental examples of emotional giving, base as some may be, watch the television evangelists at work Sunday mornings.

Personal experience is another catalyst that encourages philanthropic contributions. The stories, for example, of persons who grew up in a poor environment and later funded projects that benefited the poor are many. So are instances when a person recovered from a serious medical problem and gave to the discipline that effected the person's recovery.

A friend's wife contributes yearly to cancer research because her husband smokes cigarettes, and she hopes a cure for lung cancer will be forthcoming—just in case.

Broadly, donors are induced to make donations through a developed sense of responsibility. Couple this with circumstance and here's what can happen.

While riding a commuter train in New York City, Jonathan, a manufacturer, happened to sit beside a man who was holding his head up using a cane; the curved handle was braced under his chin. As commuters often do, Jonathan and the man began to talk.

This was Jonathan's first encounter with the disease, Myasthenia Gravis. The victim was an advertising executive and new chairman of the Myasthenia Gravis campaign in New York City.

"I never believed this could happen to me," the ad man told Jonathan. "The illness has been getting worse for years, and now I can't keep my head up without support most of the day. I never cared much about fundraising before. Occasionally I gave to some local charities, but that was about it."

In time, Jonathan got to know the ad-man pretty well. He found out more about the disease and learned about the financial help its victims needed. It wasn't long before Jonathan sent his new friend a generous donation to support Myasthenia Gravis research.

Because of choosing a railroad seat one afternoon, Jonathan discovered a terrible human problem. He came to feel a responsibility to help the ad executive stamp out a fearsome disease. That's when he decided to become a supporter.

Here are specific reasons why people make donations:

1. *Because they are asked.* Remember that expecting an unsolicited contribution because your cause is worthy is one of the earlier-mentioned great misconceptions.

2. *A person has a leadership role in an organization.* "I am a board member and giving is expected."

3. *A need to improve the quality of community life.* "I'm a member of Ridge Hill. I want to do my part to make it grow."

4. *Belief in an organization's goals.* "Our family service agency has helped many troubled people reorganize their lives."

5. *An intense interest in a particular program.* "The meals on wheels program is a great service for those who are housebound. It deserves my support."

6. *Recognition.* "I want to make a gift that is admired and remembered by my friends and the rest of the community."

7. *Peer pressure.* "My friends and business associates would never forgive me if I didn't make a meaningful gift to this drive."

8. *Admiration for a professional leader.* "Our artistic director has made this theater group number one."

9. *Good business.* "My car dealership will benefit from making a gift to this campaign."

10. *Family tradition.* "My parents always gave to this organization and so will I."

11. *Financial planning considerations* such as tax deductions.

Though almost every donor gives for more than a single reason, belief in an organization's goals is usually the primary inducement.

All kinds of people are potential philanthropic contributors: mainstays of the community, white or blue collar workers, retired persons, organization or nonaffiliated men and women. It's a matter of getting to know them . . . then getting them to know you.

How to Turn Prospects into Givers

That a potential donor has wealth is no guarantee of a substantial (or even a mediocre) gift to your campaign. It is impossible to overemphasize that *one of the most self-defeating assumptions many volunteers make is that ability to give naturally equates with desire to give.*

Having recently asked new prospects for a gift, frustrated solicitors often report something to the effect that a particular family owns a mansion, four Mercedes, a Lear jet, a condo in Palm Springs, and a Caribbean island where they recently dug up 400 barrels of Spanish doubloons.

"But they won't give us a dime!"

Well, maybe they won't now, but they might later. It's completely natural to be supportive only of the things that really matter to us personally. What generates sizable gift dollars is a prospect's *total* commitment to the aims of an organization and a keen interest in an explicit project that requires funding.

Why, then, expect a relative stranger who is unfamiliar with your organization or drive to make an extraordinary donation? Don't become indignant over what some people won't contribute. Use that same energy to plan an extensive program designed to involve prospects with your organization so they do give. The fundraiser's term for this process is *cultivation*.

Here's a concrete example of what usually happens when a prospect is not properly cultivated.

A volunteer I know met an affluent Bostonian. "I have a man who could fund my whole project," said the volunteer. "However, I think I'll ask him for $75,000, half what I need." The volunteer made two special trips to Boston to visit this man. Their meetings were affable and the volunteer was certain that he would receive the gift he requested. Two weeks following his last visit, the Bostonian sent the volunteer a check for $50. When he received the check the volunteer became outraged.

"Why are you so angry?" I asked.

"Because I showed him my plans. We had long talks. He thinks the project is great. He has plenty of money and sent me 50 bucks. That's why!"

"There's a distinct difference between this man being interested in your project and being committed to it," I told the volunteer. "You hardly know the person, and he hardly knows you or your project. You're lucky to have gotten $50."

(This is also a typical example of why the popular practice of sending solicitation letters to unfamiliar, therefore uncultivated major gift prospects usually produces little, if anything, in the way of donations.)

Bringing a major or other large gift prospect into the fold is a slow, ongoing process. It might take months; it often takes years. A campaign may start and finish, but cultivation never ends. And, since major gifts play a dominant role in your campaign, almost all the time and energy given to cultivation must be spent on influencing these and other potential big-gift donors. To some, that means foreseeing the need for multimillion dollar gifts. To a group anticipating a goal of $70,000, contributions of $700, $500, and such are large contributions. Remember, the goal defines what are considered major gifts.

When you uncover a new contributor, keep priorities in order. You have only so much time to give your organization; use it wisely. Let's presume that over the past 20 years, an affluent individual gives solely for the benefit of local team sports activities. Don't expect this person to become excited at the thought of providing funds for your underwater examination of Florida dolphins.

Another prospect may be generally interested in what your group does, but only has a peripheral view of how and why it does it. That's the person you want to get involved. If the volunteer I mentioned in the anecdote had taken the time to cultivate the Bostonian properly, he might have eventually received the contribution he was after.

Cultivation raises awareness. It's an educational process with a rational beginning, middle, and end. To foster a relationship with a prospect:

Meet the six requirements discussed earlier so that a positive setting exists: compelling goals; an easily perceived growth pattern, or a record of expertise by key leaders in a newly formed group; strong visibility; totally committed, competent leadership who are excellent fundraisers; specific, attractive campaign needs that demand immediate funding; and measurable results.

Get to know your prospect so that you have an idea of his or her values, talents, weaknesses. Try to form a positive relationship. Hopefully, you will appreciate each other's attributes, develop a mutual respect for one another, and become friends.

Introduce prospects to organizational activities that reflect their interests. Let them see first hand what your group is accomplishing. Show them, don't just tell them.

Get prospects to do something important within your organization. Best if it's an ongoing task. Depending on their interests, get them to serve on a committee or work on a project. Participation often leads to a board of directors post. In turn, many directors are major gift donors and top-flight solicitors.

Continue to communicate. Provide these people with feedback any time your organization says something new about services or programs.

The result of cultivation is to have potential prospects consider your organization or project *a part of their everyday lives.* When that happens they feel that your organization and campaign is *worth their support.* Then and only then will you really profit from their contributions.

Know that cultivation is not like dealing with computers, scientific laws, or mathematical formulas that are always stable and logical. We are talking about motivating people, putting a fire under them. People have numerous agendas, defenses, egos, eccentricities. It's simple to tell you to involve prospects in your project and to become friends. But this is often difficult to pull off because of the varied personalities involved. The secret is to cultivate people in the way *you* would like to be cultivated. Then you will find many supporters for your organization, because they are attracted by and believe in your sincerity. Don't, like some groups, create a lot of hype or glitzy cultivation programs—none of them are worthwhile. Be sincere, be yourself!

This is how one triumphant cultivation program took place, the story of a run-down, inner city public high school that boasted a special curriculum in creative and performing arts. Two highly skilled, totally committed administrators, the principal and artistic director, ran the school. The classrooms and hallways were filled with the sounds of spirited, talented kids rehearsing roles, sketching, dancing, arguing about which art form was more demanding. Academics, music and dance concerts, theatrical performances, and art exhibitions were of consistently high quality. There was a long waiting list for entry to the school. Since only the basics were publicly supported, a nonprofit "Friends" group was organized, made up of parents, administrators, and faculty. Their mission was to raise and channel funds to support programs and purchase equipment outside the school system's budget.

Meanwhile, the school received increasing attention from outside educators and the local media because of its unique status, its innovations, and high standards. Plays and concerts were consistently sold out. The school caught the eye of various community leaders and other citizens. As local support developed, the "Friends" organization began to enlarge. Still, fundraising was spotty; a major breakthrough was needed.

A generous husband and wife in this city had funded many projects over the years for the city's university, symphony, and opera company. Early on, they (mistakenly) were asked for a substantial donation to the high school and had refused. But, with typical persistence, the two administrators repeatedly courted the couple at various social functions outside the school.

One winter, a large classroom was converted into an art gallery for a student exhibition and a special preview arranged for the philanthropist and his wife. On a snowy, cold day they arrived and toured the school. At the exhibition, they became intrigued with the paintings and sculptures of the students and talked with many of the young artists. As we all know, you don't have to coach bright, talented children to make a good impression. The youngsters talked about their art, teachers, and classes, with the excitement, romance, and candor of youth. The potential donors became enthralled with the kids and their special school. A real involvement began.

Cultivation continued over many months. The couple enjoyed theater productions and concerts by the school orchestra and dance group, and helped judge student exhibitions and contests. Repeatedly, the principal and artistic director met with the couple and explained ways in which private sector funding would help the school reach its goals. When these administrators finally asked for a $10,000 grant, the philanthropist wrote a check for that amount. This was the first in a series of substantial contributions the couple made for various projects. They had developed a week-to-week concern about what happened to the school, were proud of its achievements, and vocal about letting others know how they felt. Their attitude encouraged many influential community members to become involved with the school as time went by.

The administrators of the performing arts school followed the only game plan that works: a patient, aggressive program of getting to know a prospect, showing the organization's resources to that person, and motivating the potential donor to become totally involved in its special undertakings.

Let's examine how the school adhered to the elements that make up a successful cultivation program, beginning with the six fundraising requirements:

- *Compelling goals; growth patterns must be easily perceived.*   Having designed a unique curriculum, proven it workable, attracted talented children from varied neighborhoods and backgrounds, the school had an outstanding record of achievement.

- *Strong visibility; competent, committed leadership who are money-raisers.*   Because of its curriculum and standards, the school became well-known locally and was applauded on a national level. The school's administrators, faculty members, and parents were supercharged. They accepted fundraising as a challenge.

- *Campaign needs must be exacting, attractive, and timely; results must be measurable.* The "Friends" prepared programs that required funding: grants for equipment, costumes, artists-in-residence programs, renovation of classrooms, etc. As the couple and other "friends" became involved, these were the type projects they funded. Results were easily measured. Scholarships allowed children from poor families to purchase vital instruments, art supplies, and associated equipment that they otherwise couldn't have afforded. Funding also allowed students to upgrade their training and further explore and prove their talents.

- *Get to know your prospect.* Since the couple had a long record of funding varied artistic endeavors, the administrators were aware of their interests.

- *Involve your prospects in organizational activities.* The administrators took every opportunity to show student and faculty activities to their prospects.

- *Get your prospect to do something important within your organization.* The couple judged exhibitions and competitions.

- *Continue to communicate.* The couple received all pertinent announcements of upcoming activities.

Through cultivation, members of this unique school convinced many potential benefactors that their institution deserved funding—at first a mighty task, but with handsome rewards.

Former donors are among your best prospects. Make sure that you continue to cultivate those who have given you sizable gifts in past campaigns, otherwise, "out of sight, out of mind."

A social service agency completed a building campaign, properly thanked its donors, and went about its business. The directors figured that since the campaign was over, no more cultivation was necessary. One contributor was involved in many charitable tasks. Like all philanthropists, the woman was continually courted by dozens of fundraisers. A few years later, the agency decided to begin an expansion drive because of community growth. This time she gave little because her priorities had changed.

Some volunteers won't miss an opportunity to positively influence a prospect. If nothing else, the following story shows the value of perseverance.

Hot on the trail of a major giver, Bob, a determined sort, made every effort to get an affluent but crusty prospect interested in one of his pet projects. Several others had tried and failed.

One fall day, the prospect invited Bob to go whale-watching off the Maine coast. The man figured that the trip would be Bob's undoing, and he wouldn't be bothered by him again. Although Bob was not born to the sea, this gallant volunteer gathered up his campaign materials, swallowed some antiseasick pills, and off the pair went. The boat was a small but seaworthy craft with two massive engines. At first, they motored comfortably. But, as they lost sight of land, the weather closed in and the waves soon built to about six feet. Ten miles offshore, a cold Atlantic spray whipped their faces as the pair crashed through the waves.

"Well, Bob," the prospect screamed over the wind and engines, "we ought to see some whales soon. Tell me about your project."

Bob, by now standing in cold water up to his ankles, valiantly tried to make his pitch. He had carefully prepared a terrific presentation, but couldn't say a word. Barely avoiding seasickness, he managed to hang on to a handgrip to avoid being thrown overboard. His portfolio of materials floated crazily around the cockpit as the boat pitched and rolled like a drunken hobbyhorse. All Bob could think of was getting back to shore. But he summoned up his courage and finally told the seaman-prospect about his project.

When the pair returned, it took Bob a day before his complexion turned from green to just plain pale. Not too long after, Bob received a call from the whale-watcher who invited him to his home to further discuss the campaign project. When they again met, the prospect told Bob: "Anyone who believes in his purpose the way you do deserves a proper amount of time to present all the facts."

The man later pledged $15,000 to Bob's pet project.

All About Campaigners

A question asked often is, "Does a person have to be a professional salesperson to be a good solicitor?"

"No!" is my emphatic answer. I have seen shy, quiet folks who couldn't sell hot dogs at a ball game turn into demon fundraisers because they were highly motivated and took their solicitation training seriously.

Campaigners, volunteers who solicit funds, come from all backgrounds. Because of their involvement with an organization, they tend to donate more money than other people. The best solicitors are those who are first . . . donors. Making a financial commitment nails down the investment a worker has in an organization. Once that commitment is made, rest assured that the donor wants others to follow his or her lead, and will work hard to make that happen.

Successful campaigners take the attitude that asking for donations is a challenge instead of a chore. "Look," they say, "the only way we are going to get anything done is to raise money. There are other things I'd just as soon do, but I'm prepared to solicit my prospects in the best way possible. If they are friends of our organization and can make a proper gift and don't, then I'm at fault for not convincing them that our plans are worth their funding."

The reasons volunteers campaign closely parallel the reasons they will give you money:

- First, because YOU ASK THEM! Although the word *volunteer* is used for campaign workers, remember that, unlike the literal definition, people do not often come forward and offer their services. The best way to recruit campaigners is to say how much you need them.

- They strongly believe in your goals, programs, services.

- They want to improve the quality of life in your community.

- They are high-ranking members of your organization.
- They want recognition.
- They find it difficult to avoid peer pressure.
- They seek visibility within your community.
- They admire your chief executive.
- They find it helpful in business.

Organizations that are influential and have a strong emotional appeal attract the attention of the most volunteers. It's easier to enlist fundraisers for a church or synagogue, university, prominent hospital, or symphony, than for an organization with a limited appeal or one that is not well known to the community.

It used to be that the greatest number of campaign volunteers were homemakers, the stereotype club or sisterhood woman, looking for something to do. That used to be. With women continuing to enter the work force, they have less free time, and, like men, can only allocate a portion of demanding schedules to the nonprofit sector.

Gone are the days when women were recruited by being patronized. "Honey," they used to be told, "you just bring your pretty little self down to our meeting. We'll explain everything to you. Don't you even worry about details." If you want a hardworking woman campaign volunteer, let her take part in important decision-making.

Don't overlook retired men and women. People are leaving the marketplace earlier and living longer. Many of them seek worthwhile projects to fill their time; they will bring talent and devotion to your organization.

The best way to recruit workers is to convince them that their presence will greatly aid your campaign team. Once enlisted, most volunteers are fearful about soliciting gifts. Build their confidence by:

1. Explaining the support leadership will furnish
2. Telling them how much time they must devote to the project
3. Giving them proper solicitation training

Make a continual effort to enlist and train new workers. There are never enough volunteers, and attrition is always to be expected.

What to Expect from a Governing Board

A sleepy board spells disaster. More often than not, drives don't jell because the governing body can't or won't take an active role as donors, cultivators, and solicitors.

A group of prominent physicians started up a nonprofit institute and wanted to put together a fundraising plan. They were also the Board of Directors. As our meeting progressed, I discussed the importance of their personal participation in a major gifts campaign. "Oh," they said, "we don't expect to do very much in that area."

"It's very important that you as leaders of this organization become totally involved in fundraising," I replied. "You need to identify prospects, get them interested in your . . ."

"Wait a moment," interrupted a doctor. "You don't seem to understand. We're very busy. We are offering our professional knowledge. We expect other people to do what you're asking."

"You know," said a second physician with a supercilious grin, "the next thing he'll be wanting us to do is ask people for donations."

I was astounded!

After recovering, I asked the group if they would consider expanding the board to include some lay people who understood fundraising.

"We couldn't possibly do that," the leader answered. "We don't want any outsiders on the board."

There was no way such a board could get its projects funded, and it didn't! Being a member of a volunteer governing body commits a person to many responsibilities, not the least important of which is fundraising. That's why it's common to have board members who not only have expertise in planning, policy-making, and administration, but are well known, respected, and affluent. The board needs to find peers who are major gift prospects, cultivate these potential givers, and ask them for impressive gifts. Otherwise, the major gifts portion of a drive collapses. If that happens, the entire campaign comes up short of its goal. Imagine this solicitation:

SOLICITOR: George, you've always been one of our main supporters. As you know, we're in the early stages of our campaign. I hope you will consider making a $150,000 gift.

GEORGE: I don't know. What's been donated so far? What has the board given?

SOLICITOR: They . . . well, you know they're 100 percent behind this effort. The . . . uh . . . results are not in yet.

GEORGE: They're not, huh. Well, why would you expect me to make a gift if your board members haven't? They're the leaders. Let *them* start the ball rolling.

George's attitude is typical. He is not attempting to sidestep making a donation. He has a right, before contributing, to expect more than supportive words from the organization's top leaders.

How valuable a board member is to your campaign depends on more than the amount of money the person contributes. For instance, Mrs. Wright, a woman of means, sits on a board. Her capital campaign gift is $100,000. She brings in five new major gift prospects and solicits donations amounting to $500,000.

Mrs. Dell, who is less affluent, contributes $5,000. She identifies seven new prospects and solicits gifts totaling $25,000 during the campaign.

Both women are equally valuable organization representatives. Each was totally involved in the campaign, gave a significant gift within the scope of their means, identified prospects, and each was willing and able to solicit donations from others.

Some of you might argue that by having only affluent, gift-giving board members, the diversity required to run your organization would be stifled. Okay, I accept your argument. There are cases where governing board members are unable to make consequential gifts to their campaigns. An alternative strategy exists that is discussed in the next chapter under "Who's Going to Govern Your Campaign?"

The Chief Executive as Fundraiser: Don't Be without One

"Tell us your qualifications to be our chief administrator," said a search committee chair.

"Well," the applicant answered, "I have twin PhDs, was a recipient of a Fulbright scholarship, ran a Fortune 500 company, am an army reserve general, and published a well-received book on administrative management."

"Do you have any fundraising background?" asked another committee member.

"Actually, I don't," the applicant answered.

"Thank you very much anyway," said the chair.

Sure, the example is farfetched. However, members of the clergy, organization presidents, executive directors, and other professional administrators are expected to:

- Be key campaign planners.
- Aid in identifying major gift prospects.
- Enlist capable board members.
- Enlist major gift workers.
- Cultivate individual, corporate, and foundation prospective donors.
- Solicit prospects with the largest giving potential.

A full-time job in itself? Just about, but the reasons for the professional's involvement are clear-cut:

Professional leaders have intimate knowledge of the programs, services, strengths, weaknesses, and future expectations of their organizations. They are expert spokespeople.

Like board members, professional leaders are in constant contact with affluent and influential community leaders. Chief executives can form personal relationships with those in the community who can substantially support their organizations.

Major gift contributors want to rub elbows with the head of a winning nonprofit operation. That relationship is considerably weakened if a chief executive shuns fundraising.

Head administrators have much to lose professionally (and financially) if their organization's programs remain unfunded.

Most professional leaders spend a sizable portion of their workweeks marketing their organizations. One executive employment recruiting firm reported that college and university presidents work an average of 61 hours per week, of which 20 hours had to do with external affairs, mostly cultivation of key potential donors. That's half a traditional workweek. *Chief executives are directly responsible for the success of their campaigns, despite how many staff people or consultants may be involved in the process.* The fundraising buck stops at their door.

Aiding and Abetting: The Use of Consultants

I once entered an executive director's office for a first-time meeting. Heaped upon his desk were papers, worn file folders, and cigar butts. Tie askew, feet on the desk, he held a telephone in each hand. First he talked into one phone then the other, like an entertainer doing a comic routine. At times, he held both phones together so the people he was speaking to could talk to each other.

This man has giant problems, I remember thinking.

Finally he noticed me and said, "I've got two of my board members on the line. Be with you in a second."

I nodded as he continued the phone conversations.

"Listen guys," he told the board members. "Our fundraiser just walked in. I'm sure he has more prospects than we know what to do with. When he finishes soliciting them we ought to be in good shape. I know he'll assure us that we'll reach our goal by June. Now let me tell you about . . ."

When he finally finished his calls I told him that perhaps there was a misunderstanding about what a consultant does.

"I don't have a list of prospects for you," I said, "and I'm not prepared to solicit all the prospects *you* will find. And there is no way I can promise that your goal is reachable."

"What the hell do you get paid for then?" he asked.

People who have never dealt with professional counsel often expect the person to be some sort of fundraising Lone Ranger, a hero who enters a community, personally saves the organization from certain failure, drops off bags of gold, and cheerily rides off into the sunset while a smiling crowd watches with envy.

Unfortunately, that's not the way it works.

Consultants will not come to your organization with armfuls of prospect names. Likely, not even one name, unless headquartered locally. Still, a consultant furnishes plenty of useful aid in helping the organization find prospects.

Even if consultants are expert solicitors, this ability is of limited use to your campaign. Successful solicitations require that prospects have a peer-to-peer rapport with their solicitors. Consultants do not have that relationship, and members or other potential supporters can easily be put off by their presence. Still, sometimes consultants can be helpful partners, going with you to help solicit a few top-level gifts.

No ethical consultant guarantees a successful campaign. There are too many variables about human beings and human nature to make such a promise.

So, what is their role?

- *To tell you whether you should be holding a campaign and to assess your fundraising potential.* Because of their experience, consultants can figure out if your organization can carry out a winning drive. If not, they will tell you how to prepare for a future campaign.

- *To supply a total fundraising plan.* Using experience and an objective viewpoint, advisors supply a structure to suit your organization, advising you on such things as goal setting, strategies, approaches, and procedures.

- *To give continuing direction.* Whether consultants see you each week, once a month, or are in residence during the active phases of your appeal, their task is to watch over your campaign making certain that plans are carried out, deadlines are met, volunteers are knowledgeable, and strategies are revised when necessary.

- *To contribute communications skills.* Marketing, graphic design, copywriting, and audiovisual presentations considered necessary to effectively run your campaign should be among the services a consultant furnishes. This includes the preparation of brochures, ads, reports, and film, video, or slide productions. Also, consultants will assess the efficiency and cost-effectiveness of your present communications programs and the skills of local designers, artists, printers, and so forth.

- *To troubleshoot.* Consultants are expert in diagnosing and recommending cures for a troubled campaign.

Consultants are not in business to replace existing fundraising staff or campaign leadership. Their job is to broaden the horizons of these people, allowing their organizations to become as dynamic and profitable as possible.

Major organizations usually retain consultants before and during each capital campaign, and to oversee annual-appeal planning. If there wasn't a great advantage to hiring these people, rest assured it wouldn't happen.

You can (1) have a consultant meet with you at intervals during the planning stages of your drive, (2) have he or she direct your active drive full-time if there are no fundraising staff people, or (3) combine the first two options. Get counseling during the precampaign stages, then go to a full-time schedule when the active drive takes place.

How do you choose a consultant? Here is one type you don't want—the Damon Runyon character, right out of the old musical, *Guys and Dolls*. Wearing something on the order of a white suit, black shirt, and yellow tie, this man tells you, "Look, for a piece of da action, I'll raise as much money as youse guys want."

The consultants I know are neither Damon Runyon characters, Lone Rangers, or Robin Hoods. Instead, they are businesspeople who maintain standards that protect organizations and donors from illegal, unjust, or just plain stupid campaign practices. *They also charge a fee for time spent, not a percentage of money raised.*

There are numerous consulting firms, and there are also independent consultants (I'm one of them) located throughout the United States. Thirty-five of these companies belong to the distinguished and influential American Association of Fund-Raising Counsel which has been in business since 1935. Its address is 25 West 43rd Street, New York, NY 10036.

Another way to find an advisor is by asking other organizations in your area to recommend consultants they have used successfully. Also, look in the telephone book under FUND-RAISING COUNSELORS and ORGANIZATIONS.

Expect consultants to supply you with a description of the services they offer, the contractual basis on which they work, and the clients they have served. Interview several consultants before you choose one. These people are not inexpensive, especially before you begin to realize campaign income. Daily fees for a top firm are generally between $750 and $1,250, while monthly charges for their full-time direction during a campaign range between $14,000 and $17,000. Top-flight independent consultants charge about two-thirds of these rates.

Organizations end up paying a certain percentage of their campaign goals in fees for capital drives. But don't get confused here. Charges are contracted before the campaign and do not rise or fall because of the drive. Let's look at the numbers for an example firm or independent counsel whose day rates are $900 and whose monthly full-time rate is $13,000.

Goal	Fees and expenses	Totals
$2 million	14 days on-site preparation @ $900 per day	$12,600
	Five months full-time @ $14,000	$70,000
	Expenses	$ 3,400
		$86,000

Assuming the goal is reached, $86,000 paid to consultants translates to 4.3 percent of contributions and pledges. Whether the campaign falls short, makes or exceeds the goal, the billing remains the same unless the original contract is amended.

For large capital drives with multimillion dollar goals, many thousands of prospects, and the need for a full-time fundraising director during the active phases, consider hiring a consulting company that can properly staff each phase of your effort. Think about engaging an independent consultant to mastermind smaller campaigns or specialized programs such as troubleshooting, putting foundation grants together, designing and preparing publications, or teaching workers how to solicit. An experienced professional will give you plenty of expertise and his or her fee should be lower than a full-blown firm.

Money (and time) can be saved by working with your consultant electronically instead of on site. A fax machine is an obvious way to exchange documents. Also, using compatible software, many reports, evaluations, formats, and publications, about which you will learn, can be handled computer to computer by exchanging floppy disks or transmitting information via telephone lines.

Imagine you decide to have a consultant handle the design of a newsletter template and write an instruction manual for campaign workers. Having done so in his or her office, the completed files are transferred to disk and sent by mail. A faster way is to relay the files by modem, an inexpensive device that transmits information between two computers through telephone lines. When received, all you need do is print out the completed template and manual. Your organization pays a fee for design and writing, which you'd have to spend anyway, but eliminates charges for the consultant's travel-related expenses. When there is a great distance involved between you and your advisor that can be a mighty sum.

Remember, to transfer information, word processing software must be similar. Although there are utility programs that convert one format to another, it's not worth the effort, especially in a large document. Too many strange things often happen during the conversion process and numerous glitches in the final product can leave you tearing your hair out from frustration.

Ten Prime Reasons Why Campaigns Fail

1. The drive doesn't live up to the six fundraising requirements.

2. The governing body is ineffectual.

3. An incompetent overall chair is enlisted.

4. The goal is unrealistic.

5. Not enough major gift prospects are found and cultivated.

6. Top-ranking members, constituents, and other community leaders are incorrectly assumed to be highly supportive.

7. There are not enough campaign workers.

8. The amount of money prospects can afford to contribute is not estimated.

9. Leadership does not commit itself to an action plan.

10. Solicitation training is inadequate.

The first two points I've discussed. To make sure you avoid the other eight pitfalls, take a break and then explore Chap. 2.

PART 2

Making or Breaking Your Effort: Precampaign Activities

2
Minimizing Risks

High risk is for adventurers and speculators, not fund-raisers. The less your campaign leaves to chance, the more you will win awards as a campaigner. The best professional and volunteer fundraisers know that what gets completed *before* a drive goes public greatly decreases its risk of failure.

Let's look at what the first segment of precampaign activities is about:

1. Building a case for your appeal

2. Offering the most attractive projects for funding

3. Projecting the gifts necessary to reach a goal

4. Recruiting the best leadership

5. Finding potential contributors

6. Estimating how many dollars prospects can give you

7. Investigating your proposed drive's feasibility

8. Setting a realistic goal

9. Ensuring a campaign is justified by soliciting a few key prospects

With these tasks completed, nine of the ten prime reasons why campaigns fail will not apply to your organization. That's what I call minimizing your risk of failure.

Defining the Case for Your Drive

Fundraising is so competitive that unless your campaign is considered a top priority by potential supporters, you don't have a chance of it succeeding. Jot down the following:

1. The precise reason(s) why your appeal needs to take place

2. What you will achieve if your drive is successful

3. The people who will benefit

Be pragmatic. Reduce your organization's dreams, philosophies, and plans to a few concise sentences. Here are two examples:

1. (a) We have facilities that serve 5000 people, but if given the opportunity, there are 10,000 people who could use our programs and services. (b) We must build and equip a large new facility. (c) By doing so we can serve the additional 5000 people.

2. (a) If we don't develop new audiences, serious theater will become a dying art form. (b) Since young people make up the next generation of potential theatergoers, outreach programs that bring performances and workshops to these young people get them involved. (c) A wider and more knowledgeable audience will be created to support theater, and our organization can continue as a distinguished repertory company.

The above examples form the basis for "Case Statements" that explain why organizations must hold campaigns. After you devise the case for your drive, find out if members and constituents are captivated by its message. If they are not, your effort is ill-fated. And remember, if your drive is not timely, its case is considerably weakened. Let's return to the first example.

(a) We have facilities to serve 5000 people, but if given the opportunity, there are 10,000 people who could use our programs and services. (b) We must build and equip a large new facility. (c) By doing so we can serve the additional 5000 people.

What if it read like this?

(a) We have facilities to serve 5000 people, but we believe that *in the future* we will have an additional 5000 who *might* make use of our programs and services if given the opportunity. (b) We need to develop and equip a large new facility. (c) We can then serve the additional 5000 people *when necessary.*

That's a pretty feeble argument. An obvious reaction would be: "When you're sure those 5000 people are available, then talk to me about a campaign for new facilities."

A full-blown case statement is an amplification of the three statements: the reason(s) why you must hold a drive, what you intend to get done, and who will be assisted. It's mandatory that the case statement is included in campaign brochures, grant requests, speeches, and publicity releases.

Content is important, not length. When you write the full statement, be brief, succinct, and straightforward.

This . . .

We intend to start up a fundraising drive to do away with starvation in this county.

. . . instead of this:

It has always been a precept that man is responsible for his fellow man. Therefore, at this juncture, we propose to initiate a fundraising drive to counter starvation among . . .

Let's look at expanded versions of the two sample case statements mentioned earlier: first, the membership organization that needed facilities, a Jewish community center.

Coming of Age

A modern, fully equipped Jewish Community Center is a way of life wherever there is a concentration of Jewish people. This county is one of the few regions in the United States that does not have a full-service facility. The staff receives many requests each month for programs that cannot be scheduled because of limited space.

We are no longer a bedroom community, but a financial, industrial, and professional center in our own right. Studies show that the Jewish population, which has tripled in the last decade, is here stay. The Jewish commitment to the general community and to its own community is permanent.

A focal point is needed: a community center where our 10,000 men, women, and children can explore and maintain their Jewish identity through expanded programs and services.

[Now we know why the Center's drive needs to take place and who will be helped. Let's see what the organization intends to do if the drive reaches its goal.]

As a first step toward our goal, we have purchased the former Valley School and property that includes 26,000 square feet of existing building and 10 acres of land. Plans call for completely refurbishing the present building to allow for a full complement of cultural, educational, and health-oriented programs. The surrounding acreage will provide the Center with space for a day camp, sports facilities, and nature trails.

To this end, we have embarked on a major capital fundraising program.

The next case statement was written for the theater group that planned an outreach program.

Continuing the Tradition

The history of our repertory company is a story of upholding the traditions of highest quality, professional theater while setting ticket prices the public could afford. Since the next generation of serious theatergoers will come from today's young people, we feel a responsibility to help stimulate both children and young adults to become involved in this art form.

Next season two innovative outreach programs are planned to attract a youthful audience. The first involves a tour of black communities. By using a specially equipped theater bus, members of the company will stage 40 performances of black folk stories in parks, streets, and playgrounds in some 10 upstate communities. These stories depict the imaginative folklore of black people in both Africa and the United States.

Additionally, the full repertory company will present two distinguished contemporary dramas and conduct directing and design workshops following the performances at 10 eastern seaboard colleges.

To obtain the funds necessary to produce these presentations, we have begun a major fundraising drive to gain support from individuals, foundations, and corporations.

A case statement attractively summarizes a campaign's goals. Yet, by itself, the statement rarely motivates prospects to make impressive contributions. That's a further reason why solicitation letters written to major gift prospects—essentially case statements tied to large gift requests—are fruitless. However, as we shall see, this declaration is an important beginning.

Producing a Summary of Needs

A summary of needs is a list of projects needing funding. The list can represent an entire budget or a portion of one. If the title doesn't appeal to you and you want to call it "Projects for Funding," "Current Fund-Raising Requirements," or a similar name, that's fine.

The more attractive a summary of needs is to potential donors, the more they are prompted to contribute money, especially in capital campaigns. People are not turned on—and getting them turned on is the name of the game—if they are asked to fund common, everyday items. There is a vast difference, for instance, between being asked to contribute operating budget money for office supplies and being asked to help fund a computer system for the office.

Following is a listing of needs for the midwestern college used as an example of fulfilling the six fundraising requirements in the first chapter. Notice that items are ranked within categories from the most expensive to the least.

Summary of Needs

For Program Needs:	
New Graduate Degree Program in Education	$56,000
Long-Range Planning, Research and Faculty Development	30,000
Department of Business Expansion	24,000
Audio-visual Instruction and Programs	21,000
Expanded Admissions Program	14,000
	$145,000
For Student Services:	
Scholarship Aid	$84,900
Campus Ministry and Religious Studies	51,800
Intercollegiate Athletics	29,300
Placement, Counseling, and Career Planning Programs	24,500
	$190,500
For Facilities and Equipment:	
Science Hall Roof Replacement	$50,000
Computer Management Information System Installation	35,500

Library Equipment and Acquisition	35,000
Dining and Residence Hall Renovations	22,000
Parking Lot Refurbishing	22,000
	$164,500
TOTAL ANNUAL FUND GOAL	$500,000

The college's operating budget contained many more items than appeared in the above "Summary of Needs." But it concentrated its annual appeal on three attractive areas: program needs, student services, and facilities and equipment. Within several categories were opportunities for named gifts, an example of using the capital campaign technique which names portions of a facility after the donor. Revenues from tuitions, facility rentals, and other sources made up the remaining funds necessary to balance the budget.

(Apropos of what was said about listing attractive projects in your "Summary of Needs," refurbishing a parking lot and replacing a science building roof admittedly are not terribly exciting. But reality is reality. These items were major concerns to the college and therefore necessary to be included.)

The next illustration is for a capital campaign to fund an entry into an international, round-the-world yachting competition. This is a case where the entire budget became the summary of needs because the newly formed, mainly grass roots organization lacked other sources of income. (Some descriptions of the items that follow have been shortened.)

Complete Racing Hull with Watertight Bulkheads, Ballast Tanks, Keel . . .	$160,000
Sails and Running Rigging	40,000
Architect's Fee	35,000
Deck Gear	28,000
Mast, Boom, Standing Rigging	22,000
Expenses During Race	21,000
Mechanical Equipment	20,000
Interior Joinery, Stove, Sinks . . .	20,000
Salary for Assistant	15,000
Private Weather Service	15,000
Commissioning	12,000
Insurance	5,000
Entry Fee	5,000
Office Expenses	4,000
Total	$430,000

The above listings of funding requirements illustrate organizations at different ends of the spectrum. The college was a long established, continuing institution with a broad constituent base; the race competition was a one-time capital project with an extremely narrow band of potential supporters. Because fundraising principles remain the same for all types of campaigns, from time to time the college and sailing campaigns are used as cases in point.

Does the "Summary of Needs" total become your campaign goal? It's logical to think it should be, but whether that sum is realistic remains to be seen. It depends on several factors that require exploration.

Designing a Preliminary Table of Gift Expectations

When I was a kid and our team wanted to raise money to buy baseball uniforms, we didn't need consultants to tell us how to figure out the contributions we would require to get outfitted. Here's the sort of list we came up with:

1 Parent	$ 50.00
5 Other parents	50.00
10 Other relatives	50.00
2 Candy stores	30.00
1 Pizza parlor	20.00
6 Grocery stores	50.00
	$250.00

Only $250 for an entire team's uniforms? Okay, I date myself. Anyhow, we projected the number and amount of donations needed to reach our goal. But we weren't locked into those figures. If it turned out that six parents didn't come up with $100, then maybe the other relatives would give us more than that amount to make up for it. If the pizza parlor didn't contribute $20, perhaps the grocery stores would give us more than $50.

Now that I'm a big kid we call that projection a "Table of Gift Expectations." The title is fancier, the fundraising stakes higher, but the process is the same. You can't expect to run a campaign without first having an idea of the number and size of gifts necessary to reach a given goal. Based on the patterns of successful campaigns, I'm going to furnish you a preliminary percentage formula. It's not an ideal formula because there is no such thing. But it is a guideline, one that will be refined as you come to know your supporters.

Let's review the rules of thumb set down in "Expecting the Most From the Least" that appeared in the last chapter.

Ten percent of a campaign goal should be derived from a single gift; approximately 80 to 90 percent of incoming funds are donated by 10 to 20 percent of the membership or constituency.

Always begin any gift table with a single gift equaling 10 percent of the goal, as seen in Table 1.

Table 2 shows the numbers for an organization with a "Summary of Needs" totaling $500,000.

Table 1

Number of Gifts Needed	% Each Gift	% of Goal
1	10.00	10
Continue by multiplying the "Number of Gifts Needed" by the "% Each Gift" to find the "% of Goal"		
2	5.00	10
4	2.50	10
8	1.25	10
10	1.00	10
20	0.50	10
25	0.40	10
30	0.30	9
55	0.20	11
155 gifts totaling		90%
Other gifts at		
0.10		
0.02		
and below 0.02 totaling		10%
		100%

Table 2

Number of Gifts	In the Range of	% Each Gift	Gifts Totaling	% of Goal
1	$50,000	10.00	$50,000	10
2	$25,000	5.00	$50,000	10
4	$12,500	2.50	$50,000	10
8	$ 6,250	1.25	$50,000	10
10	$ 5,000	1.00	$50,000	10
20	$ 2,500	0.50	$50,000	10
25	$ 2,000	0.40	$50,000	10
30	$ 1,500	0.30	$45,000	09
55	$ 1,000	0.20	$55,000	11
155 gifts totaling 90% of goal			$450,000	
Other gifts of				
$500	0.10			
$100	0.02			
and below $100 totaling			$ 50,000	10
			$450,000	100%

In the second table I've added two new columns: "In the Range of" and "Gifts Totaling." The table relates the initial formula to the two rules in expecting the most money from the least amount of donors. It tells you:

- A small number of gifts of 1 percent of the goal and upward conventionally account for half a campaign's income, in this case $250,000.
- As gift ranges decrease, numbers of donors increase.

For the time being, don't be concerned about how many members or prospects an organization has on its rolls. Here's an illustration for a campaign with a "Summary of Needs" totaling $1.25 million. Again, it begins with a 10 percent gift.

Table 3

Number of Gifts	In the Range of	% Each Gift	Gifts Totaling	% of Goal
1	$125,000	10.00	$125,000	10
2	$ 62,500	5.00	$125,000	10
4	$ 31,250	2.50	$125,000	10
8	$ 15,625	1.25	$125,000	10
10	$ 12,500	1.00	$125,000	10
20	$ 6,250	0.50	$125,000	10
25	$ 5,000	0.40	$125,000	10
30	$ 3,750	0.30	$112,500	09
55	$ 2,500	0.20	$137,500	11
155 gifts totaling 90% of goal			$1,125,000	
Other gifts of $500 $100 and below $100 totaling			$ 125,000	10
			$1,250,000	100%

You can see that when making up a table for a campaign whose goal is not in round figures, you will have uncommon gift amounts contained "In the Range of" column. For instance, 2.5 percent times a goal of $1,250,000 equals $31,250. Obviously, few people make gifts of $31,250. If you come up with these offbeat figures, let them be reminders that a preliminary table is only a beginning guide.

A man I know became troubled when he worked out the preliminary percentage formula for his campaign. He told me the group to which he belonged didn't have enough prospects who could give the percentages indicated in the formula. I pointed out that his table could be adjusted before it became final. It might take three of your members, I told him, to make up a 10 percent gift, or 20 of your supporters instead of 10 who will contribute a 1 percent gift. Later, we'll see how these adjustments take place.

Who's Going to Govern Your Campaign?

If you can't surround yourself with great campaign leaders, none of the techniques you've learned—and those you are about to learn—will make your campaign profitable. These people are:

1. A governing board, a special campaign committee, or both

2. A general campaign chair or cochairs

3. A campaign cabinet

Is Your Board the Best Bet?

If an organization's entire operation is geared to raising money, then the board's only function is to run campaigns; members are selected solely for their ability to give and raise funds. Board members involved in policy-making, programming, and serving on various committees must recognize that campaigning is still a major part of their responsibilities. Those who care little about fundraising, but use their talents to make an operation run more efficiently, are obviously useful. But they shouldn't be representing a campaign or making decisions about its operation. That's because *the leaders of a funding effort are the nucleus of people who contribute the most money to the drive. Additionally, they must identify, cultivate and solicit key major and other large gift prospects, and enlist others to do the same.*

A board lacking fundraising prowess must at least identify and enlist top-level campaign leaders.

I advised a research institute working in an area of heart disease not long ago. Although the group had paid stiff consulting fees in the past, only small amounts of money were raised. Were the former consultants to blame? One day I talked to a board member, a retired, high-ranking corporate executive.

"What did the professionals tell you to do?" I asked.

"Our consultants wanted each board member to recommend 20 people who would serve on a special campaign committee," the executive told me.

"Did you follow up?" I asked.

"I gave them a few names," he answered.

"But surely, with a working lifetime spent in this city, you must know many affluent people who would be challenged by this research."

"Well, not really," the executive said.

Translated, he didn't *want* to recommend 20 people.

I then asked the executive director why her group didn't follow the consultant's advice.

"This is a serious research institute," she said. "We don't like to infringe on our friends and patients by asking them to serve as money-raisers."

The volunteer's head was buried in the sand. As you might expect, the institute never approached it's fundraising potential. This is *not* an atypical story. A lack of involvement by board members in helping build a solid donor base is all too common and self-defeating.

Recruiting a Campaign Committee

A group of influential, generous, experienced campaigners enlisted to concentrate their efforts on fundraising can take over these responsibilities from a board that is not campaign-oriented. That's why, in the last story I told you, the consultants suggested that the research institute board members point out people who would serve on a special campaign committee.

Such a committee is charged with:

1. Recruiting a general campaign chair
2. Helping to decide campaign policy during the length of a drive
3. Identifying, cultivating, and soliciting major gift prospects
4. Making substantial donations to the drive they lead
5. Aiding the general chair in enlisting other key campaign volunteers

Look for these types of people as committee members:

- Board members who *are* fundraisers
- Former campaign chairs of yours or any other organization
- Past board members
- Community sages who have retired from "full-time" fundraising activities
- Present major givers
- Potential major gift donors, those in the last stage of cultivation

Besides being replacements for weak boards, special campaign committees are used extensively in capital campaigns. That's because the more community leaders an organization has to represent its drive, the more the group finds find new prospects, recruits experienced solicitors, and obtains major gifts. Since capital campaigns appeal to a large segment of a community, volunteers are more apt to become involved with these drives than with annual appeals for the same organization. As well, the governing board avoids becoming overburdened: it is still responsible for guiding the organization and often, the annual appeal. Asking them to be responsible for an additional three- or five-year capital drive is unwise.

These are typical titles for special campaign committees:

Board of Advisors

Capital Fund Committee

Special Projects Task Force

Campaign Board of Governors

The size of the committee depends on the size of the campaign and the availability of leadership. Thirty to sixty people enlisted for a large capital drive would not be unusual. Look for broad representation. Don't limit the committee by recruiting a few "in" people.

A classical music ensemble decided to build a small concert hall on a piece of donated land. Although the players were also members of first-class symphonic orchestras, as an ensemble they were exploring the outermost boundaries of atonal music. The governing board consisted of men and women, other musicians mainly, who were great supporters of the group's musical esoterica. Unfortunately, they didn't have the means to support a campaign. Through the efforts of the directors, we enlisted a Board of Advisors, consisting of 40 people who took over fundraising responsibilities for the drive. They spent the better part of a year finding prospects, then cultivating and soliciting them. It wasn't an easy job, nor did the ensemble make fundraising history. However, the new concert hall was eventually built.

Another time, a school for the visually impaired needed to improve its annual fundraising program. Though each board member was a donor, it was apparent that board donations were not sizable enough to set giving standards among community supporters. A prominent group of 55 men and women from many businesses and professions was enrolled to form a campaign committee called a Board of Governors. Its members made their gifts, identified prospects, and successfully solicited individual, corporate, and foundation donations.

Enlisting a General Chair

Your campaign must have an aggressive and outgoing volunteer boss. The boss needs a supportive, talented team for assistance, but the team cannot be the boss. Don't endanger your drive before it begins by settling for an unqualified leader. It's the responsibility of your board, special campaign committee, or both, to recruit the most competent person in town. Come up with a chief who has each of the following qualifications: a person who is:

1. Totally committed to your project

2. A thoroughly successful campaign veteran

3. Willing to make a fabulous major gift to your campaign

4. A dynamic solicitor

5. Owed more favors than he or she owes because that person supports other community projects

6. Well known, admired, and respected by your community leaders, accordingly

7. Able to motivate potential major givers to support your campaign

8. Able to surround himself or herself with a team of experienced, loyal, and supportive coworkers

9. Continually in town during your campaign (absentee management is ineffective in fundraising)

The general chair is your most important campaign asset. Don't fill the position with a second banana, or this will likely happen:

An organization had run out of experienced chairpeople. One man accepted the position knowing he wasn't fully qualified. His gift was not exemplary so he didn't have much clout when he solicited potential major givers. He couldn't enlist enough outstanding workers and was incapable of motivating workers already recruited. Because this man did not offer inspiring leadership, the $750,000 drive lost its momentum. It concluded with gifts approaching $650,000. Had the organization not been established, its campaign never would have done that well.

Successful nonprofits groom chairpeople years in advance, choosing them from among campaign-wise board or special committee members and other major givers. You can promote people to chair your drives from within, or you can find them from outside your organization. Veteran fundraisers often go to great lengths to enlist a community member who has never been a supporter. When an outsider becomes an insider, he or she brings new supporters to an organization. Again, this happens more readily in a capital campaign since it's a one-time effort with enormous mass appeal.

For instance, Mr. Briggs is a well-respected businessman. His long history of fundraising activities consists of supporting his local church as a large contributor and as chairman of many successful annual appeals. He has, through the years, developed a loyal group of followers.

The local YMCA and YWCA are getting ready for a joint capital campaign. If they can get Mr. Briggs to chair this one-time drive, he will involve his followers in the major gift portion of the Ys' campaign.

Be careful how you go about enlisting outside people. Aggressive salesmanship may be necessary, but don't cajole, intimidate, or use other drastic measures to force a person to chair your drive. You may win the enlistment but you'll lose the campaign. To expect inspired leadership, a general chair must be dedicated to your cause.

Should You Use Cochairs?

There are three reasons to have more than a single person in charge of a campaign. Two of them enhance a drive, the final one invites catastrophe.

1. Cochairs representing different donor bases give your campaign the greatest range of potential support. Lets say Mr. Jones, a luggage manufacturer, and Mrs. Baker, a telephone company executive, travel in completely different business and social circles. They are ideal selections for campaign cochairs.

2. Chairpeople are responsible for contributing standard setting gifts and soliciting them from others. You may find special people who have all the prime requisites for leadership but cannot make major gift contributions. Because of this, they are not effective in soliciting substantial gifts. If you feel these individuals would otherwise be outstanding chairs, support them with cochairpeople whose donations are on the highest level. In a campaign having three cochairs, one lady was a highly respected, experienced volunteer who, for many years, devoted her extraordinary talents to the organization. It was Joan who had a handle on fundraising strategy and fired up even the most placid prospects and volunteers. But she was unable to make a major gift to the drive. When it came time to solicit, the three chairpeople visited many top prospects as a team. Joan's role was to present a vivid picture of campaign needs. Her partners solicited the gifts—peer to peer.

3. Do not expect under any circumstance that enlisting two or more mediocre cochairpeople replaces a single qualified leader. In this situation, one-half plus one-half doesn't equal one. Delay your campaign until you find the right people for the job.

Hands-on Management: The Campaign Cabinet

When a drive is in full swing, it needs continual monitoring. You can't expect (and don't want) each member of a large board or special committee to watch over the drive regularly. Leave the week-to-week operation of an appeal to your general chair(s), key representatives from the board or campaign committee, heads of various campaign phases, professional fundraising staff, and the chief executive. These people make up a Campaign Cabinet. Its meetings are chaired by the general campaign chair(s). To put a cabinet into perspective, look at the following chart.

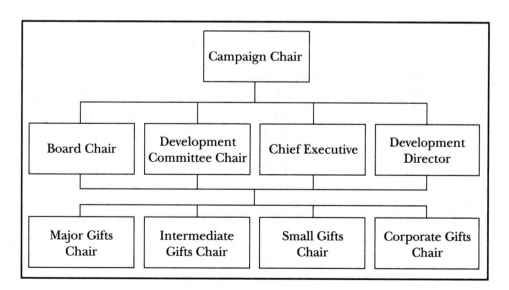

Keep in mind the difference between a campaign committee and a campaign cabinet. The committee is the nucleus of the major gift effort containing the most affluent and influential community leaders available. The cabinet, while representing major gifts, has members who are responsible for soliciting other prospects down to the smallest potential donors.

The Door Openers—
Honorary Chairpeople

Besides lending prestige and credibility to an appeal, select honorary chairpeople for their ability to put you in contact with potential donors who otherwise might not be available to your organization. Respect the title "Honorary." Don't expect these people to attend many meetings or take a load of solicitation assignments. Their contacts are mainly what you are after.

The names of honorary chairpeople appearing on a letterhead do not guarantee sizable contributions. Prospects react to active campaigners who make such a powerful case that they are driven to lend their support.

Getting a Handle
on the People
Who Might Fund You

Your best prospects on all giving levels are:

- Current and former donors.
- Users of your services who are grateful. "Your volunteer ambulance corps saved my child's life."

Other prospects can be found in:

- Your organization records. Depending on your mission, look for parents, patients, clients—anyone who has a direct relationship with your group.
- Donor listings from other organizations. The names of contributors are often published in annual reports, campaign literature, alumni newsletters, and so forth.
- Membership listings. You want corporate prospects? Ask the chamber of commerce for a list of its members. If you intend to raise money for an athletic program pick up a roster of the local country, tennis, or swimming club.
- *The Corporate Giving Directory,* published by the TAFT Group, 12300 Twinbrook Parkway, Suite 450, Rockville, MD 20852-1606. Provides a state by state listing of corporate givers, who received the gifts, and how much was given.
- *The Foundation Directory* and *National Data Book of Foundations,* published by the Foundation Center. (More on the center and foundation prospects shortly.)

- The Yellow Pages. Professionals, for example.

- *Who's Who in America,* published by Macmillan Directory Division, 3002 Glenview Road, Wilmette, IL 60091.

- The *Social Register,* published by the Social Register Association, 381 Park Avenue, New York, NY 10016.

- Newspapers, magazines, periodicals. These publications often divulge people's philanthropic and other interests.

- Rental Lists. This is a common way to find direct mail, small-gift prospects and will be discussed in Part 4.

Begin by Identifying Large Gift Donors

Large gift prospects are the lifeblood of your campaign. They must be continually identified and cultivated. Present supporters won't carry the load forever. They find new interests, relocate, their financial pictures change, they die.

The best way to find new potential major gift donors is for your top supporters to recommend them. Remember, a chief reason to enlist an affluent, influential board, special campaign committee, and general chair is because they can supply you with prospects. Concentrate on identifying individual donors since they make up over 80 percent of the nation's charitable contributors. Individuals will often expose you to corporate contributors.

One summer afternoon, 15 men and women were invited to a cookout at the home of an organization board member, an anthropologist. Many of those attending were business executives. Early that evening the anthropologist showed slides and talked about his campaign project. Some of the audience responded with tough questions about the reasons for funding, and a fascinating exchange sparked the group. The next week, the scientist wrote each of the executives and sent them follow-up campaign materials. This get-together later resulted in several substantial corporate donations.

Conversely, imagine you're a corporate contributor of mine. I ask you to suggest individuals who might be prompted to support a forthcoming project. You tell me that a new neighbor of yours, a commercial artist, has good reason to be interested in a forthcoming fine arts program sponsored by the organization. I have a new individual prospect.

Potential contributors can be recommended by any friend of an organization, but groups often miss out because volunteers don't bother spreading the word.

A painter and sculptor was a part-time faculty member of an art institute. It never occurred to the school's fundraising staff that this artist might lead them to large gift donors. One day, at her request, the artist met with the fundraisers and gave them a list of 25 wealthy men and women who had bought the artist's works. Three of those people eventually made substantial donations to the institute.

Betting on Long Shots

Long-shot prospects are affluent people, philanthropists or otherwise, whom you want to take a major part in funding your project but who have absolutely no affinity to your organization.

A retired man I know is a serious student of horse racing. I asked him to give me the odds on the possibility of long shots winning horse races. He did a study of 50 races and found that out of 500 horses less than one-half of one percent of long shots won a race. That's a little less than 2.5 horses per hundred. I would sooner bet on a long-shot horse winning a race than a long-shot prospect funding a campaign. But occasionally it happens. Newcomers have a tendency to put long shots at the top of their priority lists. Veteran campaigners spend time on long shots only after more likely prospects are approached.

Researching Individuals

The more you know about the interests of potential donors, the better chance you'll have of eventually getting the gifts you request. Corporations and foundations publish annual reports that give information about contributions and recipients; individuals do not. So make a determined effort to find out as much as possible about your new individual prospect's philanthropic, business, and social habits to detect a tie-in to one of your supporters or projects. Then cultivation can begin. Find out:

- Organizations to which the prospect belongs
- Organizations to which the prospect contributes
- The prospect's interests and hobbies
- The prospect's immediate family's interests
- The prospect's social affiliations

If for one moment you think, as some people have remarked over the years, that this information is none of your business, you'll be making an enormous mistake. In-depth prospect research should be a matter of course.

Having gathered this data, ask yourself which of your undertakings might entice the prospect to become a friend of your organization. If you don't have a reasonable idea of what captivates a potential donor, you can get into a jam when you begin cultivating the person.

During an alumni association drive, a worker telephoned excitedly. "I'm meeting a wealthy couple who recently moved here," he told me. "Both of them are attorneys, from the class of '80. They may become large donors."

"That's great," I answered. "Let's plan our next steps."

"I'll tell you what I'm going to do next," the campaigner exclaimed. "I'm going over to see them in a few minutes and get them interested in the Men's Equestrian Team." With that he hung up the phone.

Later that day he came into the office. I asked him how his visit went.

"Everything started out very well," the campaigner told me. "We talked about the old days, but then I got myself into trouble. I'm not sure if I'll ever be able to straighten it out."

"Tell me about it," I said.

"Well," said the campaigner, "When I told the couple how important the Men's Equestrian Team was to the school's image, I noticed that the man's wife was looking at me strangely. So I made sure to tell her how the team had special days when wives and girlfriends rode with the men. That did it."

"Did what?" I asked.

"The wife told me that one of her clients was the local women's liberation organization. She said it must be a great honor for women to ride with the men once in a while. Then she called me a sexist pig. Her husband backed her up."

Had the campaigner been less impatient, or had I been more aggressive with him, through research we could have discovered that the woman was sure to have had negative feelings about the men's equestrian team. There were many other alumni projects that she and her husband might have supported.

Use the following form for prospect research:

Prospect Profile Form

Prospect Name: _____ Recommended by: _____

Address: _____ Evaluation: $_____

Tel. Number: _____   (to be filled in later)

Occupation: _____

Spouse's Name: _____ Children's Names: _____

Occupation: _____

(your) Organization Affiliations: _____

Other Organization Affiliations: _____

Civic Interests: _____

Hobbies: _____

Family Members' Interests: _____

_____

	Giving Record:			Gifts to Other Organizations:	
Amt.	Type of Gift	Date	Org.	Amount	Type

Comments: _____

Tracking Down Foundations

Don't be intimidated by the thought of applying for foundation grants. After all, foundations are in business to give away money. Why not to your organization?

You're no doubt familiar with the well-known foundations such as Ford and Rockefeller, but there are many thousands of other family, special purpose, corporate, and community foundations as well. Here are the ones to consider as prospects:

1. Those whose guidelines are in accord with your organization's project. A foundation interested in supporting freedom for wildlife is not going to fund acquisitions for a zoo.

2. Foundations who have funded projects similar to yours. If you're training for the next Olympics, see who funded athletes during the last games.

3. Those whose grant ranges coincide with your request. If you need $50,000 and the foundation you discover makes grants not to exceed $5,000, then apply for a $5,000 grant and raise the rest of the money elsewhere.

Finding this information is comparatively simple. The most comprehensive source is The Foundation Center, a nonprofit organization with major offices in New York City and Washington, D.C. Additionally, there are field headquarters in Cleveland and San Francisco. Among its collection of books and computer data files, the Center publishes a large volume titled *The Foundation Directory*. By purchasing this book and its yearly supplement, you'll find out what you should know about American foundations. Such things as:

- The name, address, incorporation date and principle donor(s) to a foundation.

- Financial data. For example, assets $1,000,000; 1500 grants given totaling $990,000; highest grant $200,000; lowest grant $1,000, etc.

- Purpose of the foundation. Grants to organizations who improve the well being of senior citizens, for instance.

- Type of support. Operating budgets, new facilities, equipment, special projects, and so forth.

- Limitations the foundation might impose. For example, no support for unaffiliated individuals, or no support for other than Florida organizations.

- Grant application information. What the foundation expects your proposal to include.

- Publications produced by the foundation, such as annual reports.

- A list of officers and trustees.

The Foundation Directory is one of many publications the center offers. Write for a free catalog. The New York office is located at 79 Fifth Avenue, New York, NY 10003; the Washington address is 1001 Connecticut Avenue, NW, Suite 938, Washington, DC 20036.

If you are near either of these cities I urge you to visit one of the Foundation Centers. Its libraries are well staffed, and you don't have to be a professional fundraiser to use them.

(How to get ready for grant submissions and write proposals is covered in Part 3.)

Enlarging Gift Income
by Evaluating Prospects

It's easy to criticize any technique that suggests how much money a person should donate. But if you ask prospects to do what they can, all but a handful of people of them will make gifts far below what they are capable of giving. Instead, experienced campaigners request gifts based on what a prospective donor's contribution *might* be if that person *was extremely motivated to support a project*. Determining the amount of the gift is through a procedure called "Prospect Evaluation."

Always base evaluations on a person's *ability* to give instead of *tendency* to give, or past giving habits. Here's why:

Based on what you know about me, you believe that under optimum circumstances, I am able to contribute $100,000. My past giving records indicate that I have made gifts of $10,000, $20,000 and $35,000. Well, you think, Peter's tendency to give ranges from $10,000 to $35,000. You hope to make a breakthrough and evaluate me at $50,000. A terrible mistake! I should have been evaluated at $100,000, because I apparently have the wherewithal to give you that much money. Now when you solicit me for $50,000, here's how it ends:

> SOLICITOR: I want you to consider a gift to us of $50,000.

> ME: You make a fine case for the campaign. But I think $50,000 is too much money. I will give you a contribution of $35,000 to show you how I feel about the project. That's the most money I've ever given anyone.

If you had evaluated me for $100,000, there is always this possibility:

> ME: I'm shocked. A hundred thousand dollars is much more money than I expected to give you. I've always been a staunch advocate of yours, but $100,000 is asking a lot. I don't think I could possibly do that. Let me think about it.

The following week I make a pledge of $75,000.

The sense of the above scenario has been played out many times in actual campaign situations. Prospect evaluations lead people to think about making much larger gifts than they originally had in mind. And they get used to thinking that way. Here is something to keep in mind: *Since donating money is not instinctive, giving is something that people learn how to do. Fundraisers teach people to give by conditioning them to raise their philanthropic sights continually.* No matter how presumptuous that sounds, it's true. Once a person goes from being a $5,000 to a $10,000 donor, for example, it's unlikely that he or she will revert to repeating the original contribution to the same organization. Once that $10,000 becomes $20,000, the $10,000 level seems insufficient. Those jumps don't happen automatically. They are the result of evaluations (obviously coupled with skillfully handled solicitations) that inspire people to look at new giving horizons. Many of the greatest philanthropic contributions ever known began with lofty evaluations.

There's an ancient fundraising axiom that states: "If a prospect says yes to your first gift request, you have underevaluated that prospect." Underevaluating prospects is a common reason why campaigns fail. If an evaluated gift request is refused, it's standard to ask the person for a smaller donation. Conversely, asking for a small gift, then changing your mind and requesting a larger amount is out of the question.

Overestimating a person's gift capability is rarely insulting. Most people are highly complimented that their peers look at them as capable of making superlative contributions. (Be reasonable, however. If you evaluate prospects too far above their capacity, when solicited they may not take the dollar request seriously.)

Evaluations are confidential. But, if a person discovers he or she has been evaluated and takes offense, that prospect deserves a forthright response. Something to the effect of:

"Estimating the gifts of you and other prospects is not meant to pry into personal affairs. Our committee thinks of you as a potentially strong supporter. Its members hope that you will consider the suggested commitment because our purposes are important, and we know you are a successful person. If we are asking too much, accept my apology. I'm not here to embarrass you or tell you what to do."

If, following your statement, the prospect remains irritated, then it's most often an excuse for not wanting to make much of a gift to your drive in the first place.

The Evaluation Committee in Action

Large gift prospects must be evaluated. Try to do likewise with other potential donors as well. The people you want to serve on an evaluation committee are those most familiar with your prospects, such as:

- Friends and colleagues.
- Business and professional people who deal with and advise your prospective contributors.
- New, cultivated major gift prospects. Evaluating other people often motivates new supporters to raise their giving sights. Trust me, it works.

These are the people you don't want:

- Devil's advocates. An evaluation meeting is not the place for someone to dispute every little thing upon which the majority agrees. Devil's advocates drive everyone else crazy.
- People who don't contribute to the limit of their capabilities. Underachievers always come up with low evaluations. They put prospects on their level to justify their giving habits.

Base evaluations on as much fact as possible, and as little hearsay. When you've researched your prospects you know their:

1. Level of interest in your organization
2. Interest in a particular program that your organization sponsors
3. Past giving records

4. Gifts to other organizations

5. Form of giving (unrestricted, pledge, art work, etc.)

6. Immediate family's role in determining the nature and size of their gifts (how much influence does a spouse have, for instance?)

Bring prospect profiles and a prospect listing showing appropriate data such as past gifts and former evaluations for current donors to each meeting. There are two ways in which to evaluate people:

By Calling Names.   The committee chair calls the name of each prospect for discussion. When the members reach agreement on how much they think a prospect can give, the chair records the consensus or an average amount on a profile card or prospect listing, like this:

> CHAIR: What do you think Wesley Bell might do for us? For the last two years he's given us $30,000 and $35,000. Wesley was evaluated at $50,000 both years. He's also a firm supporter of the home for the elderly.

> MEMBER 1: He's been involved with the home for the last two years. I know he has business problems this year. Might hold him back. But I still think he can give us $50,000.

> MEMBER 2: Wes will work his way out of those problems. I think we should try motivating him to make a $75,000 gift.

> MEMBER 3: I think that's pushing it. Fifty-thousand dollars is more like it. Wes has topped out. I know his family thinks he should be paying more attention to the home for the elderly. His wife is on the board. That will influence his gift.

> MEMBER 4: Perhaps. But based on potential, $75,000 is not too much to ask.

> CHAIR: Anyone else? Okay. Let's evaluate him at $65,000 and see what we can do. [He notes the amount on his prospect sheet, then consults a prospect profile form.] What about Tom Aspic? Tom's new to the organization. He's a sports buff and is a member of the country club and tennis club. He's also a great supporter of Special Olympics. His wife is a low-scoring golfer.

> MEMBER 4: I know Tom and his wife. If we can continue to interest both of them in our physical fitness club, I'd say he could give us, oh, as much as $100,000.

That's the sense of evaluating prospects by calling their names, listening to committee member's reactions, and making a decision based on their knowledge. But see how this kind of session might get out of hand.

> MEMBER 5: I know Tom, as well. He's one of the cheapest guys I've ever known. Won't even leave a decent tip at a restaurant. We'd be lucky if he gave us $1000. And I don't think much of his wife either.

> MEMBER 4: Wait a minute. Tom's a friend of mine. Who made you such a big spender anyway?

> MEMBER 5: I give a helluva lot more money to this organization than you do . . .

The disadvantage of this format is that it's public. If someone gets started on a prospect's personality traits, look out. Yet, it's the best way to evaluate prospects for organizations *who know their prospects well and whose committee members can stick to being objective.* If the process seems unwieldy . . .

Have Each Committee Member Fill Out a Confidential Evaluation Form.
When you call the evaluation committee together, each member receives a copy of the following instructions and a prospect listing.

Prospect Evaluation Guidelines

_____

Your name

It is very important to closely follow the guidelines below:

1. Skip the names of prospects you don't know on the accompanying list.
2. In the column marked Evaluation, give your *best* estimate of a dollar amount you consider the person able to donate, or the person's giving range by filling in one of the following letters.
   AA. $50,000 or more   C. $5,000–$9,999
    A. $25,000–$49,999   D. $1,000–$4,999
    B. $10,000–$24,999   E. Below $1,000
3. When making estimates, do not use past giving as a sole reference. Many donors upgrade gifts because of factors such as increased interest in our organization and more persuasive solicitation practices.
4. This is a collective effort. You are one of a team of volunteers involved in the evaluation process. Experience shows that averaging contribution estimates parallel a person's gift-giving capability.
5. Please check the worker column if you think the prospect would be willing to volunteer as a campaign worker.

The prospect sheet can be formatted like this:

Prospect Evaluations

Name	Evaluation	Potential Worker?	Remarks
Wesley Abell	$60,000	X	Has become more involved in the elderly home.
Linda Albeit	A.		Assign to Sarah Baker.

When the forms are returned, you have a variety of evaluations for each prospect. As mentioned in the guidelines, average these figures and you'll have a reasonable idea of what each prospect could contribute if properly cultivated.

The Ultimate Risk-Cutter:
Feasibility Studies

Don't attempt a first-time annual drive or any capital campaign without first seeing if you have the major gift support and available campaigners to make it successful. By conducting interviews with community leaders (potential donors), learning what they think about your organization and project, comparing their input with known standards (norms), and interpreting the results, you are safeguarded against a campaign that likely won't fly. In fundraising, this form of market research is called a "Feasibility Study." The example college whose summary of needs you read earlier in this chapter wanted to launch a substantial capital fund drive. The results of its feasibility study showed:

- Affluent, influential community leaders were not captivated by the institution holding a capital campaign.
- There were few potential major givers.
- Many experienced, large-gift campaigners did not want to work for the proposed appeal.

Had the college held this drive, it would have failed miserably. Instead, the board shelved the idea and spent time creating more favorable conditions by expanding its role in the community. Four years later (yes, four years), the institution conducted a new feasibility study. The results were positive. A capital appeal took place and the goal was met.

The other summary of needs that we examined earlier was a $430,000 campaign for an entry in an international sailboat competition. A feasibility study showed the goal to be totally unrealistic. Because of the upcoming deadline for the start of the race, choices were to abandon the project or lower the goal. After deliberation, the project was revised, the goal dropped to $215,000, and the drive succeeded.

A cultural arts organization began a $2 million expansion drive. First reports were encouraging. The leaders of the drive solicited each other successfully. They expected the rest of the membership and community to follow suit. But despite all efforts, the leaders received only minimal donations and the campaign stalled. Had they run a feasibility study, the organization's leaders would have learned that other potential major givers in the community and most of the membership were not enthusiastic about having new facilities.

Basic to the fundraising process, most feasibility studies are conducted by highly experienced, objective fundraising consultants. There is no room for error. Even if you do everything else in-house, hire a professional for this phase of your campaign.

It will cost a lot more, in many ways, if you mount a drive that fails.

To prepare you in advance, I'm going to explain how a study is handled which will later save you time, therefore money. It will also get you thinking about whether your organization is ready to retain a consultant for this phase of your campaign.

Preparing for Interviews

Interviews are conducted in person. Otherwise, the nuances of body language that often emphasize a viewpoint better than words are missed. Here's how to get prepared for them.

A. Compile a detailed account of your organization's background, fundraising accomplishments, leadership, operating budget, staff, services, distinctions, goals, long-range plans, marketing programs, everything that will help an interviewer become familiar with its past and present.

B. List a cross-section of community leaders to be visited. Many of these people should be friends of your organization, including board members, but don't eliminate unaffiliated, influential individuals and corporate leaders who are acquainted with your group. The number of people to interview depends on the size of an organization. The more input, the more valid the results. Try to identify between 50 and 75 persons for a sizable local campaign. A larger sampling would be expected for a national drive.

C. By seeking answers to the general questions below, interviewers get a feeling for the philanthropic climate of a locale and an organization's visibility.

- To what extent is the community philanthropically minded?
- What role does the business community play in supporting philanthropy?
- What is the state of the local economy?
- What local drives are scheduled in the near future?
- How well does the person interviewed know the organization, its programs and services?

D. The answers to the next specific questions are compared to standards (norms) based on results of many winning campaigns.
  1. Does the person interviewed approve of your organization and those running it?
     Norm: 80 percent should approve.
  2. Are your needs considered critical enough to justify a major campaign to support them?
     Norm: 80 percent should think so.
  3. Will the person interviewed make a gift to help meet the needs, and does he or she think others will do the same?
     Norm: 75 percent should say yes.
  4. Will the person interviewed become a member of the campaign organization and influence other potential donors to support the organization?
     Norm: 60 percent should say yes.

5. What is the interviewer's feeling about the degree of interest shown by those interviewed? Will these people really back a campaign?

Norm: 80 percent receptive. (Not totally committed at this point, but receptive.)

This last question requires more than a statistical approach or a yes or no answer. Using a wealth of experience, the professional must interpret responses to the total interest in a proposed campaign and offer opinions that significantly affect whether to go ahead with the drive.

Interpreting Data

Let's look at the results of one study to see why an agency dismissed the notion of running a large capital campaign.

	Study Results	Norm
1. Approval and attitude	78%	80%
2. Justification of a major campaign	76%	80%
3. Will those interviewed contribute?	80%	75%
4. Will they work?	58%	60%

Based on a comparison of the percentages and additional information gathered at the interviews, the last question was answered by the interviewers.

5. Overall attitude toward a campaign?	65%	80%

The figures show the first four results to be close to or above the norms. The most positive comparison, 80 percent of those interviewed saying they would contribute against a norm of 75 percent, appears heartening. Why then did the interviewers conclude that the agency had only a 65 percent chance of conducting a successful drive against a norm of 80 percent? They knew that most of the people who said they would contribute were in no way prepared to make the standard setting gifts needed for the campaign to reach its goal.

Here's a portion of one interview with an unaffiliated community leader selected by the organization:

INTERVIEWER: Mr. Paul, I see that you have some interest in the agency we represent. I'd like to know if you'd personally consider supporting a major campaign if it decides to hold one?

MR. PAUL: I think those folks have made great strides lately, but I wouldn't possibly consider a sizable gift at this stage of the game.

INTERVIEWER: Would your company be willing to make a large contribution?

MR. PAUL: No, not now. But if the agency continues to forge ahead, I would think about some strong support somewhere down the road.

The interviewer left with more than yes and no answers.

- Mr. Paul is pleased with the agency's progress. He sees positive change taking place.

- In the future his company will likely make a contribution.

- Mr. Paul is a prime prospect for cultivation. If the agency continues to prove its worth, a major gift will be imminent.

Because of this and similar interviews, the proposed campaign was postponed.

The Written Feasibility Study

For purposes of illustration, I've prepared a shortened version of a fictitious feasibility study, beginning with a title page:

**A FEASIBILITY STUDY PREPARED FOR
THE ALPHA SYMPHONY ORCHESTRA FUND**

Table of Contents

Background
Explanation and Results of the Interviews
Analysis & Commentary
Conclusions
Recommendations
Appendix: Excerpts from the Interviews

The Background section points out:

- The organization's latest accomplishments.

- Why it needs a campaign. (The case statement.)

- The projects that need funding. (Summary of Needs.)

- Information about the feasibility study, what it consists of, and what it expects to do. (See illustration on p. 61.)

Next, the tabulated answers to the first four specific questions are compared to the norms. (See illustration at top of p. 62.)

The answer to the question, "What is the overall attitude toward a campaign?" is contained in the Commentary. (See illustration at bottom of p. 62.) Assume the interviewer felt that 60 percent of those interviewed had positive feelings. The norm is 80 percent. It is here that the professional's expertise comes fully into play, counseling the organization on how to proceed. (See illustration on p. 63.)

The final section of a feasibility report is the Appendix, which contains excerpts from the interviews. Quotations that have a direct bearing on the study results and recommendations are made without the source being mentioned: "I think the orchestra is attempting to raise too much money," . . . "I believe it's about time that the concert hall was spruced up," . . . Debt retirement should not be part of this project," and so forth.

Background

During the past year the Alpha Symphony Orchestra was involved in several new and impressive programs designed to further the symphony's goal of bringing the finest in classical and pop music to the community. These projects consisted of a special series of concerts for both senior citizens and children, a pilot program by which small ensembles performed in regional hospitals, and September pop concert program held in regional parks.

The wide audience acceptance of these innovations shows the enormous progress that the orchestra has made. However, to serve audiences more usefully, the symphony must address four important challenges:

1. The concert hall is in need of complete renovation.
2. New stage and lighting equipment is required.
3. The bandshell requires new and additional seating.
4. Relief is needed for the operating budget.

To meet these needs, a major fundraising campaign is recommended by the symphony's board of directors.

Renovation of the Concert Hall	$1,000,000
New Equipment for the Concert Hall	250,000
Bandshell Seating	50,000
Operating Budget Debt Retirement	400,000
CAMPAIGN GOAL:	$1,700,000

To learn current opinions about the symphony and its need for new facilities, 50 interviews were conducted with prominent members of the community. These interviews measured the relationship of community leaders to the symphony to show perceived strengths and weaknesses. This study determines if a positive attitude exists for holding a capital fundraising drive by comparing interview results with factors that are always present in successful campaigns. During the interviews, the answers to five important questions were sought that have great bearing on whether a major capital campaign is practical. Findings are as follows:

Results of the Interviews

	Norm	Study Results
1. Attitude toward the Symphony. Committed—30 Approving—12 Disinterested—5 Uninformed—3	84%	80%
2. Justification of a major campaign. Approved—32 Said no—12 Noncommittal—6	64%	80%
3. Willing to contribute? Yes—34 No—16	68%	75%
4. Will they work? Yes—30 No—9 Not sure—11	64%	60%

Analysis and Commentary

1. Attitude toward the Symphony. Most of those interviewed had high regard for the Symphony, considering it an enriching part of the community's cultural life.

Although all the orchestra's programs were looked upon favorably, the concerts for children were most highly praised.

Those interviewed were extremely pleased with the conductor, the quality of the players, and the symphony's management. They looked forward to the forthcoming season.

2. Justification of a Major Campaign. The majority viewpoint was that the symphony was not in an excellent position to launch a major campaign.

There were many reservations about $1.7 million being an attainable goal.

Many objections to seeking capital campaign funds for debt retirement exist.

A majority questioned whether board members could provide the financial leadership that a campaign of this size warrants.

(Continued)

3. Will they contribute? The 80 percent affirmative response suggests a positive endorsement of the symphony. Still, most of those responding positively did not feel that the major gifts necessary for a campaign of this size could be obtained at this time.

4. Will they work for the campaign and influence others? The majority of those interviewed were pleased to be involved or to become involved with a successful organization. They appeared willing to ask friends and colleagues to support a capital campaign when conditions were more favorable.

Recommendations

1. Until the symphony is assured of additional major gift donors, delay starting up a capital fund drive. Initiate a second feasibility study at an appropriate time.

2. Institute a broader cultivation program for major gift prospects. For instance, a series of buffet dinners to be held in various board member's homes where potential large gift contributors can meet with the symphony conductor, manager, and key players.

3. Eliminate one-half of the debt retirement program from the Summary of Needs and make it a part of the annual appeal for the next four years—$50,000 per year.

4. Schedule a capital campaign when there is the least amount of competition from like appeals.

Conclusions

After analyzing the results of 50 interviews with prominent community leaders, it was concluded:

The Alpha Symphony Orchestra is performing a needed cultural service for the community and, through its outreach programs, for many people within the region.

Most of the community's leadership see the orchestra as an important and worthwhile organization with an outstanding record of achievement and promising future.

There is genuine commitment by the orchestra's Board of Trustees to support the development of new ideas and programs that will continue to lead the organization forward.

Although those interviewed see the Board of Trustees as highly supportive, many people doubt that enough members will make major gifts to a capital campaign.

Many individual constituents, also those representing the corporate community, are especially concerned that two other major capital projects are now in progress elsewhere in the area. They believe that scheduling a third drive at this time is inappropriate.

There is doubt that enough major gift contributors exist at this point to mount a profitable funding effort.

Tremendous controversy exists concerning the inclusion of a debt retirement program within the framework of a capital campaign.

Summing Up

No matter how much you *think* you're ready to start up a first-time annual drive or any capital campaign, invest in a professionally conducted feasibility study.

A. Tell the interviewers about your organization's weak points along with its successes. Don't bend the truth, or you'll throw off their perspective.

B. Develop a balanced list of individuals, business leaders, and, if relevant, local foundation trustees to be interviewed. Make sure they are influential and affluent people who have the potential to support the major gift's portion of your drive as contributors, solicitors, and identifiers of other large gift prospects.

C. There are several general questions that interviewers want answered. (See page 58.) The more they learn about local fundraising conditions and the total reaction to your organization, the more intelligently they are able to draw helpful conclusions.

D. As part of each interview, five specific questions must be answered. Four of these answers are compared to norms developed after analyzing years of goal-reaching drives.

The last question requires that interviewers interpret responses to the overall interest in your proposed campaign and make a judgment that affects whether you begin a drive.

When significant negative gaps exist between interview results and the norms, it would be foolhardy to go ahead with a drive. However, rather than scrap the project, eliminate the weaknesses that the people interviewed perceive your organization to have. That may take a short time or an extended period. When you think you're ready to try again, have a second feasibility study conducted and compare results.

If your organization is advised to delay a campaign, here is something to remember that may ease the pain: *More than one-half of the organizations who hold first-time feasibility studies led by professional consultants are told to defer their campaigns.* These groups wait anywhere from six months to five years to make fundraising conditions more conducive to running successful drives. So, there is nothing to be ashamed of if your study results don't pan out and you forego a drive until later. If you want to be ashamed, run a campaign that turns out to be a failure because you thought you could hack it although the people whose support you most needed had their thumbs turned down.

What if your feasibility study figures are close to the norm, say a few percentage points off? Well, you might consider lowering the goal if you think that will cure the problem. If that's not an answer, again, the best solution is to do some collective thinking about how to make conditions more favorable.

E. When all the interview data is collected, statistics noted, and results analyzed, a formal report is submitted to your governing body, consisting of six sections.

1. Background.

- Your latest accomplishments
- Why you must have a campaign

- The projects for which you are raising the money (the Summary of Needs)
- What the feasibility study consists of, what you expect it to do for you, who ran it

2. Statistical Results of the Interviews—for example:

	Norm	Study Results
1. **Attitude toward a Campaign—**	84%	80%

     Committed—30
     Approving—12
     Disinterested—5
     Uninformed—3

3. Analysis and Commentary—Using the answers to the first four questions, the interviewers highlight opinions that many people expressed. "The majority of those interviewed, while agreeing that a campaign is feasible, thought that the drive must not begin until the board is strengthened," for instance.
4. Conclusions—This is an interpretive answer to question 5: What is the interviewer's feeling about the total degree of interest by those who were interviewed in supporting a proposed campaign?
5. Recommendations—Should you or should you not hold your drive? What should you do if the drive is deferred? It would be uncommon for a governing board not to follow these recommendations, so they had better be the right ones.
6. Appendix: Excerpts from the Interviews—A sampling of representative quotations from the interviews that illustrate why interviewers drew their conclusions. The examples point out opinions about your organization that are valuable for immediate and long-range planning.

Establishing Dollar Goals

You are now in a position to know whether the total of your initial Summary of Needs is a realistic campaign goal because:

- Your preliminary table of gift requirements gave you an idea of the number and size of gifts you'll need.
- Prospects are evaluated. You know if potential contributors can make the major and other large gifts your table suggests.
- You have the results of your feasibility study.
- You know your past fundraising achievements.
- You are aware of the economic climate of your community.

There is another factor to consider, not as decipherable as the others, but equally as relevant. We live in a totally achievement-oriented society. People do everything possible to reach greater and greater goals, and they respect others who do the same. If you want leadership and other campaign workers to be outstanding contributors and persuasive solicitors, give them a goal for which they have to reach. Just make certain your reach doesn't exceed your grasp.

Let's say an organization gets clearance to hold a capital campaign for a new building costing $2 million. Looking at its prospect evaluations and feasibility study, the group's leadership estimates $1.95 million can be raised. They set the goal at $2 million anyway because the leadership takes raising the extra $50,000 as a great challenge. Each of them contributes a little more and solicits more forcefully than ever—they are determined to bring in all the money needed.

Here's the way the competitor and his volunteers in the round-the-world sailboat race mentioned earlier reached agreement on a final goal. The original summary of needs totaled $430,000. Following the proper procedures, this sailor enlisted 25 people from across the country who became a special campaign committee called a Board of Advisors. These men and women identified and evaluated around 250 potential big gift prospects. Results of the evaluations and feasibility study showed that most of the people interviewed were not going to give at the levels shown in the preliminary table of gift requirements. Indications were that about $190,000 could be raised. That caused a great deal of disappointment, but not defeat. An alternative plan made use of an existing vessel instead of building a new one. The bottom line cost of putting this new plan into effect was $215,000. That's where the goal was set. "We're pushing too hard," many advisors said. "We'll be lucky to get $190,000," they told the resolute competitor. "No," said the sailor. "We can raise the full amount and we will." He not only got himself fired up, but his advisors also, and the reduced goal was attained.

So base your goals on the Summary of Needs, the gifts you need, the kinds of leadership and prospects you have, the results of feasibility studies, and *that incalculable striving for success that motivates people to be winners.*

Once a goal is decided upon, the preliminary table of gift requirements can be revised to make it more realistic.

Preparing a Final Table of Gift Expectations

Believing that any gift table is scientifically based is like assuming that a Las Vegas odds-maker is a scientist. There are just too many variables in fundraising to design a perfectly accurate table for any given campaign. However, based on giving patterns of winning drives, these tables are necessary for:

1. Creating gift guidelines
2. Challenging solicitors to get impressive contributions

3. Projecting the intermediate and small gifts needed to complete a drive

4. Providing campaign progress reports by comparing projected gifts to actual results

Don't get so technically immersed in designing a table that you forget its reasons for being. Let's take another look at the preliminary gift table for a $500,000 campaign.

Number of Gifts	In the Range of	% Each Gift	Gifts Totaling	% of Goal
1	$50,000	10.00	$50,000	10
2	25,000	5.00	50,000	10
4	12,500	2.50	50,000	10
8	6,250	1.25	50,000	10
10	5,000	1.00	50,000	10
20	2,500	0.50	50,000	10
25	2,000	0.40	50,000	10
30	1,500	0.30	45,000	09
55	1,000	0.20	55,000	11
155 gifts totaling 90% of goal			$450,000	
Other Gifts of		0.10		
	100	0.12		
and below totaling			$50,000	(10)
			$500,000	(100)

Adjusting the Preliminary Table

The above table follows the "% of Each Gift" formula appearing in columns 1, 3, and 5. Recall that this formula was supplied as an introduction to gift tables. To apply it to an actual campaign situation, it must be adapted because the formulas are too exacting for practical usage. Here's why. Notice that following the first three gift ranges, the numerical differences between dollar categories become small: $6250 to $5000; $2500 to $2000 to $1500, and so on. As you continue structuring your campaign, you'll want to divide it into groups of potential donors whose gift giving expectations vary by more than $1500 or $500. So, to be useful, the first of two adjustments to the preliminary table are to create broader giving ranges and revise the percentage totals for these new ranges. We'll continue to use the half-million dollar drive as an example as shown at the top of p. 68.

This completes the first adjustment to the preliminary table. By expanding the gift ranges we've ended up with a slightly more conservative guideline by projecting larger mid-range gifts that total 80 instead of 90 percent of the goal. Look at the adjusted table on its own at the bottom of p. 68.

Preliminary Table			Adjusted Table		
Number of Gifts	In the Range of & % of Goal	Gifts Totaling	Number of Gifts	In the Range of & % of Goal	Gifts Totaling
1	$50,000 (10)	$50,000	1	$50,000+ (10)	$50,000
2	$25,000 (10)	$50,000	2	$25,000–49,999 (10)	$50,000
4	$12,500 (10)	$50,000	4	$12,500–24,999 (10)	$50,000
8	$ 6,250 (10)	$50,000			
10	$ 5,000 (10)	$50,000			
	now becomes . . .		20	$ 5,000–12,499 (20)	$100,000
20	$ 2,500 (10)	$50,000			
25	$ 2,000 (10)	$50,000			
30	$ 1,500 (10)	$45,000			
55	$ 1,000 (11)	$55,000			
	now becomes . . .		150	$ 1,000–4,999 (30)	$150,000
155 gifts totaling 90% of goal, $450,000			177 gifts totaling 80% of goal, $400,000		
Other Gifts in the Range of $500 $100 and below $100		$50,000 (10%)	Other Gifts in the Range of $500 $100 and below $100		$100,000 (20%)
		$500,000 (100%)			$500,000 (100%)

Gift Expectations for a Typical $500,000 Drive			
Number of Gifts	In the Range of	% of Goal	Totaling
1	$50,000+	10	$50,000
2	$25,000	10	$50,000
4	$12,500	10	$50,000
20	$5,000	20	$100,000
150	$1,000	30	$150,000
177 gifts totaling 80% of goal			$400,000
Other gifts of $500 $100 and below $100 totaling		20	$100,000
		100%	$500,000

To find gift ranges and gift totals for your goals, use the following worksheet.

Worksheet for Determining Gifts Expectations				
Number of Gifts	% Each Gift	Gifts in the Range of	% of Goal	Gifts Totaling
1	10.00	($)	10	($)
2	5.00	($)	10	($)
4	2.50	($)	10	($)
20	1.00	($)	20	($)
150	0.20	($)	30	($)
170			80	
Other gifts at 0.10		($)	( )	($)
0.02		($)	( )	($)
and below 0.02		($)	( )	($)
			20	
			100	($)

To Complete the Worksheet

1. Use the same number of gifts as those above.

2. In row 1, place 10 percent of the goal contribution in the "Gifts in the Range of" and "Gifts Totaling" columns.

3. Find additional gift range figures by multiplying the indicated "% Each Gift" by the goal. For example, 5 percent of $500,000 equals $25,000. Place that figure within the "Gifts In The Range of" column.

4. Find the "Gifts Totaling" number for each giving range by multiplying the "Gifts in the Range of" figure you determined by the indicated number of gifts, e.g., 2 × $25,000 = $50,000.

Suppose you plan to hold a $2 million drive. You want to know what contributions to strive for and the total of these donations for each giving range. The worksheet would appear as shown at the top of p. 70.

As you work out figures for various size drives, you may arrive at unlikely "Gifts in the Range of" figures. These may be altered to fit a more common pattern. For example, if you were holding a $1,700,000 appeal:

Gift range		Dollar amount	Gifts totaling
A.	5.00% begins at	$85,000	$170,000
B.	2.50% begins at	$42,500	$170,000
C.	1.00% begins at	$17,000	$340,000
D.	0.20% begins at	$3,400	$510,000

Worksheet for a $2,000,000 Campaign				
Number of Gifts	% Each Gift	Gifts in the Range of	% of Goal	Gifts Totaling
1	10.00	$200,000	10	$200,000
2	5.00	$100,000	10	$200,000
4	2.50	$50,000	10	$200,000
20	1.00	$20,000	20	$400,000
150	0.20	$4,000	30	$600,000
177			80	$1,600,000
Other Gifts at				
	0.10	$ 2,000	( )	($)
	0.02	$ 400	( )	($)
and below 0.02		($)	( )	($)
			20	$400,000
			100	$2,000,000

Since gift tables are guidelines, for clarity there is nothing to prevent you from setting up your gift ranges this way:

Number of gifts		Gifts in the range of	Gifts totaling
A.	2	$50,000–$100,000	$170,000
B.	4	$25,000–$49,999	$170,000
C.	20	$10,000–$24,999	$340,000
D.	150	$2,500–$9,999	$510,000

Those ranges are more plausible. The important thing is to *keep the figures in the "Gifts Totaling" column the same as when you worked out the "% of Each Gift" in the adjusted formula.*

Also, feel free to amend the gift ranges, making them appropriate to your drive. For instance, if you were uncomfortable with the last range in the above example, the one that leaps from $2,500 to $9,999, you could adapt it to something more suitable. Split the 150 gifts and gift totals into two ranges, like this:

Number of gifts	Gifts in the range of	Gifts totaling
70	$5,000–$10,000	$255,000
80	$2,500–$4,999	$255,000
150		$510,000

The Final Step

The next adjustments give you a Final Table of Gift Expectations. Then, as far as numbers of gifts, percentage of goal, and gift totals go, you're on your own because the figures strictly relate to your organization. Factor in:

1. The number of members or constituents you have (this allows you to enter the figures in the last three giving ranges)
2. Any major or mid-range gifts you know are forthcoming
3. Your new campaign goal, if it was adjusted
4. The results of former campaigns
5. The results of evaluations

Here's your final gift expectations worksheet:

		Final Table of Gift Expectations Worksheet			
Number of Gifts	% Each Gift	Gifts in the Range of	% of Goal	Gifts Totaling	
( )	10.00	($)	( )	($)	
( )	5.00	($)	( )	($)	
( )	2.50	($)	( )	($)	
( )	1.00	($)	( )	($)	
( )	0.20	($)	( )	($)	
( )			( )	($)	
( )	0.10	($)	( )	($)	
( )	0.02	($)	( )	($)	
( )	and below				
	0.02	($)	( )	($)	
( )			100%	($)	

You may recall that earlier I told you of a man who thought the formula in the "Preliminary Table of Gift Expectations" was inappropriate because it didn't fit the prospects in his organization. After using his evaluations and other data, the man tailored his final table to suit the potential of his organization: a $500,000 campaign with a membership of 1800 people. His figures appear in brackets in the following illustration so you can compare them to the example.

Prepare gift tables for annual as well as capital drives. Once you adjust the table, don't revise it during the campaign if the contributions you receive don't match expectations. By comparing the results of your drive with the gift table, you can evaluate fundraising strengths and weaknesses on all giving levels.

Comparison of Expectations for Two $500,000 Campaigns				
Number of Gifts	% Each Gift	In the Range of	% of Goal	Gifts Totaling
1 [0]	10.00	$50K	10 [0]	$ 50K [$ 00K]
2 [3]	5.00	$25K	10 [15]	$ 50K [$ 75K]
4 [6]	2.50	$12.5K	10 [15]	$ 50K [$ 75K]
20 [16]	1.00	$5K	20 [16]	$100K [$ 80K]
150 [160]	0.20	$1K	30 [32]	$150K [$160K]
177 [185]			80 [78]	$400K [$390K]
( ) [140]	0.10	[$500]	( ) [14]	( ) [$ 70K]
( ) [200]	0.02	[$100]	( ) [04]	( ) [$ 20K]
( ) [400]	below 0.02	[$100]	( ) [04]	( ) [$ 20K]
			20 [20]	$100K [$110K]
( ) [925]			100[100]	$500K [$500K]

One Last Crucial Test Before You Go On

For a final check on the accuracy of your evaluations and feasibility study, solicit a handful of key supporters before starting the active campaign. This phase is called "Test Solicitations," conducted for several of the largest gifts in a drive, and requiring the most experienced solicitors available. Results of these tests should furnish a minimum of 25 percent of total campaign income.

This is no time to go after long shots. Test prospects must be the best friends you have, those with the most loyalty and the highest dollar potential. Test solicitations *set the standard of contributions for an entire campaign because donors make gifts in direct relation to those of their leadership and peers.*

Let's imagine that the Clark family, staunch supporters of the Alpha Symphony Orchestra, are asked to contribute $400,000 to the symphony's campaign during the test solicitation phase. They decide upon a gift of $250,000.

The Greens are also likely prospects. They are asked to give $300,000, but when they find out that the Clarks only gave $250,000, the Greens make a gift of $200,000.

The Baker family, also strong orchestra supporters, are not as affluent as the Clarks and Greens, therefore not a part of the test solicitation phase. But, during the campaign, it's hoped that the Bakers will donate $50,000. When approached Mrs. Baker says, "I heard that the Clarks gave $300,000, and the Greens, $200,000. They both have much more capability to give than we do. We will make a gift of $25,000."

Simplistic? Sure. However, it shows that people are highly sensitive to the amount of money their organization leaders, friends, and neighbors donate to a campaign. If test results don't live up to expectations, consider dropping the goal or delaying the drive.

Begin test solicitations by attempting to get the 10 percent gift indicated in your "Final Table of Gift Expectations," and work down from there. In a half-million dollar drive, for example, you would try to obtain:

1 gift of $50,000 totaling	$50,000
2 gifts of $25,000 totaling	$50,000
4 gifts of $12,500 totaling	$50,000
7 gifts totaling	$150,000 (35 percent of the goal)

Compare that with the rule of thumb that says a minimum of 25 percent of the goal should be gotten during the test solicitation period, and you'd be off to the right start.

Until people have made their own gifts, they are in no position to solicit others. A possible exception is the chief executive. However, nowadays more and more professional leaders frequently make personal donations although the amounts are not likely to be on a par with major givers. In any case, because of their positions, they are eligible members of test solicitation teams. Many times it is the professional leader of an organization who solicits the first contribution from a prospect and enlists that person as a solicitor.

Sometimes this phase seems interminable, but stick to the plan. It's far better to change a timetable than to ruin a campaign.

Some organizations skip the feasibility study, base the rationale for holding a drive on test solicitations, and end up with a winning campaign. If you're going to take that risk, be positive that everyone you imagine to be a major giver is one. Earlier, I mentioned the church group that didn't want to pay for a feasibility study. The top campaign leaders solicited each other and were successful in getting very large donations. However, it never occurred to them that the remaining potential big givers had only minor interest in the project—the drive never came close to reaching its goal.

3

Broadening the Base

This chapter and the remainder of the book concentrate on strategies, approaches, procedures, and formats used in mounting charitable appeals with broad donor bases. These drives are geared toward contributors with every sort of gift-giving capability. Campaigns of this sort naturally require more complex structures than those seeking gifts from limited donor categories. Look at this comparison:

Small Private Medical Institute	Private Community Hospital
Narrow constituent base.	Broad constituent base.
Goal is to get major gifts from individuals, corporations, and foundations.	Goal is to get major, mid-range, and small gifts from individuals, corporations, and foundations.
Campaign top leadership in hands of general chair, board or campaign committee, chief executive, and professional staff.	Same.
Top leadership responsible for identifying, cultivating, and soliciting major gift prospects, and submitting grants to foundations.	Top leadership responsible for identifying, cultivating, and soliciting major gift prospects. They also must recruit additional chairs to head other segments of the drive who will in turn enlist teams of workers responsible for soliciting mid-range and small gift prospects from all sources. One of these committees to be responsible for submitting grants to foundations.
Needs marketing program to attract large givers.	Needs marketing program to reach all segments of the community.
Needs basic fundraising guidelines.	Needs total action plan.
Uses person-to-person or group solicitation techniques	Uses person-to-person, group, phonathon, and mail solicitation techniques.
Needs limited worker training program.	Needs worker training programs on many levels.

The methods used in broad-based annual and capital campaigns can easily be scaled down to meet the requirements of smaller operations.

As an organization grows, it must expand its campaign structure to accept additional types of prospects. Let's imagine that the small medical institute, begun in relative obscurity, eventually develops a large following. It plans a capital campaign to enlarge facilities. The institute would then orchestrate its campaign using the same construction as the private community hospital.

When a campaign's top leaders meet for the first time, here is what needs to be pondered and discussed:

1. The campaign budget

2. How to organize potential donors so they can be solicited on a peer-to-peer basis

3. A table of organization

4. Enlisting volunteers to chair prospect groups other than large gifts

5. How many workers will be needed

6. Record keeping procedures

7. Campaign publications and other materials

8. A timetable

9. How to market the drive

10. An action plan

Let's begin by considering what campaign expenses you might have.

Preparing a Campaign Budget

"We've got more than enough money to spend on this appeal," the campaign chair told me.

"Fantastic," I responded. "But are there no limitations? Will the board approve a large budget?"

"Absolutely no limitations," the leader said. "We can spend all the money that's necessary."

It was too good to be real. I awoke in an airplane on my way to meet with the chairman I dreamed about.

Money spent on fundraising expenses is carefully scrutinized. Produce a campaign brochure that's too slick, and you'll hear about it from your constituency. Hold too lavish a solicitation dinner and some supporters will complain of overspending. I recently received a solicitation letter from an organization typically asking that I use my stamp to save it money when I returned the request envelope. Keeping expenses as low as possible is imperative, but be prepared to fund essential items that make campaigns run efficiently, such as:

- Staff salaries

- Fundraising materials—everything from campaign brochures to solicitation letters

- Office and equipment costs such as postage, supplies, telephone, typewriters, and photocopiers
- Special events—a dinner for example
- Printing costs
- Consultant's fees

This is what influences expenditures:

1. The amount of money to be raised.
2. The number of prospects you have. It's less expensive to service 2000 people than 20,000. You need fewer staff, supplies, special events, and so forth.
3. What you require for campaign expenses for such items as prospect cultivation, solicitations, consulting, and marketing.
4. Where your prospects live. If they are scattered about the country, more must be paid for telephone, postage, and perhaps special visits.
5. The length of your drive. A capital appeal usually takes far longer to complete than an annual drive.
6. Your present level of support. If you have a constant group of dedicated supporters, they will not need an abundance of materials and special events to excite them. One country club's campaigners did their fundraising during lunch hours between rounds of golf and tennis—expenses were minimal.

The table on page 77 lists typical budget items.

How to Classify Prospects

Successful fundraising practices dictate that an organization begins by soliciting its largest gifts first and concludes by asking for small contributions. To do this you need a way of organizing prospects so they are grouped and solicited in an efficient manner. There are three common ways in which to do this:

1. *By categories.* Arrange prospects by commonality such as parents, alumni, corporations, retailers. The basis of this thinking is that people who share the same profession or have like interests can motivate each other to be generous. After organizing categories, solicit the highest evaluated prospects in each group first, then work down to the lowest rated.
2. *By divisions.* Assign prospects to groups called divisions, based on giving potential. This practice is typically used by membership organizations. A group has 2000 members. Each is evaluated. The highest-rated group of potential contributors is placed in one division, the next highest group in a second division, and so on.
3. *By categories and divisions.* A combination of the first two classifications.

Typical Campaign Budget Items

Personnel
Administration Staff Salaries & Benefits $ _____
Clerical/Support Staff Salaries & Benefits   _____
Professional Fundraising Consultant Fee   _____
Travel & Expenses for Consultant   _____
Other Personnel Expenses/Fees   _____
Total Personnel Expenses $ _____

Office & Administration $ _____
Office Rental   _____
Office Equipment Purchase/Lease   _____
Telephone   _____
Postage   _____
Stationery/Supplies/Materials   _____
Other Office & Administrative Expenses   _____
Total Office & Administrative Expenses $ _____

Promotion & Solicitation $ _____
Campaign Brochures   _____
Worker Materials   _____
Planning & Organizational Meetings   _____
Kick-off Event   _____
Audiovisual Presentations   _____
Report Meetings   _____
Donor Recognition   _____
Mailings, Reports, & Newsletters   _____
Charts/Photography/Miscellaneous Printing _____
Cultivation   _____
Total Promotion & Solicitation Expense $ _____
              Total Budget $ _____

Grouping prospects by common categories is self-explanatory. How to group prospects into divisions takes some explanation, and then the last option easily falls into place.

To create divisions, you will work with an assortment of men and women whose likeness is they can make contributions within the same giving range. We know that only a handful of prospects donate major gifts, and most prospects make small gifts. Between these high and low givers is a another set of potential donors. All this can be graphically illustrated as a pyramid.

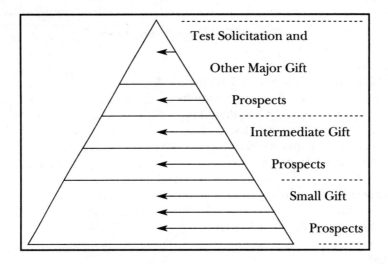

The illustration shows space for seven divisions as indicated by the arrows. How many divisions you choose to set up depends upon the number of prospects and the gift ranges decided upon in your "Final Table of Gift Expectations."

To attach gift ranges to each division, transfer the figures from your final table worksheet to the pyramid. Using our half-million dollar campaign illustration, the figures for that drive are shown below.

Gift Expectations for a Typical $500,000 Drive			
Number of Gifts	In the Range of	% of Goal	Totaling
1	$50,000+	10	$50,000
2	$25,000	10	$50,000
4	$12,500	10	$50,000
20	$5,000	20	$100,000
150	$1,000	30	$150,000
177 gifts totaling 80% of goal			$400,000
Other gifts of $500 $100 and below $100 totaling		20	$100,000
		100%	$500,000

Now let's fit these giving ranges into the pyramid:

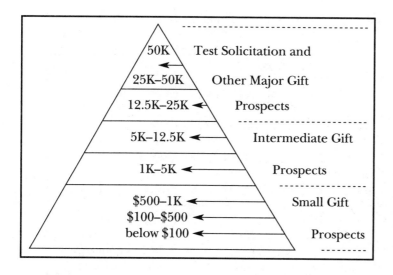

In this illustration, major gifts become contributions of $12,500 and upward; intermediate gifts from $1000 to $12,499; small gifts from pennies to $999. Missing is the number of prospects in each division. That shouldn't be a problem with major or intermediate gift prospects since they have been evaluated.

Depending on the number of small gift prospects and the way you solicit them, evaluations may be out of the question. For instance, if you run a community door-to-door campaign, you may not know your prospects until a worker visits them. Likewise, if you have members who have never given, placing these small givers in divisions is sheer guesswork.

I have set up a sample membership of 1500 people who were evaluated as follows:

Division	Range	Number of Evaluated Prospects
Test Solicitation & Other Major Gift Prospects	$50,000+	6
	$25,000–$49,999	15
	$12,500–$24,999	24
Intermediate Gift Prospects	$5,000–$12,499	40
	$1,000–$4,999	210
Small	$500–$999	250
Gift	$100–$500	320
Prospects	below $100	635
		1,500

Here is the pyramid with the evaluated prospects added:

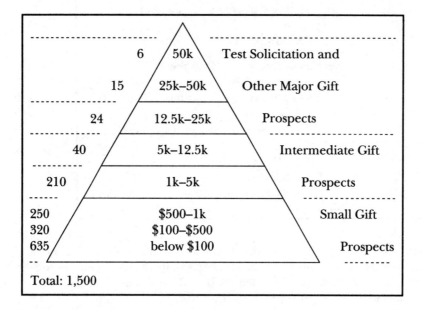

The final step is to name each division. Below, I have chosen generic names. Use these or, preferably, devise titles that suit your organization's projects.

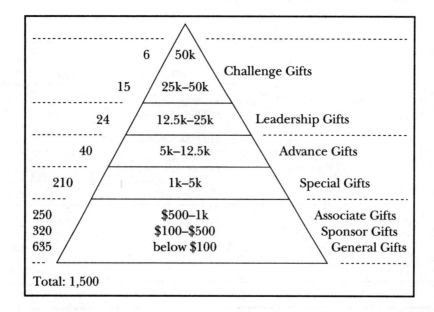

Based on evaluations and the "Final Table of Gift Expectations," 1500 sample prospects were placed into seven divisions and each group given a title.

You don't have to choose between categories and divisions under one campaign banner. It is often advantageous to combine both. Colleges and universities, for instance, usually categorize prospects as alumni, parents, corporations, and foundations. Added to those is a division called "Friends," made up of major, large, and small gift supporters who do not fall into categories.

Keep in mind that fundraisers put people of the same profession together because they know that peer pressure can spur generous donations. Mostly it does, but I have mixed emotions about assigning doctors, dentists, lawyers, and accountants into separate categories. Certainly not to indict all these people, but many professionals are more generous with lip service than with contributions. I've often observed their highly supportive colleagues, dedicated chairpeople and committee members become totally frustrated and outraged by the irrational excuses many of their fellow professionals give for not living up to their capability as donors. These same people, however, take great delight in doling out advice on what everyone else in the organization should contribute. Put one of these underachievers on your evaluation committee and you'll see what I mean. You may be better off placing doctors, dentists, attorneys, and accountants in divisions according to their evaluations. Let them relate to successful people from other walks of life. It might get rid of the self-protection which professional in-breeding can foster.

Creating a Table
of Organization

Here's why you need a Table of Organization (T.O.):

- To furnish leadership with a complete picture of the campaign chain of command
- To keep a check on worker recruitment programs
- As a worker training tool to show campaigners how their category or division fits into the total campaign picture

The general campaign chair, with the aid of the board or campaign committee, is responsible for selecting and enlisting category or division leaders. They, in turn, recruit the number of workers necessary to solicit their prospects. If a category or division has a great many potential donors, recruit cochairs to keep a single volunteer from becoming overburdened.

Following is a typical educational institution table of organization for a campaign that classifies prospects by category except for the "Friends" group which is a division.

General Chair(s)				
Campaign Committee	Marketing Chair(s) & Committee			
Campaign Cabinet				
Chair(s) Friends	Chair(s) Alumni	Chair(s) Corporations	Chair(s) Foundations	Chair(s) Parents
Workers	Workers	Workers	Workers	Workers

Next is a T.O. for an organizational campaign with prospects grouped by division.

General Chair						
Campaign Committee	Marketing Chair(s) & Committee					
Campaign Cabinet						
Chair(s) Challenge Division	Chair(s) Leadership Division	Chair(s) Advance Division	Chair(s) Special Division	Chair(s) Associate Division	Chair(s) Sponsor Division	Chair(s) General Division
Workers	Workers	Workers	Workers	Workers	Workers	Workers

Building Your Workforce

All leadership positions require the same types of individuals:

- People totally committed to your project
- Experienced fundraisers
- People who will make a gift at the top of the range to which they are assigned
- Those who can enlist others to work for them

Don't pressure people to chair your categories or divisions. I recall telephoning a newly enlisted division leader to welcome him as a member of the campaign team. I no sooner told him who I was than he became upset.

"How did I ever get myself into this," he said. "I told Bill that I didn't want to chair a division, and he said I owe him one. Let me tell you, if you can do anything for this campaign, you'll be a miracle worker. The whole project isn't that important, and I don't intend to make much of a contribution to it."

So much for Bill's enlistment technique!

When you recruit category and division chairs, make them aware that:

1. They will be part of a team effort. Nobody wants to feel he or she is only one of a few volunteers.

2. They will not be asked to do more than can be comfortably handled.

3. They will have effective training and follow-up programs available both to them and the solicitors they recruit.

Then stick to those promises.

How Many Campaigners Will You Need?

The number of workers to be recruited depends on the potential donors you have in each category or division and the way they are to be solicited. Unless extreme circumstances prevail, major and intermediate gift prospects must be asked for their gifts personally. If solicited as a group at a function, obviously you won't need a team of campaigners. As well, it's preferable to see remaining prospects in person, but that's not often practical with small gift divisions or categories because of large numbers and few workers. However, remember that:

■ A personal visit is the most forcible way to solicit.

■ Many unevaluated prospects can be upgraded into higher gift ranges. The best way to get a feeling for their potential is to spend time with them.

Attempt to assign no more than five or six prospects to each campaigner for major and intermediate gift solicitations. Getting big gifts takes time and special effort. Overloading a campaigner with prospects is a sure way to get substandard contributions.

Again, using our earlier half-million dollar campaign pyramid, let's do a worker coverage plan for the sample 1500 prospects:

Division	Gift Range	Number of Prospects	Workers Needed
Challenge	$50K+	6	2
	$25K–$50K	15	3
Leadership	$12.5K–$25K	24	5
Advance	$5K–$12.5K	40	8
Special	$1K–$4.99K	210	42
	SUBTOTAL:	295	60

About 80 to 90 percent of the campaign's income relies on comparatively few members soliciting a small number of prospects. Following the same procedure of assigning five prospects per worker, here's the remainder of the coverage plan for small gifts:

Division	Gift Range	Number of Prospects	Workers Needed
Associate	$500–$999	250	50
Sponsor	$100–$499	320	64
General	Below $100	635	127
	TOTAL:	1500	301

Enlisting 20 percent of the members to see small-gift prospects could easily be an impossibility. But understand that soliciting these donations is not as critical or complex as asking big-gift prospects for contributions. If necessary, you can safely assign more than five prospects to each small gift worker. Assigning and soliciting lower-giving-level prospects is explored in Part 3.

Let's look at the divisions in the earlier table of organization, assume we have recruited the volunteers needed, and add the worker and prospect figures.

			General Chair			
			Campaign Committee			
			Campaign Cabinet			
Chair(s) Challenge Division	Chair(s) Leadership Division	Chair(s) Advance Division	Chair(s) Special Division	Chair(s) Associate Division	Chair(s) Sponsor Division	Chair(s) General Division
4 Workers	5 Workers	8 Workers	42 Workers	50 Workers	64 Workers	127 Workers
Prospects						
6 + 15	24	40	210	250	320	635

Forms and Printed Material to Get You Started

Once prospects are classified and workers enlisted, they must be kept track of in different ways throughout the campaign. Recording data, completing reports, making accurate projections, and processing gifts used to be a ponderous, labor-intensive process. Now your organization can benefit from sophisticated computer-driven, fundraising management systems to simplify such things as record keeping, accounting, prospect tracking, reporting, and forecasting, all with incredible speed and efficiency. As you learn how small-gift canvassing programs, phonathons, and direct-mail appeals are run, you will especially appreciate what this software can do to ease staff and volunteer time. Obviously, the more the systems accomplish, the more costly they are to purchase, from hundreds to many thousands of dollars. Each year, *Fund Raising Management* magazine lists available software, and includes a description of each program, company background, policies, and prices. The publication's address appears in Recommended Reading.

To give some idea of the features that a quality, powerful, fundraising management program offers PC and compatible users, reproduced below is the Main Menu screen from "The Raiser's Edge," by Blackbaud MicroSystems, Inc.:

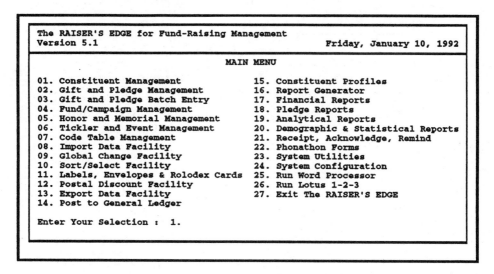

```
The RAISER'S EDGE for Fund-Raising Management
Version 5.1                                    Friday, January 10, 1992

                             MAIN MENU
   01. Constituent Management        15. Constituent Profiles
   02. Gift and Pledge Management     16. Report Generator
   03. Gift and Pledge Batch Entry    17. Financial Reports
   04. Fund/Campaign Management       18. Pledge Reports
   05. Honor and Memorial Management  19. Analytical Reports
   06. Tickler and Event Management   20. Demographic & Statistical Reports
   07. Code Table Management          21. Receipt, Acknowledge, Remind
   08. Import Data Facility           22. Phonathon Forms
   09. Global Change Facility         23. System Utilities
   10. Sort/Select Facility           24. System Configuration
   11. Labels, Envelopes & Rolodex Cards  25. Run Word Processor
   12. Postal Discount Facility       26. Run Lotus 1-2-3
   13. Export Data Facility           27. Exit The RAISER'S EDGE
   14. Post to General Ledger

   Enter Your Selection :  1.
```

Macintosh users can take advantage of such programs as Commtact/ELS and Commtact, the big brother of the entry-level system (ELS). You'll find ads for this and additional software in *Fund Raising Management*.

Before you purchase a program check out the following:

- Does the company have a proven track record? There are no guarantees, but you don't want to deal with a manufacturer who will be out of business next year.

- Will the supplier train you in operating its system?

- Does the manufacturer provide technical support if you get in a jam? Make certain it does.

- Does the vendor upgrade the program from time to time?

- Is the program truly user-friendly or will you require a special operator to enter data and otherwise manipulate the software?

- Will the software suit future plans?

- Can you mix and match existing software? The fundraising management program should interface with your present word processing, graphics, spreadsheet, and perhaps desktop publishing software.

- Will the program allow you to sort outgoing mail by carrier route and ZIP+4 codes? If you plan to do many mailings to large numbers of prospects this is an option you should have.

Don't be concerned about a manufacturer's far-off location. As good as on-site help is a modem and communications program that allows technical representatives to analyze software and user problems from any distance via telephone lines.

If you are not yet ready to go electronic, the forms below are typical of those you'll need, beginning with a data file for each prospect.

Prospect File Form

LAST NAME: CATEGORY/DIVISION:
FIRST NAME (MR.):   EVALUATION:
FIRST NAME (MS.):   GIFT AMOUNT:
ADDRESS: PLEDGE CARD SIGNED
(Y/N):
CITY/STATE: TERMS:
ZIP CODE: WORKER'S NAME:
HOME PHONE: NAMED FACILITY:
BUS. PHONE (MR.):   *:
BUS. PHONE (MS.):   *:
MEMBER: *:
TYPE OF   DATE ENTERED:
MEMBERSHIP:

ANNUAL GIVING RECORD (10 YRS.)   COMMENTS

82-	87-	
83-	88-	
84-	89-	
85-	90-	
86-	91-	

*Spares for additional information.

"Terms" means the way in which a prospect desires to pay a capital campaign pledge over several years. "Named facility" refers to a restricted gift that allows donors to have their names associated with either the whole or an explicit part of a new building—The Samuel Jones Center for Religious Studies, or the Board Room underwritten by Marion May, for instance.

Prospect Listing by Category or Division

Category or Division: _____

Name	Address	Phone	Evaluation	Assigned to	Gift	Named Facility

Worker Assignment Sheet

Worker's Name:_____   Chair:_____

Category or Division:_____   Phone:_____

Phone:_____

Name	Address	Phone	Evaluation	Gift	Named Facility	Remarks

The original goes to the worker. Retain one copy for the worker's category or division chair, keep another in the campaign office.

Name	Gift or Pledge	Date Received	Terms	PCS	Paid to Date	Remarks
Alphabetical Listing of Contributors						

"PCS" indicates pledge card signed. If it is not signed, a pledge is not considered valid.

Use your "Final Table of Gift Expectation" figures to compare actual campaign results, like this:

Comparison of Expected and Actual Gift Income

	Projected				Actual		
Number of Gifts	In the Range of	% of Goal	Totaling		Number of Gifts	% of Goal	Totaling
( )	( )	( )	( )		( )	( )	( )
( )	( )	( )	( )		( )	( )	( )
( )	( )	( )	( )		( )	( )	( )

Gift Income by Category or Division

Category or Division	Projected Income	Number of Prospects	Gifts	Totaling
( )	( )	( )	( )	( )
( )	( )	( )	( )	( )
( )	( )	( )	( )	( )
( )	( )	( )	( )	( )
( )	( )	( )	( )	( )

In large campaigns, with many category and division slots to fill, use the titles from your table of organization to make up a form to be distributed to campaign leadership so they can recommend names to fill various positions. Begin with a table of contents page.

Campaign Leadership Possibilities	
Board of Advisors	Page 1
Honorary Chair(s)	3
General Campaign Chair(s)	3
Challenge Gifts Division	4
Leadership Gifts Division	4
Advance Gifts Division	5
Special Gifts Division	5
Small Gifts Division	6
Corporate Gifts Division	7
Small Business Division	8

The pages for each category or division would simply contain job titles and numbers, allowing those involved to fill the blanks, as in the following example:

Page 7

Small Gifts Division

Associate Gifts Chair(s)
1.
2.
3.
4.
Sponsor Gifts Chair(s)
1.
2.
3.
4.
5.

General Gifts Chair(s)
1.
2.
3.
4.
5.
6.
7.
8.
9.
10.

Capital appeals ask that gifts be paid over an extended period, usually three or five years. A pledge card is a legal contract and obligates donors to pay their gift promises in a manner they select. These forms are usually printed in two panels with a perforation separating the two. One half is for the donor to fill out, the other contains confidential information for the solicitor and is detached before handing it to a contributor. A pledge card can be any shape or size, contain appropriate graphics or pictures, so long as all pertinent information appears, and it fits into an envelope. Following is a reduced example:

The Organization Building Fund Campaign **Campaign Headquarters – 1234 G Street** **(123) 456-7899**	No. _____ Category/Division: _____ Worker:_____
No. **Name & Address**	Evaluation:_____
In consideration of the gifts of others and the obligations to be incurred based upon pledges received from the undersigned and others, I/we promise to pay to the Organization Building Fund the sum of	Pledge: _____ Named Facility: _____ Remarks:_____ _____ _____ _____
_____dollars $_____ X_____ Date:_____ (Signature) Please bill me: ____Annually ____Semiannually ____Quarterly for ____years, ending 19____.	_____ _____ _____

Treat signed pledge cards with the utmost care. After gifts are recorded by fundraising staff, turn them over to bookkeeping for billing purposes. More about pledge cards in Part 3 when you attend a worker orientation session.

Those are the basic forms you'll need. Campaigners move around a good deal. Meetings are held everywhere in town and records are needed for referral. Don't lug a ton of file folders with you. Keep copies of records, reports, and other essential information in a large three-ring binder, a master campaign book.

Campaign Stationery

Stationery need not be elaborate, but it should distinctly represent your organization. List campaign leadership on the left-hand side of the letterhead in a type size that doesn't overpower the space reserved for correspondence. Try using a color stock, buff or gray for instance, instead of white, so that the envelope stands out from other mail your members or constituents receive.

Named Gift Opportunities Listings

If you are campaigning to build new facilities or to refurbish existing ones, you will offer donors the opportunity to name a building, a portion of it, or equipment within its confines. Working with your building committee and architect, compile a listing of these items and assign a dollar figure to each. For example, some items in a named gift listing for a physical education complex, which might be several pages long, might look like this:

LISTING OF NAMED GIFT OPPORTUNITIES

Gymnasium (Name Dedication)	$950,000
Health Club	500,000
Pool and Diving Area	200,000
Physical Fitness Room	100,000

The list continues by naming items *in the order of descending dollar values.* Gift opportunities listed above are obviously designed to attract large contributions. To allow smaller gift donors to take part, create less expensive items that are appealing. The example might show:

Trophy Cases	each	$5,000
Office Furnishings	each	3,500
Patron Plaques	each	500

Acknowledgment Letters

In the interest of heads-up donor relations, once a gift is received the contributor must be formally thanked in writing—the sooner the better. Acknowledging contributions is not an option; it's an imperative if you ever expect further support from the same people. If it is impractical to send original letters to everyone (large gift donors must receive them), make certain copies are well produced. Hand sign all letters. Avoid overwriting and flowery phrasing. The more personal a letter, the more it is appreciated.

Dear Sara and Paul, (or Mr. and Mrs. Brown)

Speaking for the Board of Directors and Campaign Board of Governors, I want to say how grateful we are for your generous contribution of $20,000 to support our Psychiatric Research Center.

In the past we have made slow but steady progress in studying the effects of aging on mental health. Your gift, coupled with those of other philanthropically minded citizens, goes a long way in helping us advance these trend-setting studies.

Thank you again for your outstanding gift.

Sincerely,

J. K. Ball
Executive Director

P.S. I look forward to seeing you at Chris and Janet's home next Saturday.

If you don't think a person's gift is particularly generous, leave out the word, but thank them anyway. When a donor makes a restricted gift make sure to mention it:

> Thank you for your recent gift of $5000 to our Scholarship Fund. Because of your caring and generosity, deserving students will be given the opportunity to receive a quality education that they otherwise could not afford.

or

> The Campaign Cabinet wishes to thank you for the recent gift of $500 to enter your name on the Patron's Plaque to be placed in the lobby of the new Physical Education Complex. Yours is an example of the support that will enable our new facility to be a source of pleasure for the entire community.

Due to fundraising's nature, emphasis is on major and other large gift contributors, but be sensitive to smaller givers. In many cases, their donations mean sacrificing personal pleasure. In that sense, these gifts mean even more to them than large contributions do to affluent individuals.

Campaign Brochures

The chief purpose of a campaign brochure is to introduce a drive to prospects before they are solicited. So long as you treat this publication as an aid and not a solicitation device, it will be useful. However, by itself, the most brilliantly written and produced brochure in the universe does not assure sizable gifts. Include at least these elements in your brochures:

- Your case statement
- The summary of needs (the projects you need funded and how much they cost)
- Guidelines for giving: restricted, unrestricted, matching grants, clubs and association memberships, and so on (see page 14)
- A listing of named gift opportunities
- Architectural renderings, illustrations, photographs, and other artwork
- Building plans
- Explanations and descriptions of programs, services, new facilities
- A listing of your campaign leadership
- A listing of the Board of Trustees

Only you can judge how sophisticated (therefore costly) your brochure should be. It doesn't have to be expensive or have a complex layout to be convincing. If you're running annual appeals, a spiral-bound booklet produced in black and white, updated each year, may be all that's necessary. Capital campaigns with large goals usually have full-color printed brochures. As with any campaign piece, don't go overboard with length. On my desk is a brochure for a $13.5 million campaign that is a four panel foldout, printed in color on both sides. It measures $7\frac{1}{2}'' \times 10\frac{1}{4}''$

when closed. In your text, say what you have to say in few words. Designing and laying out in-house publications is discussed in Part 6.

Here are some useful hints:

1. Feature your case statement.

2. List your board and campaign leadership at the end of your brochure, either inside or on the back cover.

3. Be sure each piece of art work tells a story. Good illustrations, line drawings, and renderings do that inherently. Photographs do not. Whether you use a volunteer or professional, find yourself an editorial photographer, a person who can set a mood and tell a story with pictures. Your most captivating photos are candid shots of recipients of your services. You can say more about the need for a new facility for the elderly, for example, by showing two lonely, aged people playing checkers in a bleak and barren room than can be said in two-hundred words of text. Snapshots and other pictures where people stare at the camera with frozen smiles will not move anyone to give you a penny. (Tips on people photography are at the end of the final chapter.)

4. Brochures often contain an open letter to prospects from the chief executive, board, honorary, or general campaign chair. If you choose to do this, don't let it smack of begging. Begin by remarking how capable your organization is and then explain its needs. Don't end the letter with a request to donate money. Instead, urge prospects to consider how consequential their support will be. That makes the next step possible: a personal, phone, or letter solicitation. Here's an example from the college we've been featuring.

From the President:

For 60 years our purpose has remained the same—to educate young men and women in the finest tradition of a liberal arts college; to give graduates the tools they need to make a unique contribution to society and to the times in which we live.

In the past fiscal year the college continued to maintain quality and diversity in education, led in the development of programs for students of many ages, and provided them with the motivation and opportunities to develop full leadership potential.

It was no accident that last year we continued a seven-year upward trend in enrollment, saw newly inaugurated programs succeed, achieved a balanced budget, and surpassed an unrestricted giving campaign goal by almost 10 percent.

If we are to continue this progress, we must face problems in the new decade— a declining student population in the state, inflation, and the rising cost of education. Solutions can only be found through the confidence, leadership, and financial support of our Board of Trustees, our alumni, our individual, corporate, and foundation friends. You are the source of our optimism.

The Timetable as a Guide

Organized by week or month, campaign timetables include planning meetings, category and division start-ups, training meetings, special events, and publicity schedules.

When to begin each category and division is based on an earlier-mentioned principle: people contribute in direct relation to the gifts of their leadership and those of their peers.

Picture yourself as a prospective donor in a division whose prospects are evaluated at $10,000 to $30,000. The campaign goal is $3 million. A solicitor comes to see you about your gift. During the solicitation you ask the campaigner, "How much money have we raised so far?"

"Well," the solicitor answers, "things are kind of slow."

"What do you mean . . . slow?"

"Well," the solicitor tells you, "the big gifts people haven't really gotten things off the ground yet. Presently, we have about $950,000 pledged. We were hoping that you might consider a gift of $20,000. Maybe our division can get this drive moving."

"The way things are going," you tell the solicitor, "I think I'll hold off until we see what else happens. Gee, that's depressing. Only $950,000."

If the leadership had done their job, your meeting might go like this:

"How is the campaign going?" you ask.

"The test solicitations went very well," the solicitor tells you. "And the Leadership Division has been going full blast. Last count, we had pledges of $2.5 million. Now it's up to us. Let's get our group started with a bang. I would like you to consider making a $20,000 donation."

That's why test solicitations focus on an organization's largest gift prospects. If you obtain trend-setting gifts from these people, you have every chance to do so from your next-highest-evaluated group of potential givers, and so on. Accordingly, if your campaign is arranged by categories, you can begin each one at almost the same time. Then it's a matter of first soliciting the highest-evaluated prospects in each category, and using the (positive) results of those solicitations to motivate each lower-evaluated group of people. The table at the top of p. 95 is an example timetable outline for an institution that classifies its prospects by category and intends to do the bulk of its soliciting personally.

Let's use the alumni category as an example of why the timetable was arranged this way. Assume their goal is $1 million. First, the major gift alumni prospects are solicited. A group of them donate $450,000. Then intermediate gifts alumni prospects are seen. Aside from agreeing with the aims of the drive, many of these graduates are impressed by what has been contributed so far and pledge $350,000. Next, the small gift alumni prospects are visited, telephoned, and written to for their donations. They are told that the alumni goal is within reach; it is up to them to support their school as did the other graduates. Those who chose to contribute do so for $200,000.

Notice that major and intermediate gift corporate prospects are scheduled to be seen three weeks after other gift categories began. Delay soliciting top corporate prospects, unless tried and true supporters, until you can first report substantial progress from individuals. Positive results lead corporate executives to see your organization as a sound philanthropic investment. The corporate phase is allowed more time to complete its solicitations because gift requests often have to be studied and okayed by committees.

Solicitation Timetable Outline by Category
(Five-Month Active Campaign)

Category	Name	Active Weeks
Alumni		1–5
Friends		1–5
	Major Gifts	
Parents		1–5
Corporations		4–12
Foundations		All Year Around
Alumni		5–10
Friends		5–10
	Intermediate Gifts	
Parents		5–10
Corporations		8–15
Alumni		
Friends		
	Small Gifts	
Parents		10–20
Corporations		
Small Businesses		

Even more than corporations, applying for grants and receiving a decision from foundations is a long-term process and must be worked at constantly.

When starting up divisions, active solicitation begins with prospects in the highest giving range. Then each lower division kicks off with overlapping starting times. How divisions are dovetailed is dependent on the number of prospects each one has and how long it takes to personally solicit them.

Here's an example:

Solicitation Timetable Outline for Divisions' Five-Month Campaign	
Division & Number of Prospects	Weeks Startup to Conclusion
Challenge (21)	1–4
Leadership (24)	3–6
Advance (40)	5–9
Special (210)	8–13
Associates (250)	12–17
Sponsors (320)	15–20
General (635)	15–20

The outline calls for solicitations to begin with the highest gift ranges and end with the smallest. Efficient campaigns are well orchestrated; volunteers play out their roles in ordered and timely ways. Both sample timetable outlines suggest specific weeks for each category to begin and end. But take these suggestions with a grain of salt. In practice, *campaigns usually fall behind schedule.* For one thing, prospects are unpredictable. Let's say a campaigner has five potential donors to see. Three of those people decide to leave town for a few weeks. That's a significant built-in delay for their solicitor.

Fundraising is not a full-time job for volunteers. With the best intentions, most solicitors, in any giving range, will see the bulk of their prospects only after various business and other high-priority obligations have been met. Commonly, the more time campaigners are given to complete their solicitations, the longer it takes them to get started. Therefore, purposely design timetables whose deadlines workers cannot easily meet. Give campaigners a relatively narrow time-frame in which to see prospects and complete solicitations. Then use the timetable to prod your workforce into action instead of treating it as an uncompromising schedule.

The number of prospects a worker can contact over a given period is not as significant as how many gifts that person can deliver in the same amount of time. As you will learn in Part 3, major and intermediate gift prospects rarely make instant decisions about their contributions. A campaigner may need to revisit a prospect several times to obtain an acceptable gift. So, if I have five assignments, allowing me four weeks to complete my solicitations is okay if there are no stumbling blocks. If there are, it could take double that amount of time. The hope is that the four-week deadline prompts me to get started at once, have some good fortune, and report most of my gifts within the allotted time frame.

Given the ramifications of human nature, a group of 50 major or intermediate gift prospects could be effectively solicited by 10 highly motivated workers in about four to eight weeks. If an organization had to see 1000 small gift prospects using 50 workers who each took 20 assignments, they could finish in about the same amount of time; smaller contributions take less time to solicit and close. Sometimes, as you'll find out later, hundreds of small gift prospective donors can be solicited in an incredibly short period by canvassing and telephoning.

As a guideline, the sample timetable outline headings as a model. Enter the weeks for each category or division based on the length of the appeal, how many prospects and workers are available, and your choice of solicitation approaches. Don't get into a position where a division starts too early because your timetable says to do so. If you have stringent time limitations, work the timetable backwards from the campaign's closing date, allowing adequate leeway.

Setting Up a Schedule

Work out a detailed weekly or monthly campaign schedule for your organization. Include category and division kickoffs, committee and report meetings, deadlines, special events, and so on. Begin with assignments like these:

Precampaign
- Enlist category and division chairs.
- Enlist challenge and leadership workers.
- Design and produce record-keeping forms, pledge cards, a campaign brochure, etc.

- Prepare training materials.
- Fill in the appropriate information on major and intermediate gift prospect forms and pledge cards.
- Enlist a marketing committee.
- Send invitations for a special event to major gifts prospects.
- Hold orientation (training) and assignment of prospects meeting for challenge and leadership gifts workers.

Week	Assignment
First	- Foundation committee meets to identify prospects and consider proposals. - Challenge gifts workers begin soliciting. - Begin advance gift worker enlistment.
Second	- Campaign cabinet meets. - Marketing committee meets to consider marketing of the small gifts portion of the drive.
Third	- Hold first challenge gifts worker's report meeting. - Hold corporate category worker luncheon. - Conclude advance gifts worker enlistment.
Fourth	- Campaign cabinet meets. - Functions committee meets to plan solicitation dinner for special division prospects.

. . . and so on.

Continue filling in your schedule until you reach the campaign's closing date, keeping the following in mind:

1. Cabinet meetings. Have your campaign's operating team start out by meeting every two weeks to discuss progress and to solve problems. As you start additional divisions, the cabinet gets together every week.

2. Report meetings. When workers are requested to attend meetings and report on their progress, they are more apt to complete solicitations on schedule. Hold report meetings every two weeks.

Conducting cabinet and report meetings are discussed in Part 3.

Whether you design timetables on a weekly or monthly basis, a printed campaign calendar with events and deadlines entered is a handy way for volunteers and staff to see a complete picture of campaign activities.

Marketing Your Campaign

Fundraisers who consider marketing tools useless are missing the boat. "Press releases won't get you major gifts," they say, or, "Posters don't bring in large contributions." Absolutely right on both counts. But most supporters are people other than big givers. You will be doing an injustice to your organization if you pooh-pooh ways to inform any prospects about your campaign efforts.

Some fundraisers have problems with elitism. To them, marketing smacks of commercialism. They believe that procedures used to sell products or business services are not in keeping with the noble, uplifting virtues of a philanthropic endeavor. Baloney! No aboveboard technique is useless if the result helps raise awareness and additional gift income. Just don't forget the earlier warning: print and audiovisual materials are not substitutes for person-to-person, phone, or mail solicitations.

These are the marketing tools at your disposal:

- Publications
- Special events
- Community relations programs
- Publicity
- Advertising
- Audiovisual productions

Adopt a Do-It-Yourself Attitude

Save money for the projects that need funding by recruiting experienced volunteers to create a marketing plan and to devise creative strategies. Then implement as many of these programs as you can in-house.

A university paid tens of thousands of dollars to a big-time graphics design firm to create a new logo (graphic symbol) for its campaign. The institution had a distinguished business and commercial art faculty, many of whom had practical experience in marketing and advertising. Many talented students also specialized in these same subjects. This university could have saved a fortune by running a contest, for instance, and awarding a prize—perhaps some scholarship money—to the graduate student who designed the best logo. It could have been judged by members of the marketing, advertising, and commercial art faculty, the general campaign chair, and the university president. I'm certainly not against hiring professionals, but if you can recruit first-rate volunteers to give you the same results, why not do so?

Allocate Your Marketing Budget Wisely

Since marketing is intertwined with many campaign activities, and you probably won't have huge amounts of money to spend on promoting your drive, produce materials that serve in more than one way. For example, if you create a newspaper ad to publicize campaign goals, design it to be used as a poster and mailing piece. As you'll see in the next chapter, I produced a six-minute slide show for a theater company by photographing a series of colorful posters, using recorded audio excerpts from productions, and adding music and narration. The presentation, which highlighted the organization's achievements, was comparatively inexpensive to put together. It was a tool that helped recruit leadership, motivate campaign workers, and cultivate and solicit prospects. Get all the mileage you can from everything you create.

Recruit the Right Committee

These are the men and women to recruit for your marketing team:

- Imaginative thinkers from any field
- Marketing, advertising, and public relations conceptual people
- Art directors, graphic designers, and commercial artists
- Photojournalists (still and video); people who can tell a story and express emotions with pictures
- Copywriters

These people don't need to be experienced campaigners, but they must understand your case, audience, campaign structure, and timetable. Don't overload the committee with members, and make sure that each person has a defined task.

Below is a sample agenda for the committee's first planning session:

I. Welcome and Statement of Purpose. . . . Marketing Committee Chair
   A. Explanation of the organization and campaign
   B. Discussion of the committee's role and responsibilities
II. The Organization. . . . Executive Director
   A. Past and present accomplishments and future plans
III. Explanation of the Case Statement and Campaign. . . . Campaign Chair
   A. Explanation of the case.
   B. The Table of Organization
   C. The timetable
   D. Marketing budget
IV. Discussion of Expectations and Concerns. . . . Executive Director & Campaign Chair
   A. Institutional marketing plan
   B. Capital campaign marketing plan
   C. Campaign materials
V. Agree on Date for Next Meeting
VI. Adjournment

Following are comments on the agenda beginning with item II.

II. Tell the members enough about your goals and aspirations so the newest volunteer committee member feels informed.

III. A. Have your general campaign chair define and explain the reasons you are holding a campaign and who benefits from its success. If committee members don't have a grasp of the campaign case, they can't be persuasive.
   B. Going over your table of organization shows the relationship between leadership and workers.
   C. The timetable indicates various deadlines.
   D. Assuming there will never be enough money available for marketing, when pressed, creative people have amazing abilities to do a great deal with limited budgets.

IV. A. Institutional marketing concerns itself with getting an organization's programs and services known by prospects.
   B. Campaign marketing concentrates on the nature, goals, and rewards of a drive.

V. The last agenda item seems insignificant but is not. Everyone needs deadlines. Make sure you schedule the next session before anyone gets away.

A marketing committee needs direction from leadership. Here are some typical requests:

EXECUTIVE DIRECTOR: What do you think we might do to upgrade our media coverage?

CAMPAIGN CHAIR: Although we try to keep costs down, we spend a great deal of money on brochures. Is there a way to have a brochure that looks good, but is more cost effective?

EXECUTIVE DIRECTOR: We would like to get some public service announcements aired. How can we go about that?

With these questions in mind, the committee can begin finding solutions:

- Plan and write a series of feature stories about campaign leaders and selected donors.

- Prepare an in-house brochure using the talents of committee members and other volunteers.

- Enlist a local TV station to donate a camera crew, and record and edit a public service announcement written and produced by members of the committee.

Commit yourself to a marketing plan once you give it the green light. Depending on the strategy, often results are not easily measured. But one thing is certain. When prospects continually see your organization's name in front of them, they are very likely going to trust its purposes. Don't change plans in midstream because you don't see instantaneous results. For instance, you approve a campaign slogan, a poster, and a public service announcement for a small gifts effort. Two weeks later you change the slogan, redo the posters, and cancel the announcements. All the changes have done is create confusion among potential givers just as they were getting to know you.

If you think your organization can't carry out a recommended scheme, drop it. More plans are ruined, more volunteers turned off because ideas are approved, then never carried through. That's insulting to your committee members, and you're liable to end up with negative feedback within the community, exactly what must be avoided.

Making a Commitment: The Action Plan

An action plan, the culmination of your precampaign activities, is like a carpenter's blueprint. If you follow it, all the pieces of your funding effort fit into place. The plan has one major purpose—to commit leadership to carry out the strategies it approved. Include full information on the following:

1. Case Statement

2. Summary of Needs

3. Final Table of Gift Expectations

4. Table of Organization

5. Campaign Leadership Roles and Responsibilities

6. Campaign Budget

7. The Timetable

8. Feasibility Study Results and Recommendations

9. Marketing Plan

When you successfully reach this point, the worst is over. You are ready to go public with a drive that should reach its goal. Here's why. Part 1 ended with "Ten Prime Reasons Why Campaigns Fail." All but the last of those negative statements can now be turned into positive declarations:

1. We have lived up to the six fundraising requirements.

2. Our governing body is committed and experienced.

3. The general chair is qualified and dynamic.

4. The goal is realistic.

5. Major gift prospects are identified and cultivated.

6. Feasibility study results are positive.

7. We have a complete workforce.

8. Our prospects are evaluated.

9. We are committed to an action plan.

The tenth item had to do with proper solicitation training. Since this subject leads off the next chapter, let's make it a positive statement as well.

10. Our solicitors are well trained and motivated.

Let all this sink in, then look at what asking people for donations is all about.

PART 3

Soliciting Major and Intermediate Gifts

4

The Case for Conducting Upbeat Training Programs

It is organizational masochism to treat volunteer training indifferently. No matter how virtuous and well organized a campaign is, most major and large gift prospects must be *sold* on how much to contribute. Only a romantic believes otherwise. To obtain the largest donations, your organization must develop a team of highly trained salespeople—solicitors. Can you possibly imagine a corporate sales staff not receiving in-depth training regularly? Unquestionably, the essential differences between professional salespeople and nonprofit organization solicitors is the level of training received and how seriously sales education is taken. The professional's financial success depends on knowing the product and how it is to be marketed; the volunteer's does not.

There are all kinds of excuses for a ho-hum approach to training. One campaign leader said, "Let's not spend much time and energy on education. My workers are very bright people and their time is limited. Besides that, we've always had a hard time getting volunteers to training meetings." What he didn't understand was that bright people with limited time still need training, and that his group's instructional methods were not appealing or his workers would have attended previous sessions. If you can enlist people to campaign for your project, you can get them to training sessions.

Why so intense about this subject? Because many drives go right down the drain, and with them endless hours of intense preparation, because of mediocre solicitor training. I don't want your organization to follow that pattern.

Picture this situation:

A group begins a campaign by holding a major gifts worker training session, in fundraising parlance an "Orientation Meeting." It's 8:00 P.M., midweek. A dozen volunteers troop into a classroom. The well-meaning teacher, a talented, able solicitor, stands before a blackboard, chalks in campaign needs, and passes out a booklet entitled, *Great Ways to Get Gifts*. Then, for the next hour, the trainer bombards the class with facts about the organization and campaign. At first they are attentive, but as the lecture proceeds, their eyes glaze. Somebody yawns. It's catching. The session finally grinds to a halt at 9:30 P.M. with everybody but the lecturer half asleep.

A few days later, a worker who attended the meeting calls the campaign office. The man is terribly upset because he couldn't get to first base with a prospect. An analysis reveals that he couldn't respond to several objections to the campaign that the potential donor had raised. "Didn't you read the material we gave you?" the staff person asks.

"No," said the worker, "I thought I remembered everything from the orientation meeting."

This volunteer was no dummy. His teacher knew the elements of solicitation. What happened?

1. During the long lecture, workers were expected to grasp and retain many facts and statistics. They also had to absorb the many elements that make up a convincing solicitation. There was no time for role playing—rehearsing a solicitation—which is the way newly trained volunteers practice what they have just learned.

2. The meeting was held in the middle of the week, at night, after a busy day. Energy levels were low, concentration was at a minimum.

Let's make some assumptions:

- Because a person has made a gift to you, it doesn't mean that the donor automatically becomes a knowledgeable solicitor. You don't become a super salesperson because you've bought a product.

- Soliciting is not among most workers chief priorities. Because *you* may look forward to asking for gifts, don't think for a minute that every volunteer has that same motivation . . . so

- . . . On its own, lecturing is not the ideal way to teach volunteers soliciting. Granted, there are persons with extraordinary ability who could speak all day and continually entrance their students, but they are the exceptions, not the rule.

- Providing workers with guidebooks on proper solicitation practices is, by itself, a grossly inefficient way of teaching them to obtain any type of gift.

- To receive maximum benefit from a training session, volunteers should be taught in a proper setting and atmosphere.

Let's look at what can be done to make these sessions communicative and stimulating.

Don't Be Cheap with Training Time

I've conducted sessions for veteran campaigners that lasted several hours, and run seminars for less seasoned and new campaign workers that lasted the better part of a weekend. Many training meetings last about an hour and a half—for everyone. Although this may be standard practice for these organizations, I am totally uncomfortable with such a short period when working with anyone other than the most seasoned volunteers. *Insufficient training does not serve an organization's best interests.* I advocate a minimum of four hours to train new and inexperienced major and intermediate gift solicitors, and allow them to practice what they've learned. Rehearsing, or role playing, is essential. Memorizing rules does not a convincing solicitor make!

Weekend mornings are a good time to begin orientation sessions. Workers are fresh and not concerned about business appointments. Begin at eleven, finish at three. Provide lunch and make at least half that period part of the work session by assigning table captains and discussing the material covered beforehand. If you must train on a weekday, and have only minimum time, avoid evenings. Schedule an early breakfast or an extended luncheon.

Group interaction is an important factor in motivating workers and teaching soliciting. Do everything to get volunteers to attend orientation meetings. If attendance is poor, those who turn up will feel that fellow campaigners didn't care enough about the project to appear. They will go through the session in a down frame of mind.

A successful training meeting does more than instruct: it inspires. If, following their indoctrination, workers are not immediately ready to go out and champion your cause, consider the meeting unsuccessful.

When you hold orientation meetings:

- Use appealing speakers.

- Vary the speakers. Unless you have an incredibly short presentation, or a professional trainer, don't let one person run the entire program. A change in personality and delivery keeps workers stimulated.

- Don't use long-winded commentators. It takes very little to lose a volunteer's concentration.

- Attach time limitations to each agenda item and abide by them. Don't tell your workers that you'll be finished by three and send them home at cocktail time.

- Try using a solicitation instructor from outside your organization to liven the atmosphere. You know the old saying, "You're never a hero in your own hometown." Workers pay more attention to strangers than local teachers they know very well. Either choose a dynamic fundraising pro (for whom you'll have to pay), or an experienced, talented volunteer from out of town.

- Use audiovisual shows as part of the program to appealingly illustrate your case and train workers in proper solicitation practices.

Training Presentations That Cut the Mustard

Industry has for years educated sales forces using sophisticated slide, film, and video presentations. These productions are not prepared because there is extra money to spend. Executives know that audiovisual teaching devices help increase sales. Accordingly, everything you can do to beef up a training program comes back to you in increased gift income. Reduce lecturing to a minimum. Replace it with a trainer who understands group interaction and with dynamic productions.

If you have a choice, meaning if you have enough money, create two separate shows. One that tells the story of your organization's accomplishments, plans, and goals—an institutional piece. Aside from spurring on campaign workers, it can and should be used for cultivating prospects, recruiting leaders and new members, and helping to spark big gift prospects during a solicitation. Get the most mileage possible for your investment. Prepare a second presentation strictly to teach soliciting. Here are some options for both:

Produce a Quality Slide Show.   This is a comparatively inexpensive but impressive medium to use if the slides are first-class and the order of presentation tells a moving story. Use photographs of your facilities, but concentrate on pictures of people you serve or hope to serve. Combine these with illustrations, graphs, and drawings to point up campaign needs or explain solicitation techniques.

Slide presentations that run too long turn from enlightening to boring. It may be okay for Uncle Harry and Aunt Jane to treat you to two hours of slides about their trip on the Orient Express, but your show need not be over eight or ten minutes. You could easily present 80 to a 100 slides in that amount of time. (After about six seconds most slides lose the viewer's interest.) Make sure the person who narrates the show keeps the pace lively.

A more exciting way of promoting your organization and campaign is to use both slides and a complete audio track—narration, music, sound effects. Look at the following example, excerpted from the opening of a show I put together for the repertory company whose case statement you read at the beginning of Chap. 2.

Audio	Slides
(Sound: Clock ticking, sustains then fades under for . . .)	*Varied Phoenix Theater logos from past to present, slow changes between slides.*
NARRATOR: Often the passage of time establishes traditions. However well founded these traditions may be, for them to continue requires adaptability and a sensitivity to fulfilling current needs.	
(Clock fades out. A plaintive flute theme is established in background.)	
NARRATOR: Those logos you see are familiar friends to thousands of theater goers . . . symbols of our company through	

the years. Many curtains have been rung up
for productions of great distinction,
for productions of special appeal . . .

(Flute out, montage of lively voices, sounds,   *Lively sequence of slide changes:*
all from productions.)   *photographs of colorful posters*
                                                         from various productions.

(Sound and music fades under for . . .)

NARRATOR: One year ago, a new idea began
to germinate . . . it was necessary more than
ever to foster communication with young
people . . . We placed six professional
directors in residence in six New York   *Shots of directors in residence*
high schools last season [etc.]   *and school children in action.*

In the simplest of productions, once the sound track is completed, it's the responsibility of the person who changes the slides to match them to the audio track, a matter of practice. The advantage of a recorded, rather than live, audio presentation is that professional narrators can be used, the commentary is constant at each showing, and the music and sound create moods and stimulate attention.

Put some added visual zip into your shows by using two or more projectors and dissolving between them for slide changes. Twin projectors, and a dissolve and audio unit can be rented, but if you intend to use the show often you may want to own the equipment. The latest units allow you to store audio and visual commands so the whole show plays back automatically.

Assuming excellent layouts, slides combining text and graphics or photographs have high audience impact. Computer buffs will know that software exists which allows the operator to electronically create such slides. *Persuasion, Freelance,* and *Harvard Graphics* are examples of current programs on the market. Since software undergoes such rapid changes, it pays to find the program that best suits your organization's requirements.

Once slides are created and the information transferred to floppy disk, the material can be handed over to a professional for imaging—the process of making 35mm slides from computer text and art. Software manufacturers often include a brochure from one of several national companies who specialize in imaging. Likely, it will be more economical to find a local production house for this service. Look in the phone book under "Audiovisual Production Services." Before choosing someone to image your slides, be certain their software is compatible with yours, and the person understands your project. Be sure to look at samples of their work.

If you design slide layouts yourself, be alert to three common pitfalls:

1. Using incorrect backgrounds. White is terrible, for example. Use a color that emphasizes and is in harmony with the text and graphics.

2. Reproducing whole pages of text. A full page of copy is near impossible to digest when projected. Instead, break up each page into several slides. Better yet, summarize each page.

3. Using too many statistics. Use graphs.

In short, simplify each slide so it only makes a few points.

If you want to start from scratch, there are firms that not only image but devise original, compelling visuals for slide presentations. One top-notch company I know presently charges about $7 to $10 per word slide and $15 to $40 for each graphics slide, assuming you provide the text and artwork. Obviously, costs vary greatly based on the complexity of the finished product. But, as a practical example, if you hired the same firm to put together a presentation using your script, photographs, and graphics, a perfectly respectable, eight-minute piece designed for a single projector could cost as little as $1500. Let's say you spend $5000 or even $10,000 for the production. The question which needs to be answered for this or any other presentation is: based on your goal, will the investment help increase visibility, cultivate prospects, inform and motivate workers in a more dynamic way than other techniques?

Two black-and-white reproductions of computer-generated, imaged color slides appear on page 111, opposite.

Produce a Videotape.   In the hands of professionals or experienced amateurs, a videotape can create masterful scenes and a powerful audio track to point up your needs, demonstrate services, and teach soliciting. For training, video is far preferable to slide productions which cannot imitate actual solicitations. Consider an institutional videotape for capital campaigns where you can justify its cost and make use of the show over an extended period. But beware. Charges for a professionally executed eight-minute institutional piece (as much time as you need) could amount to between $20,000 and $80,000. However, if you can recruit volunteer professionals to help with such things as scriptwriting, photography, and editing, you can cut these expenses considerably. Just don't sacrifice quality for cost. *A poor production may hurt more than help if viewers equate its amateurish quality with an organization's other methods of operation.*

Having said that, not many organizations can or should pay a fortune for a training videotape. But the difference between telling workers how to solicit and letting them view the solicitation process in action is enormous. So, even if high-quality production values must be sacrificed, produce a training video if at all feasible. Remember, it's for viewing by your "in" group, not your broad public. Since many scene changes and settings are unnecessary, perhaps you can convince a local station, cable outlet, or educational institution to donate studio, staff, and equipment time.

To show a videotape to a large group of people, such as at a training meeting, have it transferred to film so that it can be projected onto a large screen. Again, refer to "Audiovisual Production Services" in the phone book.

Since VCRs are common, you can send both institutional and training tape cartridges to members or constituents for varied purposes. Suppose you are soliciting a

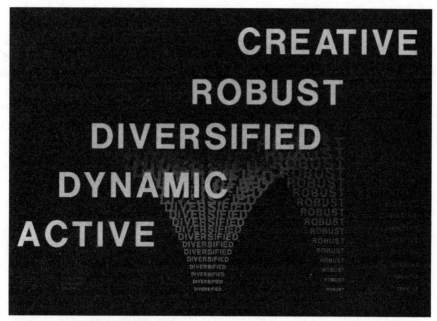

(Courtesy of Rindsberg Digital Photography)

(Courtesy of Rindsberg Digital Photography)

major or large gift prospect who tells you she will make the requested donation if an out-of-town relative can be prompted to donate a portion of the gift. As a cultivation device, the woman sends her relative a videotape cartridge of the institutional presentation. Or perhaps a school alumni campaign is in session. On the day of training, an out-of-town alumni chair shows a training videotape to assembled workers.

With all that videotape offers, think carefully about producing or having a company create a multiprojector slide presentation to show off your organization and illustrate its case. Besides the obvious savings (that alone may be enough), here's why:

1. Everyone sees the ultimate in production values on commercial and public broadcasting television. We are saturated with magnificent graphics, award-winning photography, the best spokespeople. It all takes on a visual and aural sameness, but . . .

2. Most people rarely see highly developed slide shows. That makes them distinctive and attention-getting.

3. Motion isn't everything. The emotional impact of well-photographed slides, the large images, brilliant color reproductions, and persuasive layouts command a viewer's total concentration.

4. A slide show can be videotaped, at low cost. Granted, it loses some quality in the transfer process, and because of the small TV screen, it also loses some impact, but it can be easily sent to distant places for viewing by workers and potential contributors.

Slide and video productions add stature to your organization, excitement to your campaign, turn volunteers and prospects on, and teach effective soliciting. Presentations should be well worth the investment so long as you think of them as tools, not substitutes for solicitors.

When you plan an audiovisual production, consider:

- Its life expectancy. How soon must it be updated? How much will it cost to update?

- The best mood to represent your project. Will the piece be somber or upbeat, slow or quick paced?

- What pictures best illustrate your point of view?

- How best you can put slides or scenes together to tell a story.

- Saying what must be said in the shortest possible time. The most common fault of audiovisual presentations is unnecessary length.

- The dynamics of your visual information. Does each picture or scene relate to your campaign case? If not, drop it.

- Using photography to full advantage. For instance, you may want to photograph a facility to show it at its best or worst, depending on the impact you want to leave on the audience.

- Graphics to illustrate important statistics.

5

Training Your Salesforce:
The Power of
the Personal Visit

If you build a reputation for holding informative and engaging training sessions, volunteers will come back repeatedly. Three topics must be discussed at each orientation meeting:

1. Organization and campaign updates. Don't take for granted that workers know about current needs or goals. (This is where an audiovisual presentation can strongly illustrate your case.)
2. Solicitation training and role playing.
3. Assigning prospects to workers. The most practical, efficient time to give out assignments is when campaigners are together and keyed up from a training session. That's when your drive has their full attention.

Feel free to invite major and intermediate gift workers to the same meeting. The principles taught apply equally to all upper-level solicitors who will see prospects in person. Begin the orientation meeting with a review of the organization and campaign:

 I. Organizational Background & Achievements, Campaign Needs & Goals
  A. Welcome by chief executive or board chair
  B. Show institutional presentation. (If none exists, have one or more of your leadership tell volunteers about your organization and campaign.)
 II. Campaign Progress. . . . Campaign or Division Chair
  A. So far, _____ prospects have pledged or contributed $_____. This represents _____% of our campaign goal which is $_____.
  B. This category or division [the one at the session] has _____ prospects. Its goal is to get $_____ by _____(timetable cutoff date).

III. Solicitation Training & Role Playing. . . . Trainer

IV. Assignment of Prospects. . . . Division Chair

At this point, simply supplying a list of components that make up a successful solicitation leaves no realistic idea of how these sales techniques are applied in real life. So to teach you how to solicit, I'm going to illustrate the process by using a script format for these reasons:

1. To give concrete examples of how group interaction and changing pace is superior to lecturing

2. To portray the give and take that really happens between solicitors and prospects

3. To furnish guidelines for producing a training presentation of your own

Now imagine you're attending an orientation meeting for volunteers who are going to solicit upper-level gift prospects for a capital campaign. (Other than emphasizing numerous named gifts to stimulate contributions, annual appeal campaigners are trained in the same way.)

In the meeting room is a blackboard, projector, and viewing screen. Assume the first part of the agenda is complete, and it's time to learn how to ask people for the type of gifts that make or break a drive.

Training is conducted in three phases:

Phase I—Creating Group Interaction

Phase II—How Solicitations Are Developed and Concluded

Phase III—Rehearsing a Solicitation: Role Playing

Visit to an Orientation Session

Phase I—Creating Group Interaction

To start juices flowing, workers are made to express themselves right from the start. Let's let the trainer take it from here. [My further comments will appear in brackets.]

TRAINER: Our organization has a solid set of goals that deserve total community support. But we're not going to get that backing until prospects are convinced that our case is so strong that they want to be an integral part of the project. A successful solicitation begins with understanding or finding out where a prospective contributor's interest in the organization lies. In the commercial world you call that . . . knowing your customer. Think about why people donate large gifts. Generally, they are driven by a conviction that being philanthropic helps furnish a better way of life for themselves or other people. But to make a top-notch presentation, you must have more than a general idea about what prompts a prospect to contribute. Tell me, what do you think are the specific reasons why people make donations?

[The aim of this discussion is to let students know that most people make contributions for several reasons. Then, they will realize that solicitations must be tailored to the precise interests of each prospect. Using a blackboard or flip chart, the trainer jots down the workers answers and comments on their reactions to this question.]

CAMPAIGNER 1: I think people contribute because they care deeply about a particular cause.

TRAINER: Good. (*Writes on the blackboard*) "Belief in an organization's goals." That's a high priority motivation. Most people give for more than one reason. What are some others?

CAMPAIGNER 2: Because a particular program interests them.

TRAINER: Give me an example.

CAMPAIGNER 2: I'm interested in speech therapy because I stuttered when I was a kid.

TRAINER: Fine. Think what would happen if your solicitor was unaware of this interest and his presentation was built around sports activities. How about another reason?

CAMPAIGNER 3: Because my friends are involved with the organization and want my support.

TRAINER: Absolutely. That's peer pressure, a strong consideration in giving.

WORKER 4: My father and mother taught me that it was traditional for our family to make donations to charitable organizations.

TRAINER: That motivation is inherited from biblical times.

[The discussion goes on. The completed list contains the following:

Belief in an organization's goals

An intense interest in a specific program

Peer pressure

Family tradition

A person's leadership role in an organization

A sense of wanting to improve the quality of community life

Recognition

Admiration for a professional leader

Tax deduction

Good business]

TRAINER: Let me give you an illustration of how knowing a prospect's reasons for giving greatly aided one solicitor. A board member who took his responsibility seriously decided to make a large donation to name a facility. During the solicitation he remarked that the executive director was doing an outstanding job and deserved his and other's support. I have just told you three distinct reasons why that contribution was made: (1) the board member had a leadership role in the organization, (2) the man desired recognition so he named a facility, and (3) he had great admiration for the chief executive officer. Before the solicitation took place, the campaigner assigned to that gentleman discovered these were the motivations that would most influence the board member. So, during the presentation, the worker:

1. Pointed out how much the success of the campaign relied upon outstanding board support
2. Suggested three named gift opportunities, one of which the donor chose
3. Told the prospect how much the executive director was counting on him to set a trend with his donation

No successful solicitor sees a prospect without first determining what might compel the person to make a suitable contribution.

[Continuing to involve his students in discussion, the trainer next asks the workers to verbalize a feeling that makes most campaigners anxious.]

TRAINER: How do each of you feel about asking a prospect for money?

CAMPAIGNER 5: It isn't my favorite sport. But we have to solicit if we want our projects funded.

CAMPAIGNER 6: It scares me to death. I find it extremely difficult.

CAMPAIGNER 7: (*To* CAMPAIGNER *5 and 6*) I thought you two loved soliciting. I guess you're just like everyone else.

TRAINER: Sure they are. We're all in the same boat. Asking people for donations is difficult. A large part of the problem is self-image. Nobody wants to be thought of as a beggar, or to be turned down. You may never get completely rid of the anxiety caused by asking people to donate money. But, remember, you're part of a team of people asking those who are thought to be friends to help support a worthwhile project that will enhance the community. You have an absolute right to do that proudly and enthusiastically. If someone turns you down, don't take it personally. A donor is as close as your next appointment.

[When the question is put to them, most workers admit being apprehensive about requesting donations. The trainer's task is to ease these fears by putting soliciting into perspective.]

TRAINER: A final question. Picture yourself as a prospect. How do you like to be solicited?

CAMPAIGNER 8: I like an aggressive solicitor who can have it out with me.

CAMPAIGNER 9: That kind of person turns me off. I'd prefer somebody who is laid back and intellectual.

CAMPAIGNER 10: Not me. I'm affected by an emotional request.

TRAINER: You seem to have different ideas about being approached for your gifts. Please listen carefully. I want to tell you the secret of reaching your full potential as a volunteer. When you see prospects, solicit them just as *you would like to be solicited*. Taking that approach, you will be comfortable with yourself, therefore confident and believable. Prospective givers will respect you so they will carefully listen to what you say and seriously consider the gifts for which you ask.

Every solicitor has an individual way of communicating with a prospect. One fabulous money-raiser I know is a woman who never raises her voice above a whisper. She speaks slowly and always smiles. Those mannerisms aren't for effect. This woman conducts her successful business and relates to her family in the same way.

Another winning campaigner I know is like a tornado, loud and aggressive. He wears a perpetual frown and pushes hard for every extra dollar he can get a prospect to donate. He isn't playing a role. This high-strung man cuts his lawn with the same intensity as he solicits. If either one of those people tried to emulate the other's approaches when he or she solicited, each would be an ultimate failure.

Before we discuss the best ways to ask people for donations, I have a request. I understand that although you've been solicited, several of you have not yet made a personal gift to the campaign. Please make your contribution before you visit prospects.

[The trainer's point is well made. In the fundraising theorist's world it's assumed that before a training and prospect assignment meeting takes place, workers are solicited by their chairs and make donations. It's a perfectly logical assumption. But let's remain in the real world where too many campaigners who have not contributed to their drives are assigned prospects and told to solicit them. Except in isolated cases, it takes a great deal of chutzpah for solicitors to ask people for donations without first having made one of their own. What an incredibly weak starting position!

Worse yet, how can any general chair, or category or division leader, *allow* workers who haven't contributed to solicit? The campaigner can't properly say to a prospect, "*We* need to commit *ourselves* to this project," or, "It's up to *us* to support this campaign." They would have to tell the potential donor, "*You* must be committed to the project, *you* must support the drive." What the worker-donor says is, "To prove how seriously I believe in this project, I have agreed to donate *x* dollars or help fund *x* facility and want you to consider a contribution of . . ." That is coming from a position of strength.

Here's a rule I hope you won't need to break: *no major or large gift solicitor will approach a prospect until his or her gift has first been made.*]

Phase II—How Solicitations Are Developed and Concluded

TRAINER: (*Continuing*) There is a thoroughly time-tested, organized way to go about soliciting funds. (*Trainer passes out a sheet of paper to each worker that contains the following information:*)

1. Know Your Campaign and Prospects
2. Make a Personal Appointment
3. Describe the Organization's Needs and Relate a Personal Viewpoint
4. Request the Gift
5. Counter a Prospect's Objections
6. Close the Solicitation

Now I'm going to show you a short film that illustrates the six points. Then we will practice what has been learned.

[Assume the film was originally produced on videotape and transferred for large group screening. Because the medium creates a different atmosphere, the group remains totally attentive. Feel free to use the following material as a model for your organization's presentation.]

(Fade up on exterior shots of an organization's headquarters. Theme music up full. Dissolve to interior shots of people busily engaged in activities that the organization sponsors. The narrator enters and the camera stays with him as he walks into a small, comfortably furnished room. On the walls are various photographs of the organization's facilities, past presidents, awards, and artist's renderings of planned new facilities. The narrator sits on a corner of a desk. Theme music fades out. Superimpose the following title for three seconds.)

Know Your Campaign and Prospects

NARRATOR: (*To camera*) Before making an appointment to see a prospect, familiarize yourself with every aspect of your organization and campaign case. *A solicitation is not a one-sided event with the solicitor talking and the prospect listening.* Much of what occurs is discussion. You will not only present your campaign's objectives, but also be asked to answer questions about these purposes. Then you most likely will have to respond to various opinions or negative comments about your project. If you are up on the facts, none of this will catch you off guard. Begin by finding out:

1. What portion of the campaign commands your prospect's interest
2. Specific reasons for giving that motivate the potential donor
3. The way in which the prospect can profit from making a donation to your drive

When these questions have been answered, using the prospect's gift evaluation, list items from your summary of needs or named gifts options that the prospect might consider funding.

For example, a potential donor assigned to you is a physical fitness enthusiast. You know he can be encouraged to make a first-rate donation if he becomes interested in your organization's athletic program. Knowing the prospect is evaluated at $50,000, you review the listing of named gift opportunities and find three options that would best suit his interest:

1. Gymnastics equipment costing $50,000
2. Naming the Physical Fitness Director's office which requires a donation of $35,000
3. Exercise equipment costing $25,000

Now you are ready to solicit. If, during the visit with the prospect, you've done everything possible to persuade him to underwrite $50,000 worth of gymnastics equipment and can't, then the second option can be suggested. If the prospect doesn't find that feasible, perhaps he will consider making a contribution for exercise equipment costing $25,000. During the height of a presentation and gift request is no time to search for ways to inspire a prospect or find projects that you suspect the person might fund. (*Superimpose the following title for three seconds*)

Make an Appointment

NARRATOR: Many seasoned campaigners will tell you that getting an appointment to visit a potential contributor is often more difficult than it appears. After all, you're not about to make that would-be-donor a business deal he or she can't refuse. You're not calling for social reasons. Prospects have every sort of excuse for not seeing you. But since people can't be solicited as forcibly over the phone as in person, you must be persistent and get prospects to see you face-to-face.

Often, when trying to make an appointment, you run into a person who attempts to make a donation on the spot, one far beneath the prospect's evaluated gift. Listen to our solicitor's reaction to this approach . . . (*Scene changes to interior of executive office. The prospect, Jack Straight, sits at his desk studying a report. The telephone rings and he picks it up.*)

STRAIGHT: Jack Straight here.

VOICE OF SOLICITOR: Hi Jack. This is Harold from the organization campaign committee. Haven't seen you in quite a while. Last time we talked was at the youth hall banquet. I want to get together with you and . . .

STRAIGHT: (*Interrupting*) Harold, good to hear from you. Don't even concern yourself. I know why you're calling. I read the letter and brochure you sent me about the campaign, and I intend to make a gift of $10,000 this year. Don't even waste your good time coming to see me.

HAROLD'S VOICE: I appreciate your early thinking about our campaign, Jack. But there are several things about the project I'd like to discuss with you personally. Can we visit for an hour or so?

STRAIGHT: Well, I'm pretty busy. I have some big meetings coming up, and I'm going out of town soon. Why don't we just take some time on the phone?

HAROLD'S VOICE: Jack, you are someone who our organization counts on. I want to go over some special plans and layouts. Our building committee has spent many weeks getting these designs together. They knew you'd be interested in seeing them. This is a major undertaking. Please agree it's worth a small amount of your personal time.

STRAIGHT: Okay Harold. Let me look at my schedule. (*He consults his schedule book*) (*Cut to narrator in meeting room*)

NARRATOR: When phoning for an appointment several things may occur.

The prospect is a friend or colleague and agrees to see you because of that personal relationship.

The prospect tells you he or she could care less about your project and hangs up. That's not a likely scenario in the upper gift ranges because of the evaluation process.

There is initial resistance, as in Harold's case. A personal appointment is often made by pointing out the significance of the campaign, its serious consequences to the membership or community, and its benefit to recipients.

The response to initial resistance should be figured out *before* you call for an appointment. The way Harold got his meeting illustrates how prospect research comes in handy. Let's listen to Harold's approach one more time. (*Cut to replay of Straight listening to Harold*)

HAROLD'S VOICE: Jack, you are someone who our organization counts on. I want to go over some special plans and layouts with you. Our building committee has spent many weeks getting these designs together. They know you'd be interested in seeing them. This is a major undertaking. Please agree that it's worth a small amount of your personal time. (*Cut to narrator*)

NARRATOR: Knowing that Jack Straight is a loyal supporter, Harold emphasizes that Straight can be counted on. He also knows that his prospect, like most of us, is sensitive to peer pressure, so he mentions that members of the building committee have high expectations for Straight's involvement. Then he points out the magnitude of the campaign. Harold is prepared: he didn't leave anything to chance.

Now that Harold's prospect has agreed to see him let's follow along. (*Cut to Straight's office*)

STRAIGHT: Okay Harold, why don't you come down to the office tomorrow about ten. Or I'll buy you lunch at noon.

HAROLD'S VOICE: I appreciate that Jack. But I wonder if it might be convenient for you to come to my house for coffee one night this week.

STRAIGHT: My nights are pretty well booked. Don't you eat lunch?

HAROLD'S VOICE: Sure, but I thought it might be quieter if . . . (*Cut to narrator*)

NARRATOR: What's gotten into Harold? He finally got an appointment and he's frustrating the prospect by not wanting to visit his office or accept his luncheon invitation. Well, Harold's not being obstinate. Let's imagine he accepted Straight's invitation. Directly at 10 A.M. he arrives at the office . . . (*Cut to Straight's office. In the background are sounds of typewriters, office machines and telephones ringing. The door opens.*)

SECRETARY: Mr. Straight, Harold from the campaign committee is here to see you. (*Straight nods his approval*) (*To Harold who is off camera*) You can go in now, sir.

HAROLD: (*Entering*) Good morning Jack.

STRAIGHT: Good morning Harold. Take a chair. Want some coffee?

HAROLD: No thanks. I appreciate you taking the time to discuss our campaign. This year we are taking on a major challenge by . . . (*He is interrupted by Straight's secretary over the intercom*)

SECRETARY: Excuse me Mr. Straight, but did you want to talk with Boston?

STRAIGHT: No. And please hold my calls unless it's Jed or Doris. I'm sorry Harold. Fire away.

HAROLD: As you know, when we first built the Youth Wing we thought that about 1500 children would make use of the facility. We have outgrown ourselves. Our only option is to . . . (*Harold is interrupted by a knock on the door and Straight's telephone ringing*)

STRAIGHT: Excuse me, Harold. Come in. (*Picks up phone. Door opens and Doris appears.*) (*Straight speaks into phone*) Yes Jed, any changes? (*Looking at Doris*) Do you have that report ready? (*To telephone*) No, not you Jed . . . (*A bit of office mayhem—voices, sounds, all happening at the same time. Then picture and sound fade. Shot of narrator.*)

NARRATOR: This is a typical example of what can happen when you try to solicit someone in an office or public place like a restaurant. The solicitation becomes fragmented because the prospect can't concentrate solely on what you have to say. Unfortunately, many gift requests take place in these environments. Offices and restaurants are expedient and convenient for busy volunteers and prospects; business and social engagements are often carried out in such places. However, if possible, stay clear of them when meeting with prospective large givers. A major difference between selling a commercial customer and a nonprofit organization prospect is that you, the fundraiser, have the opportunity to choose where to make the sales presentation.

Earlier Harold was trying to get Straight to come to his home because he could control the atmosphere. There is a distinct psychological advantage to seeing a prospect on your turf. Consider setting up a room within your facility that is given over to high-level campaign meetings and solicitations. Decorate it with photographs, models, illustrations, awards you have won, and anything else that will impress your prospective upper-level prospects favorably. If you have a slide or video presentation to promote your organization, this is the place to show it. (*Superimpose following title for three seconds*)

Present Your Needs and Personal Viewpoint

(*Cut to shot of Straight and Harold entering the room from which the narrator has been speaking. The camera follows as they seat themselves in comfortable chairs. Straight looks at the various photographs and renderings on the walls.*)

NARRATOR: (*Off camera*) Let's go on with the solicitation. Don't assume a prospect is totally familiar with your campaign needs. Tell the potential donor why you are campaigning and about the people who will be assisted—put the case statement into your words.

HAROLD: Jack, as you know, this year our organization is facing a major challenge. We have more kids who need our services than we have space. We need to expand and renovate the youth wing. There is a major problem with asbestos removal in the oldest part of the building. Equipment is outmoded. Here we are growing faster than ever, and we don't have proper facilities to handle that growth. Look at this set of plans and drawings for the new wing. (*Harold shows Straight several drawings that both study.*)

STRAIGHT: Well, it seems like a remarkable project.

NARRATOR: (*Off camera*) Because he is up-to-date on organizational expectations and campaign rationales, Harold can tell his prospect all about the proposed new facility. After Straight digests the information, Harold begins the second part of his presentation.

HAROLD: Jack, I want to tell you a story. The other night I was on my way to the organization for a meeting. About half a block away, I heard six teenagers arguing. I knew two of the kids, members of our youth group. They were trying to get their buddies to a class in creative computer graphics instead of hanging out at the mall. With much determination, the two teenagers convinced their friends to attend the class. When I left the meeting, the six of them were completely absorbed by what they were learning. A year ago those two boys wouldn't have thought about computers or graphics. And their friends would never have come near the place. It made me feel very good to be a member of our organization. I was even more willing to help get our project funded so that other children can have the same opportunity as those kids. (*Straight nods in agreement*) Let me show you the rest of these drawings. (*They go over the drawings*) (*Camera zooms back to reveal narrator*)

NARRATOR: Harold has made the need to upgrade and add facilities come alive by telling a story about real people involved with the organization. *Philanthropy is not a technological business, it's a people business.* Nobody's going to give you an outstanding gift because you have a demanding summary of needs or require several million bricks for a new building. If you want prospects to be moved by your mission, give them a first-hand example of how people down the block, on the other side of town, or across the ocean have been or will be aided by your organization's services.

Let me illustrate another instance of how a personal viewpoint can help sway a prospect. Part of the reason this college trustee secured a major gift for scholarships from a potential donor is because he told the person . . . (*Cut to trustee in different setting who speaks to the camera*)

TRUSTEE: Because of my college education, I've become financially successful. When I was a teenager, our family was poor. I worked very hard in the West Virginia coal mines to attend college at night. I would never have made it through without the help of student aid. I promised myself that if I ever made any money I would do everything possible to help kids from the same background as mine. I've spent 20 years doing just that. We have a duty to share with others not as fortunate. Without student aid I don't know where I'd be. But I know I wouldn't be a board member of this great institution. And I wouldn't have the pleasure of asking for your gift to our scholarship fund for disadvantaged students. (*Cut to narrator*)

NARRATOR: Let's return to Harold's solicitation of Jack Straight. Harold concludes his presentation on a strong note by announcing his gift. (*Cut to Straight and Harold*)

HAROLD: (*Pointing to the drawings*) Jack. I am totally committed to this project. That's why I decided to make a donation of $30,000. (*Cut to narrator*)

NARRATOR: Harold has shown that his commitment to the new facility is more than lip service. His next step is to request a gift from Straight who is evaluated at $25,000. If Harold had not made a contribution of at least that amount it would have considerably weakened the gift request; people make donations in relation to those of their peers. (*Walks over to a chart*) Let's review the solicitation process so far.

Know Your Potential Donor

See Your Prospect in Person

Choose the Right Place in Which to Solicit

State the Case Powerfully

Tell a Personal Story Related to the Project

Use Your Gift as an Example

(*Walks away from chart. Superimpose the following title for three seconds*)

Request the Gift

NARRATOR: Rarely, if ever, will a large contribution come to you gratuitously. You must ask for one. The gift recommended by your evaluation committee can be found in the materials relating to your prospects, such as on pledge or gift cards. Before Harold shows us the correct way to request a donation, let's look at some disastrous methods of asking for money. (*Cut to a worker in different setting who speaks to camera*)

WORKER: I think that brings us up to date on what we are trying to get done. What do you think you might do for us?

NARRATOR: (*Off camera*) Giving the prospect a choice of how much to contribute is a typically simple and unproductive way out. The person will give the smallest possible donation. Some workers avoid asking for a set amount of money in this way . . . (*Cut to worker*)

WORKER: I know you're a supporter. Take some time to think about our project. Here's your pledge card. Fill it out and send it to the campaign office when you make a decision about what you want to give us. (*Cut to narrator*)

NARRATOR: Leaving a pledge card for a prospect to complete without an agreed gift is inexcusable. It offers the person another perfect way to make a gift far beneath his or her potential. Here's the correct way to ask for a donation. (*Cut to Straight and Harold*)

HAROLD: Jack, our project must be successful. I want you to consider making a gift of $25,000 to fund the counseling room in the new youth wing extension. (*Cut to narrator*)

NARRATOR: Did you notice how Harold petitioned the gift? He asked the prospect to *consider* making a $25,000 contribution. Potential donors are not insulted when asked for large gifts in this way. Contrast Harold's wording with I *want* you to give or you *should* give $25,000. The only time you can possibly be demanding is when the prospect is someone close to you.

What happens next? The campaigner has made the case, given a personal viewpoint, and declared his or her support. The potential donor now understands how much money the leadership would like to have donated. What more needs to be said for the moment? Nothing more. Yet many campaigners become embarrassed or insecure at this point so they chatter away, like this. (*Cut to worker and a prospect in different setting*)

WORKER: And so everything I've said leads me to ask your consideration of a $50,000 contribution this year to help fund the museum's new study program. Now I know that seems like a great amount of money, but the committee is really counting on you. Ted Rose, the chairman, was asking about you the other day. If you can bring yourself to feel a sense of true involvement I know you will make a generous commitment. As I said, the reason behind the study program is . . . (*Cut to narrator*)

NARRATOR: Hold it! All those words following the gift request are unnecessary. The prospect has been placed in a decision-making position. There is no reason to qualify the request, nor will repeating the case induce the prospect to say yes. Instead, the person has no time or immediate need to ponder the seriousness of the moment. The prospect might easily avoid the entire issue of making a gift and come back with . . . (*Cut to solicitor and prospect*)

PROSPECT: Say, I haven't seen Ted in some time. How's the old bird doing? Give him my regards. Ted and I worked on many committees together. He's a good man. I thought he was finished campaigning. What made him change his mind?

NARRATOR: The gift request is put aside. Now the volunteer is in the position of having to answer a question before rerequesting the contribution. Let's try it Harold's way. (*Cut to Straight and Harold*)

HAROLD: . . . leads me to ask your consideration of a $25,000 gift to fund the counseling room of the new youth wing extension. (*There is silence. Harold looks directly at Straight, waiting for an answer. Straight looks around the room thoughtfully.*)

STRAIGHT: Well, that's quite a request. (*Harold looks at Straight hopefully. There is silence.*)

STRAIGHT: I told you over the telephone that I would give $10,000. (*Continued silence*)

NARRATOR: (*Off camera*) Harold's silence is not risky or intimidating. He is not casting an evil eye on his prospect. He is letting Straight contemplate a $25,000 donation. Silence is an ally, although difficult to maintain. When there is tension we prefer to have sounds around us. Here's how Straight responds to Harold's request. (*Narrator exits. Superimpose the following title for three seconds.*)

Counter a Prospect's Objections

STRAIGHT: Harold, I had my mind made up to give you $10,000. The economy has been pretty bad, you know. It's affecting my business. And I do support other organizations.

NARRATOR: (*Off camera*) Jack Straight has delivered two common objections. It's Harold's responsibility to respond to them.

HAROLD: Jack, I understand how you feel, but you're a successful man. You've been that way for a long time. I have confidence that you will deal with the problems of the economy. Believe me, I'm certainly not asking you to drop your other giving programs. I also support other causes. But funding the new youth wing extension is a one-time project, an investment for children of every age and background in our community. That's why I've made a special effort to make a larger gift than I might have otherwise and ask you to do the same.

STRAIGHT: Well . . . (*He leafs through the brochure*)

NARRATOR: (*Off camera*) First, Harold told Straight that he understood his feelings. That is essential. It takes away the opportunity for a prospect to become defensive, therefore argumentative. Then Harold began nullifying the objections. The first one was simple. Telling Straight that he is successful and will continue to be so neutralizes the complaint. Second, most philanthropists give to more than one organization. Never tell prospects that they must give to your drive at the expense of another. Let's replay the last scene with a less talented solicitor.

STRAIGHT: . . . the economy has been pretty bad, you know. And I do support other organizations.

SOLICITOR: Jack, let me stop you for a moment. Which other organizations do you support?

STRAIGHT: Well, my college, for one. The alumni fund and . . .

SOLICITOR: That's fine. But you know, they've got thousands and thousands of grads. We're smaller and local. We deserve it more.

STRAIGHT: (*Becoming irritated*) I don't think that's the point.

SOLICITOR: And who do you blame for the economy? The party in power, I'd say. Can't do much about that for the moment. It's not my party.

STRAIGHT: Well, dammit, it's mine. I didn't think we were here to discuss politics. (*Cut to narrator.*)

NARRATOR: This solicitor is about to destroy any chance of getting an upgraded gift from Straight. He doesn't listen and chastises the prospect for his beliefs. Every solicitor must realize that *overcoming objections are as much a natural part of the solicitation procedure as stating the case or asking for a donation.* Complaints are most often encountered when you ask for a decision about a suggested gift. An objection can represent a prospect's true feelings about an issue, or it can be an excuse that covers up a potential donor's real feelings. Never, never engage in an argument with a prospect. Instead, listen. Let the person say everything that needs to be said. Then attempt to change these viewpoints by turning them into positive statements or easily answered questions. To do that efficiently you must be mentally prepared. Before the solicitation takes place, decide what objections might be encountered. Then have responses prepared for each. Following this presentation your trainer will tell you more about surmounting objections.

   If you believe an objection is an excuse for another problem that a prospect may have, find its source. Then come up with a logical and reasonable response. Like this. (*Cut to a worker and prospect in a different setting*)

PROSPECT: I appreciate you taking the time to visit, but I think it's time that someone else took over for me. I'm feeling burned out. I told my husband just last week, "The organization and I seem to be going at cross purposes." (*Pauses*) Please have some coffee. (*She pours a cup*)

NARRATOR: (*Off camera*) A solicitor who has studied the prospect's background sees through the veneer.

SOLICITOR: (*Taking coffee cup*) Thank you. I think this would be a terribly inappropriate time for you to step down as a leader. At a campaign meeting the other day, I was talking to our executive director. He is puzzled because he doesn't know why you haven't been to the organization lately. Has he called you?

PROSPECT: Well, he phoned yesterday, but I wasn't home.

SOLICITOR: I'll let him give you details, but I know he wants to discuss the new elderly program. He needs your input.

PROSPECT: (*Now more kindly*) That's interesting. I was insulted by the shabby way he treated me last time we spoke.

SOLICITOR: He didn't mean to be insulting. He respects your opinion and always has. Let's call him right now and get things straightened out.

NARRATOR: This campaign worker had done her homework. When she heard the objection, the solicitor knew it had nothing to do with the prospect being burned out. The real reason the potential donor was being uncooperative had to do with being snubbed by the executive director. Her feelings were hurt. Prospects with hurt feelings are not moved to make large contributions. The campaign worker had to first soothe the wound before the solicitation could go forward.

Closing the gift, attempting to get the highest possible donation from a prospect, is by far the most difficult stage of a solicitation. But if you can't close, all the effort put forth before that point is wasted. Let's see how Harold makes out as he enters this final phase. (*Cut to Straight and Harold, superimpose the following title for three seconds*)

Close the Solicitation

STRAIGHT: Harold, I suppose you're right. I'll pull my way out of this business slump. But I think I'll pass on your request. I'm concerned about overextending myself.

HAROLD: I know times are tough, but I also know how much this project means to you. Twenty-five thousand . . . $5000 a year for five years would be an extraordinary leadership gift to the community's children. It also would induce many others to upgrade their contributions. Please take some time to think it through. I'll come by the first thing next week and we can talk again. (*Cut to narrator*)

NARRATOR: Harold will not conclude the solicitation during the first visit if his prospect's offer doesn't match the amount he requested. Some of you might be thinking, "I wouldn't turn down Straight's $10,000 gift." You'd be making a mistake. It's a proven fact that *succeeding visits to supportive prospective contributors eventually lead to donations equal or close to a requested gift.* The next visit may go something like this. (*Cut to Straight's office*)

STRAIGHT: Harold, I've given your request much thought and I think the contribution you're asking of me is too high. Here's what I will do. Instead of making a gift of $10,000, I'll up that to $15,000.

HAROLD: I appreciate your generosity, Jack. But our studies show this is the year we must totally fund renovations and new facilities. The organization is committed to this campaign. Earlier, you agreed with its priority nature. We don't govern needs, the community does. It's our job to respond to them.

STRAIGHT: (*Somewhat angrily*) Harold, I am responding! I believe in this project as much as you do. I just don't think I can make a contribution of $25,000. I have real respect for you. You're a giver and a hard worker, but you're pushing too hard.

HAROLD: Jack, don't be angry. You know I'm not pushing for myself. I'm fired up about the kids who will make use of the counseling room I'm asking you to fund. I know you're totally sold on the project and care about the future of youngsters in our community. I'm asking you to set a standard. (*Cut to narrator*)

NARRATOR: Notice that in both closing statements, Harold mentioned Straight's affirmative attitude toward the project and his desire to help make the planned youth wing a reality. *During the close, repeat everything that a prospect agreed with during your case presentation.* Doing this lowers a potential donor's resistance to making the requested contribution. *Then repeat how the prospect will personally benefit from making a donation.* Harold told Straight his contribution would not only support the youth wing, but motivate others to make exemplary contributions.

Harold has said all he can about needs. He can accept the $15,000 offer or continue attempting to motivate the evaluated, $25,000 contribution. He chooses the latter. There is another tactic left to him, a method equally at home in corporate board rooms and social situations—peer pressure. (*Cut to Straight and Harold*)

HAROLD: Jack, I'm not making light of your generous offer. But I ask you to rethink your gift. You've been living in this community as many years as I, and have been an integral part of its growth. We are older now, but that doesn't mean our obligations are less. We must shoulder more responsibility because we have become more successful over the years. Our chairman and the campaign committee, people you know very well, hope you decide to reach deep down and make the greatest contribution of your career to name the counseling room. Tell me you'll do that for the children and for your friends.

STRAIGHT: (*Not unkindly*) I told you that would be stretching it.

HAROLD: I understand. The entire leadership of this drive has stretched its gifts to support our project. We were all thinking about smaller contributions than we ended up making. We're not asking you to do more than we have done ourselves. If you need some more time to think about your gift that's fine. Monday I have a campaign cabinet meeting and I would like to report to our leadership that you have agreed to name the counseling room. Tell me you'll do that.

STRAIGHT: Harold, what I will do is contribute $4000 a year and pledge $20,000. That's final. Can we go over that list of named gifts opportunities again? There are a few items in the area of counseling that I'd like associated with my name.

HAROLD: Absolutely. Thank you, I'm grateful. I know the campaign committee will be very excited when they hear about your contribution. (*Straight and Harold scan the named gift list. Camera zooms back to include narrator.*)

NARRATOR: Harold is an aggressive and persuasive solicitor. His job was to get Jack Straight to give maximum dollars. He knew his prospect's loyalties and sense of responsibility to the organization. He was also confident that the gift he was after would not alter the lifestyle of his prospect—Harold's use of peer pressure was not out of line.

When a solicitation is completed, thank the donor. Tell the person that a formal acknowledgment letter will be forthcoming. In a capital campaign, this would be the time to present the prospect's pledge card for signature. The solicitation is then officially concluded. (*Narrator walks over to a chart*) Let's review what happens after you tell the prospect about your donation.

Request the Evaluated Gift for an Explicit Purpose

Use Silence to Focus the Prospect's Attention on the Request

Counter Objections

Allow the Prospect Time to Consider the Request, If Necessary

Set Up a Second Appointment

When Closing, Restate What the Prospect Found Positive about Your Presentation and the Benefits of Giving

Use Peer Pressure to Upgrade Gifts

(*The narrator moves to another part of the room and seats himself down at a table where a solicitor is already seated.*)

NARRATOR: For the past few minutes you've watched a campaigner upgrade his prospect 100 percent, bringing him from an initial offering of $10,000 to a gift of $20,000. This is an example of what can happen if you have a supportive prospect and orchestrate the solicitation correctly. But not everybody you'll run across is as pro-organization or generous as Jack Straight. What happens when you ask for a gift and prospects tell you they don't intend to give a penny to your drive? Here's one response. (*Cut to solicitor*)

SOLICITOR: (*To camera*) You're not serious are you? Why, you are the biggest cheapskate the world has ever known. I can't wait to tell everyone what a nonsupportive skinflint you are. (*Cut to narrator*)

NARRATOR: Berating a prospect may give you great satisfaction, but that person will be lost as a donor for future drives. Unless you're absolutely positive that a prospect cares nothing for your project, there may be many reasonable excuses for that person not to make a contribution. However, next time you hold a campaign—in fundraising there's always a next time—that same person may be one of your most valued contributors. So swallow your hurt feelings and say something like this. (*Cut to solicitor*)

SOLICITOR: I understand. We will miss your support. But we want to keep you up-to-date on what we are doing. And I hope you won't mind if I contact you again next year. (*Cut to narrator*)

NARRATOR: Potential supporters are too hard to come by. Don't immediately give up on prospects who say no. Invite them to special events, send them newsletters, attempt to continue their cultivation.

Less agonizing is a capital campaign prospect who says he or she will make a contribution but not a pledge. Here's how you might handle that one.

SOLICITOR: This new facility will be here for many, many years to come. This is the only campaign we will hold to support this project. To raise the enormous amount of money we need, we are asking for a three-year commitment from each of our supporters.

NARRATOR: In a capital campaign, concentrate on the one-time effort. Another problem you might face are prospects who tell you they can't presently make the three- or five-year pledge for which you asked, but might be able to do so in the future. Imagine a prospective donor was solicited for $5000. This is what the solicitor might remark:

SOLICITOR: I have some suggestions for you to consider. Instead of making yearly payments of $1000, could you donate $500 this year and then make payments for four years of $1125. Or you might want to defer the first year's contribution and pay $1250 for the second, third, fourth, and fifth years.

NARRATOR: Don't give up trying to obtain a pledge from a prospect while the campaign is under way and the person's feeling of support for the organization is greatest. Offer them optional payment schedules. If that doesn't work, attempt getting a first-year cash gift.

What happens when a prospect tells you, "I would like to contribute to the capital campaign, but do you also expect me to give to the annual fund?" If you don't have support for your operating budget, you can't keep the doors open. Yet you need funding for your capital project. Here's how to handle the problem.

SOLICITOR: Without our annual giving program we would not be in business. I'd be foolish to tell you to donate to our capital funding effort at the expense of the ongoing drive. What I'd like you to consider is maintaining your yearly donation and also making a pledge to our one-time building fund campaign.

NARRATOR: (*Theme music in background*) The most skillful campaigners look at asking for money as a challenge instead of a nerve-wracking, awkward chore. When a solicitation is completed successfully, volunteers feel a tremendous sense of accomplishment and fulfillment. Those responses stimulate campaigners to continue being unrelenting and masterful as they go from assignment to assignment, often persuading prospects to make contributions far above what they planned to give.

Using correct solicitation practices won't guarantee trend-setting gifts from every prospect you see. But not using these established methods greatly diminishes your chances of receiving the large contributions that all campaigns need to succeed.

Thank you for joining us. (*Music and picture fade out*)

TRAINER: The narrator in the film made a point of saying that objections are an integral part of the solicitation experience. These complaints can ruin a solicitation unless you're aware that they will occur and feel confident that you can counteract them. In the film you just saw, if Harold was not able to respond to Straight's objections he would not have been successful. (*He passes out a sheet of paper on which is written:*)

How to Handle Objections:

Always Hear Them Out

Never Let an Objection Lead to an Argument

Classify Objections as Valid or Invalid

Respond with Solutions to Objections

Convert the Objection into an Answerable Question

Find a Common Ground with the Prospect

Turn Negatives into Positives

TRAINER: Ignoring objections only builds them up in the prospect's mind. Allow potential donors to verbalize opinions and criticisms. Remember that objections can be used:

To express true feelings

To cover up real feelings

As a way to vent frustrations

As an excuse for not making a requested gift

Arguing with prospects causes resentment. So even if you know that a potential contributor is dead wrong, keep your wits. Focus on solutions to the objections.

Break objections down into two categories—valid and invalid. Give me an example of an invalid objection.

WORKER 1: Disliking a board chairman.

TRAINER: No. That's an opinion that may be unwarranted to you, but not to a prospect. Personalities are common objections. How would you handle that one?

WORKER 2: First listen, then point out that our drive is beyond personalities.

TRAINER: Exactly. Now someone give me an invalid objection.

WORKER 3: Our drive will hurt other campaigns that deserve support.

TRAINER: What do you tell the prospect?

WORKER 4: That our drive is more important.

TRAINER: By doing that you've given the objection validity. Here's why that objection is unjustified. Since giving is something that people learn to do, experience shows that the more people contribute, the more they continue to do the same. So if there have been successful drives run in a community, you can expect that yours also will be successful. Counteract invalid objections with facts.

Converting an objection into a question is an excellent way to avoid arguments. What if I tell you I don't care for your young adult programs?

WORKER 5: "What changes would you make?" I would ask.

TRAINER: (*Acting as the prospect*) I would like to see more intellectually stimulating activities take place.

WORKER 5: I'd be more than happy to talk to the head of the program committee about your request. There is always room for change and for additional projects. I will see to it that your suggestion is taken seriously by the committee.

TRAINER: Excellent. You've neutralized my objection.

WORKER 6: That didn't seem so difficult.

TRAINER: It wasn't. *None of the common, rational objections you'll hear from prospects are difficult to overcome.* It's a matter of you staying ahead of the prospect. Try to remember that you are soliciting people who either belong to your organization or have reason to support it as a constituent. If they are totally antagonistic they shouldn't be bona fide prospects in the first place. The kind of objections you will face are not like those of a proabortion advocate trying to change the views of an antiabortionist. Don't get paranoid about objections. Just identify them in advance and have responses or answerable questions ready.

Another way to water down an objection is to find a common ground between you and the prospect. If someone tells you, "Our family makes no use of the facilities that you want us to fund," what do you say?

WORKER 7: I understand. We too use for the facilities infrequently. But I don't think we should dismiss the families that *will* use them.

TRAINER: Right. By first saying that you understand the objection, and then pointing out how people will be aided, the objection loses its strength. Now think about turning negatives into positives. How do you turn around this common complaint? "I don't want to fund salaries and other administrative expenses."

WORKER 8: I agree with you. If I thought that was all my contribution was going for, I wouldn't have made one. But remember that the largest proportion of donations supports programs and services—85 cents on the dollar. We must be realistic. Without the staff and other expenses needed to run the operation, we wouldn't have the activities that our community needs.

TRAINER: That's the correct response. Here is something else to contemplate. The best solicitors know how to go directly from responding to a complaint or negative opinion into the closing. It's called "closing on the objection." For instance, a prospect tells you that membership rates are too high and fees are too steep. You answer by saying, "If we get the fundraising support we need, we won't need to adjust the fees. That's exactly why I'm asking you to consider a contribution of x dollars to support this project."

Let's look at objections in another light. Many of them can be dispensed with before they occur. When you plan your presentations, build in answers to the objections you think may be raised. For example, if you tell a potential donor during your presentation that fees have steadily risen, but can remain the same depending on the outcome of the campaign, you have neutralized the objection before it is stated.

That ends the scripted portion of the training session.

Dear reader, you will have the greatest chance of getting suitable contributions if you remember to do one thing—*think like your prospects*. No matter how much money or power they have, these people have many of the same interests, problems, fears, and anxieties as anyone else. See them as human beings and not as names on an assignment list. Then you can anticipate and cope with their responses, tough questioning, fence-sitting, and the other factors brought out during a solicitation.

Understanding solicitation theory is the first step to becoming a successful fundraiser. The second is for volunteers to put theory into practice, to develop a flowing presentation and a personal style.

Phase III—Rehearsing a Solicitation: Role Playing

Role playing is *essential* for beginners and inexperienced volunteers. It also hones the skills of veteran solicitors. Set up a video camera so each role play can be recorded. By seeing and listening to themselves during the playback, workers quickly learn what is good and bad about their solicitation techniques. Dream up several imaginary prospects and jot down a few important facts about their backgrounds and interests. Here's an example.

Helen Goodperson

This prospect is a 50-year-old advertising executive. Her avocation is painting. Evaluated for $150,000 dollars, her record of giving to the organization, over the past three years is:

$100,000
$70,000
$70,000

Mrs. Goodperson is aggressive and independent. Her affluent husband, to whom she is very close, has only a passing interest in our organization. He prefers to spend his free time delving into personal computer software. The couple's other community interests are in the arts.

Have highly experienced solicitors play the prospects, conjuring up responses similar to the person whose roles they play. Approaches are based on information provided by the prospect sheets:

TRAINER: Based on what you just found out about Mrs. Goodperson, how should she be solicited?

WORKER 1: With an unromantic, no-nonsense approach because that's in keeping with her character.

TRAINER: What projects would you try to get her to fund?

WORKER 2: Our artists-in-residence program.

WORKER 3: Since she and her husband are close, we could ask her to subsidize new equipment for our computer laboratory.

TRAINER: Okay. I'm going to ask some of you experienced campaigners to play the role of prospects. Give the solicitors as tough a time as possible. We'll begin with making the appointment.

When each solicitation is completed, the trainer replays the tape and comments on technique. The more times a person has to role play, the better a solicitor he or she becomes. Here are the main points trainers look for when they evaluate workers following a role play:

1. *Appointment Making.* Did the volunteer get right to the point? How did the worker handle excuses for not holding a personal meeting?

2. *Presentation of Needs.* Did the solicitor gain the prospect's immediate attention? Was the case stated strongly enough? Was an exciting or moving personal story presented?

3. *Requesting the Gift.* Did the solicitor announce his or her gift? Was a particular gift requested for a specific item? Was silence used as an ally following the request?

4. *Countering Objections.* How logically were objections overcome? (There should have been plenty of them.)

5. *Closing.* Did the solicitor offer valid rationales why a lesser gift than requested would be unacceptable. Was peer pressure used as an aid? Were points that the prospect agreed with during the presentation restated? Were the benefits of giving that the prospect will receive repeated?

Additional Ideas to Be Discussed

Solicitation training is completed. Before assigning prospects, certain policies and pledge card information must be made known. These subjects can be covered by the trainer or one of the leadership.

Jointly Named Gifts.   Sometimes two or more families want to share a single named gift. For example, the "Brown, Jones, and Smith Swimming Pool." Generally, this method of joint giving dilutes the amount of money which each family donates. This is a leadership decision, the result of which is announced at training sessions.

Joint Family Contributions. This system of giving has the opposite effect of the above: it should increase a family's total contribution. Suggesting to certain prospects that they contact an out-of-town family member and ask them to add to the prospect's donation often means the difference between getting a portion of a requested gift and the whole gift.

Challenge or Matching Gifts. Perhaps you've gotten a donor who agrees to make a gift that is only valid when the amount is matched by other contributors. Challenge or matching gifts stimulate volunteers as well as prospects.

Corporate Matching Gifts. Many corporations match donations made by their employees. For example, an employee donates $2500. His company donates a like amount and the organization receives a total of $5000.

Spouses Working as a Team. It depends on the people involved. It's not a good idea when one or the other is intimidated by their mate's prowess as a solicitor, or if both are weak solicitors.

Soliciting Friends, Relatives, and Acquaintances. Let's face it, we are more dynamic and confident soliciting people close to us than those we don't know.

Don't give your workers a full set of solicitation materials until the end of the meeting. You don't want them referring to handouts instead of paying attention to the trainer. When the materials are distributed, the workers receive:

1. A list of why people give
2. Types of giving (restricted, unrestricted, named gifts, challenge grants, etc.)
3. A named gift opportunities listing
4. Campaign brochures and a copy of a cover letter sent to prospects
5. A list of common objections and responses (tailored to your organization)
6. Example gift or pledge cards

Pledge cards are used in capital campaigns and obligate a donor to pay his or her donation as indicated by the terms noted on the card. (See sample pledge card on p. 134.)

With a sample pledge card before them, tell volunteers:

1. Prospect names and addresses will be filled in by campaign office personnel.
2. Directly beneath the name is a sentence that begins, "In consideration of the gifts of others . . ." The statement means that a pledge must be paid only if

enough other people also pledge to the campaign so that an organization can go ahead with its project.

3. The prospect must sign and date the card after making a gift, and fill in the billing information.

4. The information on the second panel is for the solicitor and campaign office. The file number and name will already have been completed, and each prospect will have a dollar figure next to "Evaluation."

5. The "confidential" second panel must be separated from the other portion of the pledge card before giving it to the prospect for signature.

The Organization Building Fund Campaign **Campaign Headquarters – 1234 G Street** **(123) 456-7899** **No.** **Name & Address** In consideration of the gifts of others and the obligations to be incurred based upon pledges received from the undersigned and others, I/we promise to pay to the Organization Building Fund the sum of _____dollars $_____ X_____ Date:_____ (Signature) Please bill me: ____Annually ____Semiannually ____Quarterly for ____years, ending 19____.	No. Category/Division: _____ Worker:_____ Evaluation:_____ Pledge: _____ Named Facility: _____ Remarks:_____ _____ _____ _____ _____ _____ _____ _____

How You Can Be the Best One-On-One Solicitor Around

General Ways

1. Solicit your prospect as you would like to be solicited so that your commitment is clear and your believability is never in question.

2. Don't beg. Invite the prospect to be part of your project.

3. Make sure the potential donor knows that he or she will be one of many supporters.

4. Don't dominate the solicitation. Draw out your prospect and listen to what the person has to say.

5. Never underestimate the power of eye contact and other body language.

Specific Ways

1. Make your generous gift before seeing prospects.

2. Know your prospect's interests in the organization and his or her reasons for giving.

3. Make a personal appointment to see each potential donor.

4. Hold the solicitation on your turf.

5. Present the case thoroughly and enthusiastically.

6. Tell a personal story about your relationship to the project.

7. Use you own gift to help persuade prospects.

8. Ask a prospect for the dollar amount suggested by the evaluation committee.

9. Ask the prospect to fund a particular part of your project.

10. Use silence to let your request sink in and to elicit a considered response.

11. Have solutions to common objections in mind before soliciting.

12. During your presentation, build in answers to typical objections.

13. Don't argue with a prospect's objections. Begin by telling the person that you understand how he or she feels. Then turn the complaint around, neutralize it, or make it into an answerable question.

14. When closing, repeat the points that your prospect agreed with during your case presentation to lower resistance to the gift request.

15. During the closing, repeat the benefits of giving that the prospect will receive.

16. Learn how to close on an objection.

17. Don't accept a donation you don't approve of until you've tried everything possible to upgrade it.

18. Use peer pressure, when indicated, to help elevate contributions.

19. Don't lose a potential donor because he or she won't make a gift. Continue to cultivate the prospect.

20. Get your prospect to consider optional payment schedules, when necessary.

6

Assigning Prospects and Getting Solicitations Underway

Remember that people will more likely make major and other significant gifts if they are asked by a peer who belongs to and handsomely contributes to your organization. For instance, I may know a lot about solicitation and understand your case, but that doesn't mean that on my own I can successfully negotiate trend-setting contributions from your biggest prospects—we are not on a peer-to-peer, hometown level. Having said that, there are times when out-of-towners, perhaps celebrities of one kind or another who represent the same cause, can motivate huge donations by their presence in a community. More commonly, however, the most dynamic results will be assured if you assign prospects to local volunteers in the same socioeconomic circles.

If you have trained workers from more than one category or division, separate each group for prospect assignments. A team of two campaigners has a better chance of getting a top-level gift from a prospective donor than a single worker does because a team can be more persuasive. However, assigning upper-level gift prospects to more than one volunteer is not an iron-clad rule. If you are short on workers, use the team method for some prospects, let other campaigners solicit on their own, or assign a few more than the recommended five potential donors to your teams.

Sometimes it's advantageous for more than a pair of workers to visit a prospect. The committee approach works well with some people because it shows them the importance of their potential support. Use your judgment. If you know your members and constituents, odds are you will make the right choice.

Two common ways of self-selection exist when assigning major and intermediate gift potential donors. Although workers choose their prospects, try to exhibit some control over assignments by seeing that each volunteer selects both known supporters of your organization and reluctant dragons. One large gifts division worker chose only the toughest of the tough prospects to solicit. At each report meeting, his campaign energies fading by the week, he told of turndowns and minor gifts from these people. After a while he stopped attending the meetings because he gave up. *No salesperson can continually deal with rejection—especially volunteers.*

This is how to distribute prospects:

By Calling Names

Have the category or division chair announce the name of each prospect and let the workers choose who they wish to solicit. Give a team member a copy of the prospect's file card or, in a capital campaign, a pledge card, and record the assignment on a prospect listing. This is a straightforward procedure, logistics are simple, and workers who are familiar with a prospect offer valuable advice on approaches. Here's an example:

> CHAIR: Let's get started. I'm going to call out the names of the leadership division prospects alphabetically. Carl Best.
>
> ERIC: I'll take Carl. What's his evaluation?
>
> CHAIR: Fifty-thousand dollars.
>
> LEWIS: That's pretty steep.
>
> SARAH: He'll be a tough one this year, Eric.
>
> ERIC: Why is that?
>
> SARAH: He's taken some bad licks in the market.
>
> JOE: Yes, but things are looking brighter. I think he's ready to make a large gift to the education program. I'll take him with you Eric. (*Chair gives Carl's pledge card to Eric*)
>
> LAURA: Wait at least two weeks before you see Carl. The market's picking up and maybe then he won't use it as an objection.

Distributing Lists

This alternative method eliminates the interplay between workers; it also takes more time to get gift or pledge cards distributed. However, if it is impractical to call out each prospect's name:

1. Give each volunteer a copy of the appropriate category or prospect list and ask them to check off the names of people they want to solicit.

2. Ask each worker to choose double the amount of prospects (ten instead of five, for instance) since duplications of requests are inevitable.

3. Collate the listings, make a choice of workers, and send the workers their prospect's gift or pledge cards.

Avoid letting workers take lists home to choose assignments. By the time choices are finally returned and assignments made and mailed, motivation will have ebbed considerably.

When volunteers begin to make solicitation appointments depends on how your drive is arranged. The quickest way is to urge workers to arrange meetings with their prospects directly after they receive assignments. This procedure is used most effectively in drives for groups whose workers and potential donors know each other very well and are highly supportive. If you choose this practice, *be sure prospects are sent a letter* and perhaps a brochure in advance introducing the campaign and mentioning that a volunteer will soon call for an appointment. Time the package to arrive a few days before the orientation meeting takes place. Since fundraising deadlines are often used more to stimulate volunteers than to delineate rigid time schedules, the letter not only alerts prospects but also puts pressure on workers to get started. During the assignment portion of the meeting, review the letter with your workers. For instance:

> CHAIR: Three days ago we sent a campaign brochure and cover letter to your prospects. When you call for an appointment it will come as no surprise to them. You have a sample of the letter in your training materials that I would like to review.

> Dear Carl,
> For some years it has been painfully apparent that our present facilities cannot cope with the demands of a continually expanding community. The enclosed brochure outlines a complete building and renovating program that, when funded, will fully serve our growing population.
> Shortly, one of our volunteer campaigners will contact you to answer questions, furnish additional material, and ask your participation in this community effort. I know you will extend every courtesy to them.

A Century-Old Process That Still Works: Campaign Kickoffs

Instead of handing out assignments and asking volunteers to call for appointments immediately, many organizations running capital campaigns use a practice developed by YMCA fundraisers that hasn't changed much since the turn of the century. It's a remarkably effective program to get prospects charged up about a forthcoming funding effort. At the same time, it creates a deadline for category and division chairs to enlist, solicit, and train workers, and to assign them prospects.

The climax of the program is a sophisticated social event attended by prospects and workers called a campaign kickoff. Kickoffs are the result of two converging plans that begin weeks before an event takes place. Depending on the number of potential donors involved, these gatherings range from a banquet to a series of cocktail parties. Usually the organization picks up the tab, and no solicitation takes place at the event. Let's imagine that a college first plans to solicit its board of trustees, followed by major gift friends, alumni, and corporations. Each of these groups would have separate kickoff events. Or perhaps the corporate group should be invited along with major gift friends. Several options exist.

Keep in mind the purposes of holding these events:

- To bring a capital funding project to the attention of influential and affluent members of a community
- To provide a sense of urgency for funding a project
- To make prospects aware of when they will be solicited
- To conclude a cultivation program
- To inspire campaigners and give them deadlines

Here's an example of how these two action plans, one for workers and another for prospects, converge:

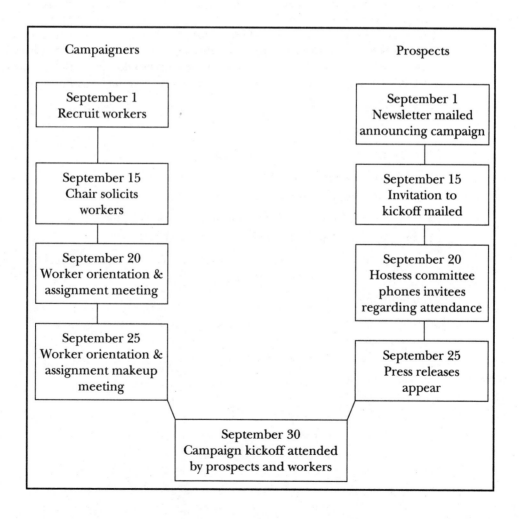

What happens next?

1. Immediately following the kickoff, a letter and campaign brochures are sent to all prospects. Letters to those who showed up thank them for being present, reiterate the campaign case, and announce the name of the volunteer(s) who will be calling for an appointment. The only major difference in the letter to nonattending prospects is to say how sorry the organization is that the person was not present at the kickoff.

2. A copy of the prospect letter is mailed to the appropriate worker. Following receipt of the copy, workers immediately call their prospects for solicitation appointments.

Attendance at a typical kickoff is roughly 25 percent. But even if prospects don't show up they have been made aware of the magnitude of the funding effort and realize their strong support is desired.

The type of event you choose is only limited by your imagination and pocketbook. Whatever form it takes, be certain the program is informative and provoking so that prospective donors leave the kickoff wanting to champion your organization. How to do this is discussed in Chap. 8 that deals with similar special occasions used in annual and capital efforts where solicitation actually takes place during the event.

Following is a sample kickoff agenda for an educational institution:

1. 6:00–7:00 Cocktails (two open bars; student quartet to play background music)

2. 7:00–8:00 Dinner

3. 8:00–8:05 Welcome. . . . Board Chair

4. 8:05–8:15 Slide Presentation Promoting the Institution

5. 8:15–8:30 President's Message. . . . President

6. 8:25–8:35 Outstanding Support Awards. . . . Board Chair

7. 8:30–8:35 Introduce Guest Speaker. . . . Board Chair

8. 8:35–9:00 Guest Speaker. . . . Dr. Dogood: *The Need for Philanthropic Support of Higher Education*

9. 9:00–10:30 Dancing

7

Keeping Workers Energized

Following a properly executed orientation meeting or campaign kickoff, workers are enthusiastic and raring to go. As the days and weeks pass, eagerness dwindles. The natural tendency for volunteers to let down must be counteracted. First, your campaign cabinet must stay on top of things.

Campaign Cabinet Meetings

Recall that a campaign cabinet is a group of leaders responsible for the week-to-week operation of a drive: the general chair who presides, key representatives from the board or special campaign governing committee, heads of categories or divisions, the chief executive, and professional fundraising staff. The cabinet's weekly task is to examine all areas of the drive, to troubleshoot, and to adjust tactics when necessary. Following is a sample agenda and a sense of what happens at one of these meetings.

I. Overall Campaign Progress. . . . Campaign Chair

    CHAIR: So far, we have gifts totaling $650,000 toward our goal of $1 million. This is an increase of $150,000 since last week at this time. Ruth, give us a progress report on the major gifts division . . .

II. Category or Divisional Progress Reports. . . . Chairpeople
Each category or division head reports gift income, the number of prospects who have been visited, and whether the category or division is on schedule. Don't get into long discussions of problems at this point. That's next on the agenda.

III. Discussion of Problem Areas. . . . Campaign Chair

    CHAIR: For the most part your reports are encouraging. Let's hear some negatives. Dick?

DICK: I can't move several of our best corporate prospects off dead center. I know they're interested, but they won't make a commitment. Specifically, I mean Randy and Barbara.

EXECUTIVE DIRECTOR: Neither of them has been to the agency for some time. Maybe if Dick were to invite them over for lunch, we could put together a program to pump up their enthusiasm.

AMY: I'm going to a dinner next weekend and I know Barbara will be there. Let me speak to her.

DICK: Good idea.

JOHN: Randy's having some problems with a new acquisition. Give him a little more time. I think he'll come through.

CHAIR: Okay. We have another matter to discuss. Many small gift canvassers are slow to see their prospects. I think we need better worker follow-up . . .

A bright, energetic cabinet has its eye on every phase of a campaign. It is flexible and ready to adapt plans, find new resources when called for, and stimulate workers under it to live up to their potential. Especially when campaign times are the toughest.

Category and Division Report Meetings

Category and division leaders are responsible for the proficiency of their workers. Hold report meetings to:

- Keep workers charged up.
- Update volunteers on progress.
- Share solicitation experiences. Workers learn a great deal from each other.
- Review solicitation techniques.
- Reassign prospects when necessary. If volunteers come to feel they can't get appropriate gifts from a potential donor, it won't happen, and they will avoid contacting the person. The only cure is to change solicitors.

Schedule report meetings every other week. Attendance is usually high at first, then it begins falling off. Hold the meetings anyway. Even if a worker doesn't attend, receiving a notice reminds he or she that solicitations are to be made and reports are expected.

Campaign Newsletters

Publications are another way of keeping campaigners up-to-date and reminding them of their responsibility to a drive. A monthly or twice-monthly report need not be elaborate, but neither should it look grossly amateurish. Produce it on a single 8½″ × 14″ sheet of paper, folded to become a self-mailer. Note the text on desktop publishing beginning on p. 267. Newsletters contain the following information:

- Campaign financial updates.

- A review of solicitation procedures. Select different examples for each mailing and base them on actual solicitations.

- Pictures, graphics, illustrations. Break up text by placing artwork between subjects.

- Short, upbeat feature stories about solicitors, prospects, donors, and committees.

Here's a brief example:

THE ORGANIZATION BUILDING FUND CAMPAIGNER'S NEWSLETTER

Campaign Update

Campaign Chair Jody Brown reports that $450,000 was raised in gifts and pledges toward our goal of $950,000. That figure represents a 12 percent increase in gift income during the past month.

With almost half the goal reached, three campaign divisions are in full operation with another three scheduled to begin during the coming weeks.

What Works and Doesn't Work When You Solicit Prospects

Red Greene told us that he recently got caught between a rock and a hard place. Red made the mistake of writing a letter to a prospect requesting an appointment. Several days later he received a letter from back the man and a check for $1000. The prospect was evaluated at $10,000. *Make your appointments by telephone. Don't give prospects a chance to make unsolicited contributions.*

Jan Brown had different experience. Her research showed that one prospect was a former medal-winning college diver. Jan convinced the woman to make a donation to fund diving equipment for the new swimming pool. *Named gifts are a powerful factor in getting prospects to make donations far above what they originally intended.*

What's New

We have a secret that we won't have to keep from you much longer. By next issue we hope to announce an impressive challenge gift from one of our members. Details are presently being completed.

The Foundation Committee, chaired by Dorothy Ring and Paul Escay, has completed three proposals requesting funds for the cultural arts center, scholarships, and athletic equipment. These proposals will be in the hands of foundation representatives shortly.

REMEMBER TO ATTEND REPORT MEETINGS

Telephone Follow-up

Campaigners may skip report meetings, but they can always be reached by phone. Have category and division chairs get in touch with their workers weekly. If you know your volunteers, you know how to stimulate them. "Come on Marion, let's get on the ball," works for some people. Others must be comforted: "John, I know how busy you are. But I would appreciate it if you could make an appointment with Bill."

Here's the gist of a representative telephone conversation:

CHAIR: Hi, Jane. How are things going with your solicitations?

JANE: Well, I have two appointments next week. I've just mailed you two completed pledge cards although I'm not pleased with either result. Bernice gave us $75,000 and we'd hoped for $100,000. And Bob Davies donated $35,000.

CHAIR: I don't think you should be disappointed. Those are two tough prospects. You've done very well.

JANE: I also saw Fred and Suzie and they won't budge. They seem interested enough, but won't make any kind of commitment for the moment.

CHAIR: Let me bring up Fred and Suzie for discussion at our next cabinet meeting. Maybe you need some help with them.

JANE: I'd appreciate it. I'll wait to hear from you. How are things going otherwise?

CHAIR: Very well. We have some stumbling blocks, but all in all the large gift phase is about two-thirds completed.

JANE: That's great.

CHAIR: I want to thank you again for your time and effort Jane. We really appreciate it.

At report meetings or by telephone, let volunteers know their efforts are recognized by leadership, and that support will be given when needed.

Audio Cassettes

Recordings containing the case statement, requirements for giving, examples of successful solicitation techniques, and a short motivational message help campaigners recall their training, build confidence, and make them aware that leadership is counting on them to get the job done.

You cannot compete in the fundraising marketplace unless you can convince people to give you noteworthy gifts. To do so, volunteers must be exceptionally well trained. Even professional salespeople must learn how to adapt their skills to the nonprofit fundraising experience.

Once volunteers are trained and assigned prospects, stay on top of them until all solicitations are completed. Badger them, pamper them, just don't ignore them. Keep enthusiasm on a high level and they will live up to your expectations.

There is an additional solicitation method that membership and constituent organizations can employ to raise substantial funds. Properly orchestrated, it motivates a gift income almost equal to that obtained by personally visiting prospects. Let's examine that idea next.

8

Group Solicitation: Difficult, But Less Risky Than You'd Imagine

The very notion of asking people to contribute sizable gifts in front of each other throws many volunteer leaders into a state of shock, then outrage.

"How vulgar can you get?" I've been asked.

"Absolutely tasteless," people say.

I admit that the first time I was a party to this method of raising money, you wouldn't have easily spotted me because I was hiding in a dark corner of a large room. Yet I learned that group solicitation, properly treated, can raise vast sums of money, and not hurt anyone in the process.

A big gift fundraising event, commonly called a function, is a luncheon, dinner, cocktail party, or other gathering where prospects attend by invitation and *are aware they will be solicited.* No tickets are sold and expenses are usually not underwritten. The essential difference between a function and the motivational event called a campaign kickoff described at the end of Chap. 6 is that functions count on mass solicitation to bring in huge gift incomes. (Prospects attending kickoffs get solicited individually following the event.) It's a proven and feasible method, but *not* for every group. As you become familiar with how functions are organized and run, you will know whether your organization should get involved with this solicitation option.

Functions Versus Benefits

Although gala social events called benefits have nothing to do with group solicitation (unless there is a secondary fundraising program at the benefit itself), the question is often raised, "Why not hold a benefit instead of a function?" Since functions and benefits cater to groups of people instead of individuals, these gatherings are often thought of in the same framework. Nothing could be farther from the truth. Doubt-

145

less, large benefits can raise great sums, give an organization needed visibility, and attract new supporters. But expenses are usually high and often dig deeply into profit.

Best to consider a benefit within the structure of an annual appeal because it can dilute a capital campaign's traditionally run big gift effort by asking the same prospect for two donations: one to the campaign and another to the benefit. "So what?" you say. The combination of both gifts would equal that of a single gift. No, it wouldn't. Only a portion of the benefit contribution would be available to fund projects. A large part of it would go toward expenses. Compared to benefits, functions are simple and inexpensive to produce. A skillfully run benefit can take as long as a year to plan and organize, often at the expense of other campaign events.

Many times benefits turn out to be merely giant parties for people who can't remember why they are attending. If your capital campaign is solidly organized and its needs compelling, a benefit should be last on the list of fundraising methods—you will have maximized your gift income by the means noted throughout this book. Save your talented, special event organizers for a series of functions.

Here is a comparison of functions and benefits:

Functions	Benefits
Functions are educational, motivational, social events held to help fund a project. Those attending know more about their cause when they leave than when they walked in.	Benefits are social events to help fund a project.
Gift income is a result of the function.	Gift income is received before the benefit based on a projection of income against expenses.
The cost of large functions is paid for by the organization.	Benefits must be heavily underwritten to be profitable.
Expenses are low compared to the return.	Expenses are high, thereby lowering profits.
Functions are after maximum giving of evaluated prospects. Properly strutured, gift income can be overwhelming. Functions work equally well in annual and capital appeals.	Benefits are after preplanned net profits. Donations, often in the form of ticket sales, are the same for each contributor and do not approach the possibility of function gifts. Benefits should be considered one phase of an annual appeal.
Functions rely on inspirational formats and group dynamics to stimulate giving.	Benefits rely on social pressure to stimulate giving.
The responsibilities for scheduling, the type of function, whom to invite, and the program contents are in the hands of the general chair, governing board, or special campaign committee.	The responsibilities for the type benefit, who to invite, and the program contents are mainly in the hands of benefit chairs.
Several functions may be held for each drive.	A single major benefit can be held each year.

Some Function Basics

A function is a sound alternative to face-to-face soliciting because group interaction motivates prospects to donate exceedingly large contributions. Gift income that may take weeks of personal soliciting can be obtained during a single event.

Group solicitation is feasible only when known supporters including current and former donors and those at the top of the cultivation ladder are present. Otherwise, the whole affair will be a disaster in terms of income.

Functions are easily interwoven into several campaign stages:

As Category or Divisional Kickoffs

- A campaign category, professional women, hosts a fundraising luncheon for 60 of their members.

- You evaluate 150 persons to be in a major gifts division of your campaign. Fifty of them are first visited personally. The remaining group is solicited at a special dinner.

As Small Gatherings
Called Parlor Meetings

- An alumni committee holds a special luncheon in which solicitation take places for 20 key graduate-prospects.

- Your general chair invites 10 major gifts prospects to his home for cocktails and a buffet, to be followed by a guest speaker and group solicitation.

Functions rely on group dynamics to stimulate maximum giving; a follow the leader, "join the bandwagon" approach. To get prospects highly enthused and their adrenalin flowing, you must rely on a well-balanced, dynamic program led by knowledgeable, respected, and talented speakers. They can be soft-spoken and intellectual, thunderous and emotional, so long as they keep prospects on the edge of their seats and get them to stand up and be counted as outstanding contributors. Those who also solicit must be especially electrifying and persuasive.

Choosing a Solicitation Method

Depending on the nature of your organization and the makeup of its members or constituents, there are three solicitation methods from which to choose. First, the ground rules that apply to each:

- The persons you invite to a function are highly supportive.

- Those invited *realize that fundraising will take place at the event.*

- The group solicitor is well respected and has made an outstanding gift to the project, or has gained an outstanding reputation for supporting the cause, or, hopefully, both.

- At least one-third of the persons attending the function have already made significant donations to the project and are prepared to announce them at the event.

1. Calling the Names of Individual Prospects.

This is the least genteel, the most difficult to pull off, but by far *the most successful way to solicit funds at a function.* Here is an example of asking prospects for their gifts directly.

A group solicitor concludes her talk stating that it's her family's intention to make the largest donation in its philanthropic career to the organization's capital campaign—$200,000. She then calls on the major gift chair to make his gift announcement. Then several others *who are prepledged* make their support known. The solicitor asks for additional responses. A prospect stands and says she will make a gift of $175,000. There is applause. Another donor makes known his *prepledged* gift after being called upon. Next, the chair calls on a person in the audience who makes a pledge of $125,000 to the drive. The solicitor continues to call prospect names, interspersing them with known givers. She trusts the earlier program and gift announcements to continue motivating notable donations.

This procedure, used in the right situation, can produce major and intermediate gifts about equal to those gotten by person-to-person solicitation. It works when prospects are emotionally energized about a cause and proud to express their feelings about supporting a project. Picture a pent-up ball team sprinting out of the locker room before the start of a game. Their coach has them pumped up; they can't wait to play. That's the sort of group spirit that allows this technique to raise extraordinary sums of money. The reason for having known givers announce their gifts is, as I've stated earlier, because people tend to make gifts in direct relation to those of their peers. If you use this method, here are the main things to remember:

- When names are called, the fundraiser must choose a sequence that prompts maximum giving by starting with several known donors who have provided the largest contributions. Then the person requests gifts from prospects who have the greatest potential. Additional prepledged supporters are called on when there is a lag in prospect announcements.

- If there are persons in the room whom the solicitor believes are not likely to contribute acceptable gifts, they shouldn't be called upon. The fundraiser is under no obligation to call everyone's name.

2. Calling for Gift Announcements.

If the first method is too strong, consider leaving it up to the prospects whether to announce their gifts.

A chairman concludes his fundraising talk by stating that he intends to make a contribution to his organization's annual drive of $75,000. He then asks members of the audience to make their support known. No names are called. As before, the first people to respond are known givers. They set an example. Others in the crowd follow suit and make gifts or pledges, spurred on by the contributions of their peers.

Calling for gifts is still public, but a milder form of requesting contributions than directly calling on a person. There is another important difference: the solicitor lacks control over which prospects announce their gifts, and in what order. Prepledged givers who have made the highest gifts must announce them immediately. If less affluent donors begin the announcements, the risk of having potential top givers emulating gifts of the smaller contributors is high.

The third method is not nearly as dynamic or profitable as the first two.

3. Announcements from Pledge Cards.

Here, the fundraiser asks prospects to write down their donations on pledge cards. The cards are delivered to the microphone and the solicitor reads the contribution and donor's name to the audience. The inherent weakness in this method is that prospects have no chance to be captivated by a donor's announcement. Realize that when people respond aloud to a group solicitor, they often do more than stand up and name a contribution. They also mention the personal, and sometimes moving, reasons why they are giving. Those responses help convince other people to do likewise. You'll get a better idea of how individual gift announcements can spark a group when we visit a parlor meeting shortly.

Known givers play a different role in this method of requesting donations, that of table captains. Their task is to influence prospects seated at their tables positively before the solicitation portion of the program. The gifts or pledges of table captains are announced by the solicitor to help spur on the prospects seated with them.

There is an additional method used to solicit group donations, but compared to the others it is unproductive. Use this alternative when other options are out of the question and person-to-person solicitation is impossible.

A chairperson concludes her fundraising talk by mentioning her contribution. Then she says something to the effect of:

"The table captains will now pass out an envelope containing your pledge card. You've heard our guest speakers and I'm sure you are moved by what they had to say. The goals of our drive are evident. In the spirit of the evening, please take a moment to fill out your cards and one of our volunteers will pick them up. Thank you."

Remember person-to-person solicitation training? One rule you learned was: don't leave a pledge card with a prospect until after the gift is made. By doing so you enable the potential donor to fill in the smallest pledge possible. Now you are forced to break that rule.

Let's say the event is going beautifully. The program was well received and everyone seems stirred up about supporting the campaign. Prospects open their envelopes and remove the card. Often they gaze at it, then stuff the card in a pocket or handbag. They will sleep on their decision on how much to give. Having done so, much of the impetus to make an exemplary gift will have passed. Others sign up for relatively small gifts.

Instead of asking for donations this way, you'd be far better off holding a campaign kickoff event, then personally soliciting prospects in the days following.

If what you've read so far is totally discomforting, don't be concerned. Obviously, you don't want to offend supporters. Many organizations have declined to use these methods and campaigned successfully. If you're prepared to have a go at group solicitation, testing is the best way of seeing whether it works for your organization. Don't start a function program by renting the largest banquet hall in town and wining, dining, then soliciting a few hundred top supporters. Begin with a small, inexpensive gathering, a parlor meeting for those who are turned on by the campaign's goals. Here's an illustration.

Ж Visit to a Parlor Meeting

Fourteen committed, large gift prospects are invited to a buffet dinner in the home of a distinguished community and campaign leader. It would be difficult to refuse this gentleman. Twelve of these people, evaluated between $100,000 and $200,000, consent to attend. One-third have been personally solicited by the host and consent to announce their gifts at the dinner. When the prospective donors received their personal invitations, it was clear that the gathering was a fundraising event:

> Dear (first name),
> I would be grateful if you would join me for a buffet dinner at my home Thursday, April 4, beginning with cocktails at 6:00 P.M.
> The purpose of this get-together is twofold. First, to receive a confidential briefing on drug abuse and its associated crimes in our city. Second, to declare our personal financial commitments to support the communitywide campaign to build a treatment center.
> I am pleased to tell you that author and activist Dr. Alice Blue will bring us up to date on the latest issues facing the city and nation. Alice, as you may know, is a member of the Federal Committee for Drug Enforcement and has just returned from a fact-finding mission that took her throughout the United States.
> Knowing your concern with the city's substantial problem of fighting substance abuse, I urge you to attend this important dinner meeting. Please let me know if you can be with us.
>
> Best Regards,
>
> J. K. Johnson

An agenda to follow dinner is worked out with the campaign chair, one of the prepledged attendees.

1. Cocktails—6:00 P.M.
2. Dinner—6:30 P.M.–7:15 P.M.
3. Welcome & Statement of Purpose. . . . J.K.J. (5 min.)
   a. To update the campaign
   b. To receive the latest update on the national and local drug problem—who it affects, projections for the future, and possible solutions

    c. The need for immediate financial support
4. Campaign Update and Case. . . . Campaign Chair (5 min.)
    a. At conclusion, introduction of Dr. Alice Blue
5. Briefing. . . . Dr. Blue (30 min.)
    a. Report on national and local drug abuse
    b. The role of the private sector in supporting drug treatment and education programs
6. Questions & Answers. . . . (20 min.)
7. The Need to Support the Project. . . . Campaign Chair (5 min.)
    a. Call names for gifts (approx. 25 min.)
8. Adjournment—8:45 P.M.

On Thursday, a pleasant dinner hour comes and goes. Following the campaign update and case presentation, Dr. Blue speaks. She is knowledgeable and compelling. The questions put to her are answered with expertise. Then the campaign chair speaks.

> CHAIR: I am overwhelmed by Alice's report. I had no idea that drug abuse was so widespread. We in this city cannot solve the problems of the whole country, but we definitely can help ourselves. Let me tell you a story.
>
> A friend's son goes to college. I've known him since he was a small boy. One day the youngster tells his parents that he wants to quit school. They know the boy's been edgy and getting poor grades during the last semester. What they don't know is the kid's a cocaine sniffer. Here's a boy who wouldn't touch a cigarette or a drop of alcohol, and he's a confirmed addict. His dad is an attorney, his mother runs a retail store. They never suspected that this could happen to one of *their* children. But it has happened. And it's happening to many sons, daughters, and adults, both wealthy and poor. One way or another we are all affected by drug abuse. There are streets in this small city that aren't safe to walk, even in the daytime.
>
> Our organization's campaign to build a private drug treatment center and start up the most dynamic education program available will turn the tide in this city. As Alice said, our taxes can do just so much. We've got to meet our civic responsibility and see this massive project to its conclusion. As you heard in the campaign update, we have started the ball rolling. What better way to follow the lead of our board of directors and governors than to make our own financial commitments now.
>
> When I consented to chair this campaign, I thought long and hard about making my donation. I wanted it to be substantial, to be an example to those who care about this project. I am proud to tell you that tonight I will make a five-year pledge of $250,000 to our campaign.
>
> Now please. I ask that each of you join me in announcing your donations. J.K., will you begin? (*The host stands*)
>
> J.K.: We in this room can strike out against drug abuse by providing facilities for victims and educating those who could become victims. This is a time for action. I will match that $250,000 pledge with mine.
>
> CHAIR: Thank you J.K. Thank you very much. Barbara?

BARBARA: I too have thought about this drive and about what I've heard here tonight. I will give $100,000.

CHAIR: That is an exemplary gift Barbara. Thank you.

[Until now, gift announcements were from prepledged supporters. The following three are not. These prospects were captured by the mood and momentum of the evening.]

CHAIR: We have commitments so far of $600,000. A fantastic beginning. Sam?

SAM: Alice, I was taken with what you had to say. I am also impressed by the level of giving that I've heard so far. I've been behind our drug treatment project from the start. This city has been my home for a long time, and I have no intention of seeing parts of it become disaster areas. I consider it a responsibility to pledge $200,000 to this drive. (*Anna stands*)

ANNA: I've been a volunteer in our hospital and seen the babies that were born from addicted mothers. What tragedy! We'd better do something about this situation as quickly as we can. Our family will give $150,000.

CHAIR: Thank you both for your generosity. Mike?

MIKE: When I was on my way here tonight I decided to make a $125,000 donation. After listening to Alice and those that pledged before me, I will contribute 200,000 over a five-year period.

CHAIR: Mike, that's a fine gift. Thank you very much. (*Names are called and gifts are announced to conclusion*)

What you have just read mirrors a successful group solicitation. It gives you a firm idea of how one gift announcement spurs another. I know that this scenario leaves some of you upset at the very thought of being in the same room with my characters. Yet I have often watched this form of solicitation take place with astonishing success. There is no embarrassment to anyone if:

- Prospects are completely committed to and emotionally involved with their cause.

- Donors are proud of the contributions they make. (If they are not, don't expect a public announcement.)

Gifts are propelled upward by the dynamics of group interaction, resulting in an organization gaining outstanding income. The illustration was for potential contributors of six figures. If upper-level givers are those capable of donating only four or three figures, believe me, the process works the same.

I'll tell you a secret. I felt sorry for the prospects when I was first involved in arranging parlor meetings and large solicitation events. What pressure they had to endure in front of their peers! How naive I was. These people came to the functions willingly. They knew giving was expected and were delighted to support the organization to which they donated.

The other solicitation variations—calling for gift announcements, and filling out pledge cards and having the donations announced—don't pack the punch of calling on prospects directly.

Qualifying Your Organization

If you're still intrigued by functions and want to know if your organization is ready to run them successfully, here are some questions to answer.

1. Would you be better off if you solicited these same prospects in some other way? Recall that group solicitation is a close second to face-to-face solicitation.

2. Can you hold a function that is in line with your organization's image? For example, what would you think of this invitation?

> The Revolutionary War Ladies Sewing Circle
> cordially invites you to a fundraising bash at
> Sneaky Pete's Saloon and Disco
> to benefit the Annual Campaign.
> Fun for All   A Hell of a Night

Ludicrous? You bet. But many fundraising events are minimally attended because an organization attempting to be creative invents a get-together that is totally out of sync with its membership.

3. Will your governing body approve expenses? Renting a hall, hiring a food service, providing entertainment, printing and mailing invitations, insurance, and so forth can amount to a substantial sum of money.

4. Will your supporters attend a fundraising function?

5. Do you have an experienced special events chair(s) and workforce to organize the event?

6. Do you have a proper time frame in which to hold your function? It may take several months to plan and organize, and must not conflict with other campaign activities.

Exercising Control

Once you plan a function be sure you have control over as many of its elements as possible. Picture this situation.

A summer night. In the distance, lightning flashes continually. Inside a small amphitheater, the stage contains a podium, a microphone, and chairs for a choral group. A trio unpacks their instruments, ready to accompany a well-known baritone who has consented to donate a concert to the Chorale Club Campaign.

The rain sweeps in with a freshening wind. Twenty-five diehard supporters are scattered around the rear of the amphitheater where, like the stage, there is overhead protection from lighting platforms.

The program begins with the campaign chairperson. She reports on the drive, then introduces a state senator. Thus begins a rambling denouncement of the opposing political party, the town's mayor, and the White House. Unable to take any more, two members of the audience shout obscenities at the politician who is led offstage by the chair.

The trio plays an interlude.

The chairperson returns and makes a depressing announcement. While offstage, she received a message from the baritone's manager. Another singer, scheduled to perform a paid concert, has lost his voice and the baritone must replace him at once. After all, the baritone has to make a living.

The rest of the program is lost to the rain.

When you trust a function to bring in all or a portion of big gift income, leave nothing to chance. Obviously you can't depend on the weather being friendly. I recall a fundraising dinner that was held on the grounds of a lovely estate. A backup plan called for moving everything indoors if the weather threatened.

Be extraordinarily careful of the speakers you book. You are totally dependent on these people to set the tone for fundraising. If a professional entertainer or artist is scheduled to appear on your program, make sure to have a valid contract with that person. Take nothing for granted and your fundraising events won't be diffused by mistakes that didn't need to happen.

Putting a Function Together

All functions begin with leadership decisions:

Board, Campaign Committee, or Cabinet Responsibilities
- Scheduling the function (it must fit into the complete campaign timetable and not interfere with other fundraising plans)
- Deciding on the type of function
- Determining the people to be invited
- Enlisting chairs
- Creating an agenda and program
- Determining which method of solicitation to use

Function Committee Responsibilities
- Enlisting key committee leaders
- Budgeting
- Creating a function timetable
- Handling arrangements and decorations
- Handling invitations
- Handling telephone followup
- Handling publicity

Scheduling the Function

Schedule functions during the planning stages of a drive and build them into your campaign timetable. There are times, however, when gatherings must be put together rapidly in response to emergencies or other special situations, like these examples:

A freak storm destroys a wing of a home for the elderly funded by a social service agency. Insurance does not pay all the damage. A meeting is quickly arranged for known supporters of the home. Its purpose is to raise funds that cover the difference between the insurance payoff and the cost to fix the wing.

You plan to solicit donations of prospects assigned to an intermediate gifts division in your campaign personally. Somehow worker enlistment is not what it might have been and you are short on campaigners. A series of parlor meetings is held—luncheons and dinners—to solicit prospects in groups.

The People to Invite

The options for a full-scale function depend on how many people are in a category or division and the method of solicitation. Too large a group, and prospects get lost in the crowd when making gift announcements. If you're holding a parlor meeting, analyze which of your supporters would best respond to being solicited in an intimate group situation.

Don't be concerned that you will insult anyone by asking them to attend. Since the invitation shows fundraising will take place, if prospects don't want to be solicited publicly they won't show up. It's easy to leave someone off an invitation list accidentally, so comb prospect files carefully. People's feelings get hurt when they're not invited to special events—even if they don't chose to attend.

Enlisting Chairs

A large function demands many organizational skills and talents. The volunteers who qualify to run your functions must be:

- Experienced organizers
- Creative and imaginative
- Well respected with unending energy levels
- Able to attract talented volunteers and delegate responsibilities
- Able to control a budget

Creating a Program

Nowhere is it written that people should not enjoy themselves at a fundraising event. *The best functions are celebrations,* people coming together to show their support. Balance the educational side of your program with festive settings and entertainment of one kind or another. If you can book speakers who are both entertaining and thought provoking, so much the better.

Your program must have drawing cards. Look for speakers that not only have a command of the subject, but communicate in an upbeat way. A dull, long-winded lecture will not stimulate anyone to make the gifts you'll be after.

Choosing a Solicitation Method

Again, the choices:

1. Calling the names of prospects and letting them respond
2. Calling for gifts from whomever wants to make them
3. Asking prospects to fill out gift or pledge cards and announcing results from the podium

Key Leaders and Committees You'll Need

Depending on the size of the function, the chair(s) may want to enlist cochairs to handle different portions of the event. They in turn enlist their committees. Following are five essential positions that must be filled for any sizable function:

1. *Arrangements and Decorations Cochair.* Takes care of table groupings, food and beverage service, entertainment, and decorating the room or hall in which the function takes place.
2. *Reservations and Seating Cochair.* Handles incoming reservations from invitations and places prospects at appropriate tables. Follows up on unanswered invitations.
3. *Publicity Cochair.* Markets the function to prospects and, if applicable, to the press.
4. *Invitation and Printing Cochair.* Writes invitation and mailing pieces, sees to design and printing.
5. *Mailings Cochair.* Takes charge of addressing, stuffing, and mailing invitations.

Preparing a Budget

It's easier to spend money than raise it. Once a tentative budget is drawn up, it must be approved by campaign leadership. Then each function cochair is held accountable for seeing that expenses are kept in line.

Here is a budget format for your functions that you also can use for the campaign kickoffs discussed in Chap. 6.

BUDGET FOR _____   DRAFT #_____

   1. Facility rental $_____
   2. Food service   _____
   3. Beverages   _____
       Liquor $_____
       Wine   _____
       Other   _____
   4. Decorations   _____
   5. Printing   _____
   6. Postage   _____
   7. Promotion   _____
       Photography   _____
   8. Entertainment   _____
   9. Equipment rental   _____
       Sound system _____
       Lighting   _____
       Other   _____
10. Speakers   _____
       Fees   _____
       Expenses   _____
11. Licenses or permits   _____
12. Insurance   _____
13. Miscellaneous   _____

   _____ _____
   _____ _____
14. Contingencies (5%)   _____
            Total Expenses $_____

Wanting a function to be first-rate, but not having enough money to assure that it will be, is a common problem faced by planners. Another fear is that if everything is top notch the organization will be accused of spending money that should be used for programs and services. What's more depressing than hearing a prospect say during a function, "I thought we are desperate for funds. Everything is lovely, but it seems to me that you should have used the money for our project." On the other hand, if the room is barren, the same person might say, "What a cheap outfit, what a terrible evening." Somewhere a compromise must be made.

Buying everything at discount prices reduces your budget significantly. Donated materials are even better. One man went through a long diatribe accusing a function chairperson of overspending. She took as much of his lecture as she could, then said . . .

"Let me tell you, Mr. X, that the flowers on your table are from the garden of one of our committee members. The caterer charged half what she usually does, the musicians played for union scale, and the sound system was borrowed from my brother. I hope you enjoyed yourself anyway."

The man was leveled. (The mistake the chair made was not to highlight these contributions in the program given to guests.)

Let's look at each budget item and see where expenses could be saved.

1. *Facilities.*   Assuming you don't have or don't want to use your meeting hall, book a hotel or restaurant meeting or banquet room. Shop around. For example, you will find hotels and restaurants that do not charge rent if you purchase a certain number of meals.

2. *Food service.*   Be conservative with the money you spend on meals. That doesn't mean salsa and tacos from the local Mexican joint, but it also doesn't mean pâté, filet mignon, and champagne for 200. Investigate different caterers (if you're not locked into a menu by a facility) and find out the cost per plate and the quality of the food. Make sure you know the charges for items such as waiters, tablecloths, dishes, gratuities, and so forth.

3. *Beverages.*   Will you have an open or paid bar before dinner? Will you offer wine during dinner? Buy known but not top shelf brands of liquor, good but not great wines. Your supplier or bartender will know how much to stock. Make sure unopened bottles are returnable.

4. *Decorations.*   Strive to create the atmosphere you decide upon using as few expensive materials as possible. Creative people can do incredible things with a few yards of this and a bagful of that.

5. *Printing.*   Design, lay out, and otherwise prepare notices, invitations, response cards, and envelopes in-house. (See Part 6, "The Frugal Way to Smashing Layouts.") Strive for a quality appearance at an economical cost. Get bids from different printers and inspect examples of their work. Don't expect a printer to reprint your order for nothing if there are mistakes. Proofreading is an organization's responsibility.

6. *Postage.*   Anything handwritten requires first-class postage. If on an invitation you write, "John and Sara, I look forward to seeing you at the dinner," it must be mailed first class. Consider sending personalized invitations to at least your top supporters, since the more intimate invitations are, the more likely a prospect is to attend a function. The least expensive way to send invitations for large groups is by bulk mail, requiring a post office permit and a two-hundred-piece minimum mailing, or using carrier route or ZIP+4 codes. Check with your post office.

7. *Promotion and photography.*   Use the function to gain visibility for your organization. Whether you want the press at your event is up to you. Assuredly, they shouldn't be there during the fundraising portion of the program.

   If you can't get services donated, don't scrimp on hiring an editorial photographer. You want someone who can shoot appealing, candid, action photos of your leadership, guest speakers, and top donors. Use these pictures for future publicity, and give copies to key leaders and top givers.

8. *Entertainment.* If you use professional musicians, entertainers, or speakers, be certain to have a proper contract with them specifying fee, performing time, travel, and other expenses you must pay. Also find out if they need props, sound, or lighting equipment.

9. *Equipment rental.* Speakers must be easily heard and seen, so a public address system and perhaps a spotlight may be required. If you plan to show a film as part of your program, be certain the projector is adequate for the number of feet it is away from the screen.

10. *Guest speakers.* (See item 8 above.)

11. *Licenses or permits.* Depending on where you're holding the function, check to see if a liquor license or an occupancy permit is required. Find out if there are other local rules or regulations that apply.

12. *Insurance.* Find out if you need any special policies or riders to cover the function.

13. *Miscellaneous.*

14. *Contingencies.* About 5 percent of the budget is enough to build in for surprises.

Arrangements

A function chair can be likened to a theatrical producer, the arrangements chair compared to director and set designer. If you're not familiar with the facility in which the function is held, get hold of or make up a floor plan. You need it for seating, placement of decorations, and crowd movement. Make sure people can move about freely and not bump into one another coming and going from buffet tables or bars.

Decorations don't need to cost a fortune to be impressive. For instance, a creatively arranged, huge basket of fruit on a buffet table can be extremely appealing and cost little. Put your major decorations where they will be most noticed. Imaginative arrangements people will save you money.

Invitations and Mailings

Save the Date. This is a teaser to get known friends to reserve your function date well in advance. It can be a flyer, a postcard, a memo, and so on. For example:

> Exactly between Halloween and Christmas
> A very special fundraising dinner will occur
> With a guest you all know but have never met.
> Help begin the Lend-A-Hand Agency Drive by
> circling your calendar this very moment.
>   November 27, 6:00 P.M.
> Your personal invitation will follow.

Invitations.   Personalize invitations as much as possible. Make people feel that you really care to invite them.

The Campaign Committee of the Herring Society
invites you to attend
a fundraising dinner to support the Annual Campaign,
to be held September 24th at Fisherman's Hotel

Ho-hum, you say. Wouldn't the invitation be more appealing if a few words were written in longhand at the bottom? Like this:

John and Jody, please make sure to come. Haven't seen you since last summer and we've asked that you sit at our table.

Jim and Sandy

Remember, a personal note requires first-class postage. To save money you might opt for a generic, printed version of a handwritten message on your invitation, but it won't be as effective.

When writing invitation copy, always include journalism's five "W's": who, what, when, where, and why. Don't forget to mention that fundraising will take place. You don't need someone jumping up in the middle of your request for gifts saying, "Wait a minute, nobody told me I was supposed to make a pledge tonight. What sort of rotten organization is this?"

Coordinate your graphics and printing. Stick to various alternatives of the same typeface. If your invitation is burgundy and gray don't make the return card blue and white.

Return Cards.   How formal the return card appears is dependent upon the formality of the invitation and event. Here's an example of a typical return card:

Annual Major Gifts Kickoff Dinner
The Hometown Center

Will Attend_____Will not Attend_____
No. Attending_____
The favor of a reply is requested by
by May 7, 1992

Bulk Mail.   To get discounted mailing rates you must have an organization permit and at least 200 identical pieces. Contact your local post office for information on such things as rates, the proper forms to use, and how the pieces should be banded. You also will need a nonprofit indicia printed on the top right of the envelope.

Use bulk-rate stamps, bought in rolls of 500, to make an envelope appear as if it is mailed first-class. If you want to assure that everyone gets an invitation and that your prospect listings are up-to-date, have "Address Correction Requested" printed on your envelopes. You will be charged first-class postage for the pieces returned, but it is worth the cost to keep files updated.

Perhaps more suited to large direct-mail programs, *Carrier Route and ZIP+4* are cost saving options if coded for each are part of a mailing list computer database. Many rules and regulations apply to both of these programs. It is best to check with your post office for up-to-date information. If you don't maintain a database but have your prospects computerized, there are list management services available to format these programs. Look in the phone book under "Mailing Services" and look at ads in the periodicals listed in "Recommended Reading."

Telephone Follow-up

Don't depend entirely on invitations to get people to a function. Have a telephone squad call each invitee shortly after the mailing is delivered. If a prospect is wavering, a phone call often convinces the person to attend the event, as in the following example.

> CALLER: Hi, I'm calling about the leadership gifts luncheon. We haven't heard from you. You are planning to come, aren't you?
>
> PROSPECT: I'm not sure. I'm incredibly busy. What day is it again?
>
> CALLER: It's noon on Thursday the twenty-third. Trust me. You don't want to miss this program. The organization's new plans are spectacular and our guest speaker is formidable.
>
> PROSPECT: Well, I've got a three-thirty appointment I can't break on the twenty-third.
>
> CALLER: I'll have you out of there in plenty of time. Please come. John Brown and Alice have been asking about you. They said they would pick you up. Everyone's expecting you.
>
> PROSPECT: Who can turn you down? I'll be there.
>
> CALLER: Thanks. I'll fill in a blank reservations card for you. But do me a favor. After we hang up, put the date on your calendar.

Picking the right person to make the call is essential—assign peers to call peers.

Putting a Function Checklist Together

A checklist serves two major purposes: it trusts nothing to memory and gives chairs and committee workers deadlines.

For purposes of brevity, the following checklist, most of which also can be used for a campaign kickoff, combines items that fit within the same category. Separate them for an actual event.

OPERATIONS TIMETABLE

ACTION	RESPONSIBILITY
Preliminary	
( ) Campaign leadership to schedule the function, set the agenda, enlist chairs and committees, and draft a budget.	Board or campaign committee, campaign chairs, function chairs
( ) Known donors recruited to attend function.	Campaign committee or division chair
( ) Prospect list compiled and updated.	Category or division chair(s)
( ) Save-the-date cards, invitations, and associated mailing pieces designed, proofed, printed, addressed, and stuffed.	Printing
( ) Save-the-date card mailed.	Mailing
( ) Prospect pledge cards filled out.	Campaign staff
( ) Facility booked, caterer engaged, and menus chosen.	Function and arrangements
( ) Licenses or permits secured.	Arrangements
( ) Decorations, table placement, and equipment rental planned.	Arrangements
( ) Speakers and/or entertainers booked and contracts signed.	Arrangements
( ) Press invited and press releases sent.	Publicity
( ) Engage photographer	Publicity
Four Weeks Before Function	
( ) Mail invitations and reservation cards. (Allow additional time for bulk mailings.)	Mailing
Two to Three Weeks Before Function	
( ) Begin making table assignments via return cards.	Reservations
( ) Begin master attendance list.	Reservations and seating
( ) Make attendance followup calls.	Reservations and seating
( ) Prepare seating plan for guests and head table.	Reservations and seating
( ) Check with suppliers	Arrangements
( ) See that name tags are ready, if appropriate.	Reservations and seating
One Week Before Function	
( ) Inform caterer of approximate number of meals to prepare.	Arrangements
( ) Make sure equipment is in order.	Arrangements

Two Days Before Function

( ) Give final attendance count to caterer.   Arrangements

( ) Tables set up; equipment moved in.   Arrangements

( ) Liquor and wine delivered.   Arrangements

One Day Before Function

( ) Set up registration table   Arrangements

( ) Install decorations   Arrangements

Day of Function

( ) Check sound system and lighting.   Arrangements

( ) Set tables; set up bar.   Arrangements

( ) Set up registration table; place name cards   Arrangements
in alphabetical order.

( ) Place organization materials to the right of   Arrangements
the place settings.

( ) Make last minute seating changes.   Arrangements and seating

( ) Greet the press; distribute handouts   Publicity
describing the event (press kits).

Postfunction

( ) Send acknowledgement letters to those
who made gifts or pledges.

( ) Plan how to solicit those who did not
attend.

( ) Send thank-you letters to function volunteers.

( ) Send pictures taken at the event to
selected guests.

( ) Evaluate the function.

- Did you get the kind of gifts you expected?
- What were the strong and weak points?
- What was the feedback from those who attended?
- How would you modify the event if it were held again next campaign?
- Did you run over budget?
- Did you receive the press coverage you wanted?

Reminders

1. Although functions can be used to solicit any gift range, the time expenditure
   and expenses are usually justified for prospects capable of making major and
   intermediate gifts.

2. Make sure those you invite are committed to your project.

3. Be certain your program is educational and provocative. Your speakers must inspire the audience to support the drive at the highest giving levels.

4. Select prospects carefully. When you call names, don't mix $1000 givers, for instance, with $150,000 contributors at the same meeting. Neither group will be comfortable.

5. Keep the program moving. Time your agenda and try to abide by the time schedule.

9

Shedding Light on Grant Procedures and Proposals

Research and Perseverance Pay Off

Assuming your cause is worthy and timely and your submission acceptable, getting proposals funded is difficult because of competition. Let's imagine that 500 organizations aid a particular cause. It's reasonable to think that over a year's time a foundation making grants to this cause could receive proposals from each of these groups.

Still, don't let rivalry put you off. And don't be timid about seeking funding if this is your first campaign. Many foundations prefer to make grants to worthwhile new organizations.

Before sending out proposals, thoroughly research each foundation to find out if:

- The aims of your proposal are in keeping with a foundation's interests such as those published in *The Foundation Directory*. If you can't find these guideposts, write the foundation and ask for them. Its staff won't think you ignorant if you do so.

- The gift amount you request is realistic. You'll have egg all over your face if you request $100,000 from a foundation who states it never gives more than $50,000 in individual contributions.

After you've submitted a proposal, be patient. Don't expect an immediate response. Typically, your presentation is first screened by a staff member who decides if your project is compelling and meets guidelines. Then the proposal is forwarded to the final decision makers—the foundation's officers and trustees. They may not meet often, so you may have to wait months for a foundation to notify you one way or another about a request.

The worst thing that can happen to your proposal is that it's rejected. If so, don't get defensive and cross the foundation off your prospect list. Instead, consider the long-range picture and be persistent:

- Write the foundation and thank the officers and trustees for considering your request. If your project remains timely, ask if you can resubmit the proposal in the future. Perhaps your submission was just edged out this year and it might be approved next time around.

- Ask the foundation if it would be interested in a similar project.

- Continue communicating. Relate your latest activities and accomplishments.

- Submit additional proposals.

Cultivate foundations as you would individuals. Establishing a rapport between a member of your organization and a foundation representative stands you a better chance of eventually receiving a grant. One aggressive development vice president running a $106 million capital campaign brought his staff together and outlined a plan to bring distinguished faculty and foundation administrators together to discuss various departmental needs. A year later, foundation support showed a large upswing that was directly attributed to these personal visits.

I recently phoned a corporate foundation executive to see if a proposal that was soon to be submitted was on the right track. The staff person in charge was extremely helpful, suggesting several ideas to improve the execution of our grant request.

When you research a foundation, study its list of officers and trustees to see if someone in your organization knows these people. In one campaign, a committee met to identify prospects. It came across a family foundation which none of our advisory board had heard of before, but whose grant guidelines were right down its alley. When the chairman read off the names of the trustees, an advisor remarked, "I went to college with one of those men. I'll give him a call." The organization had an inside track to that foundation.

When you receive an appointment with a foundation spokesperson, send the people who have control over both the project and its budget.

Preparing for Grant Submissions

A resounding "yes" to the following questions means your organization is ready to write and submit proposals.

1. Can you justify that your project is *important enough to be immediately funded?*
    (During the past two years, homelessness has increased over 75 percent in our city. The downtown area has 2000 homeless persons located mainly in the Alltown area. City and state funds cannot totally handle the problem.)

2. Do you have a *practical solution* to meet a need or solve a problem?
    (Our first year's pilot program calls for two ways of dealing with the homeless. The first is to provide low-cost shelters by renovating existing structures in the Alltown area between second and tenth streets. At the same time we will provide a job placement service for the unemployed. They can use the housing so long as they qualify as homeless and work at jobs offered to them.)

3. *Can results be measured* when your project is funded?

(Renovations by volunteer craftspeople will provide three hundred shelters during the next six to eight months. Those homeless entering the job market and earning adequate wages will seek more permanent housing, thereby making room for new homeless persons.)

4. Does your staff have the *necessary qualifications* to conduct the project?

(Our agency has provided social services to the city for 20 years. Its professional staff of skilled social workers and many volunteers has been responsible for scores of programs that have aided people in distress. This project will be headed by Dr. Joe James, a sociologist, who has distinguished himself in the field of personal self-help for two decades.)

5. If your project is funded, *can it continue to operate?* It's one thing to raise startup dollars, another to raise operating funds.

(We have projected maintenance costs for renovations and the cost of starting up a special placement service. Each is included in the agency's operating budget after the initial year.)

6. Can you provide a detailed *"summary of needs"*?

7. Do you have *support documents* available? Such as:

Resumes or biographies of your project staff and key board members

Your operating budget

Annual reports

A copy of the IRS statement granting your organization the right to solicit tax exempt funds

Endorsement letters from professionals in the field or from potential recipients who will profit once your project is funded

Working Up Proposals

Here's how to organize proposals:

Subject	Action
Title Page	Name the project and the sponsoring organization.
Introduction	Establish credibility by stating your organization's background, the case for your campaign, and the time frame.
Overview	Describe the specific reason(s) why you need a grant.
Summary of Needs	List budget items related to the gift request.
Proposal	Ask the foundation for a specific gift for a definite purpose.
Appendix	Support materials. Include the previously mentioned addendum as it fits your organization.

Proposal writing is not romantic prose or bureaucratic rhetoric. It is clear and concise business writing, without frills, so . . .

1. *Keep your presentation brief and to the point.*   You don't get good marks for length. An overwritten proposal may be taken as a sign that your project is not well thought out. For the most part, proposals, not including an addendum, need not be over 10 or 12 pages. Many excellent submissions are far less. One example of overwriting is the story of a gentleman who was trying to raise foundation money for an educational project and wasn't getting anywhere. A friend asked me to see what I could do to help. Part of our long distance phone conversation went like this:

> ME: From what you say, you seem to have a very appealing project. I'd like to see your proposal. Tell me a little about it.
>
> CAMPAIGNER: It's certainly complete. Nothing is left out, and it has plenty of rationales.
>
> ME: How long is it?
>
> CAMPAIGNER: Sixty pages.
>
> ME: Sixty pages? That's far too many.
>
> CAMPAIGNER: (*Angrily*) You don't understand. My subject is very difficult and complex.
>
> ME: No! Doing away with hunger is difficult. Doing away with AIDS is complex. And proposals for those subjects wouldn't need to run sixty pages. Your project is not at all hard to comprehend. You might try cutting it by 75 percent. Foundation people expect the point to be made rapidly, no matter what the subject.

This man refused to edit his proposal and was lucky to receive one small grant in two years of trying.

2. *Compose in an active voice, and be positive.*

Our project meets community demands that are in total accord with your foundation's guidelines.

instead of . . .

It is hoped that this project will, in accordance with your foundation's precepts, meet certain needs that our community thinks to be of a priority nature.

3. *Avoid bureaucratic language.*   There's no need to "prioritize, structurize, indoctrinize," and so forth.

4. *Be specific.*   "Our classrooms hold 200 students and we have 300 people who have signed up for classes," not, "We have more students than classroom space."
   Make sure the first page captures the reader's interest or the person will not pay full attention to the remainder of the text. Let's look at two introductions; notice how each organization presented its case.

THE DEPARTMENT OF AUDIOVISUAL RESOURCES
AT THE UNIVERSITY MEDICAL CENTER

Introduction

The University Medical Center, as part of its commitment to continuing excellence in patient care, education, and research, has recently embarked on a major development program.

A significant component of the program is the establishment of the Department of Audiovisual Resources that will provide the institution with an opportunity to realize the full potential of audiovisual aids.

Audiovisual resources already play an important role at the medical center, but a comprehensive and fully equipped department is not yet a reality. The objective of the department is to develop and coordinate the most effective and comprehensive audiovisual aids in all aspects of medical education, research, and patient care. The department will be a major educational resource for the School of Education and the Postgraduate Medical School. It also will provide specialized training for paramedical personnel, nonmedical personnel, and patients. These audiovisual aids have the further advantage of conserving the precious time of the physician to the advantage of his or her patients.

There was no need for the medical center to state its institutional credentials because of its well-known reputation. Neither would other similarly entrenched nonprofits have to detail background. The case for the medical center's new audiovisual department appears early, in the second and third paragraph of the introduction. An organization or individual with less visibility must provide essential background material before stating the case. For example, in the introduction to the proposal for the around-the-world sailing competition, often referred to in this text, it had to be made clear the race was first-rate, and the sailor a worthy competitor.

A PROPOSAL FOR FUNDING
THE AMERICAN FLAG CAMPAIGN

Introduction

The BOC single-handed round-the-world sailing race is perhaps the toughest sporting event in the world. Akin to conquering Mount Everest, the race is a unique test of determination, endurance, and resourcefulness. In addition, the competition is a tough physical challenge that demands consummate skills. Not only do entrants have to guide their vessels through tropical calms, but they must fight the roaring, icy gales of the Southern Ocean.

(Continued)

Each competitor—a single person—functions as captain, navigator, and crew. Alone at sea, the racers must deal with many months of constantly changing dangers and other confrontations while often combating frustration and loneliness. More than 500 people wrote to the race committee to ask about the last BOC Challenge. Twenty-five sailors from nine countries actually started the race. Sixteen completed the circumnavigation. The race was divided into four legs. Starting from Newport, Rhode Island, the yachts, etc . . .

American sailor, author, and adventurer Hal Roth placed fourth in class and sailed 27,500 miles over a period of nine months during the race. In his career, Mr. Roth has logged over 145,000 miles of ocean sailing in small sailing yachts (including two circumnavigations and two trips around Cape Horn). He has written seven widely acclaimed books on high adventure, and joins a select group of sailors whose great voyages began when they were in their fifties and sixties, such as Joshua Slocum and Sir Frances Chichester.

[The background information led up to a brief case statement.]

The third BOC challenge begins during September 1990. Race organizers anticipate 40 starters from 12 countries. It is Mr. Roth's intention to make a second bid to win this race that in the past has been won by French sailors who have competed in specially designed and extremely well-equipped vessels with heavy shore support. We believe that American designers, builders, and sailors are the best anywhere, and with adequate financial support can fit out a winning vessel and prove the leading edge of United States technological leadership and advancement.

To this end, we have embarked on a major fund-raising program sponsored by the Oceanus Institute, a nonprofit organization.

When a little-known organization or project must be fully described, as in the above example, make sure qualifying information relates to the six fundraising requirements mentioned in Part 1.

1. *Compelling organizational goals.*   In the circles for which this proposal was written, the notion of a highly regarded United States sailor winning this international competition was of great interest.

2. *Background of key leaders must reflect a record of experience and expertise.*   Roth's credentials were briefly but concretely established. (An introduction is not the place for a résumé or curriculum vitae. Those belong in the appendix.)

3. *Key leaders must be strongly visible relative to their markets.*   Roth had previously participated in a similar event, written seven successful books on ocean sailing, published many articles, and frequently lectured on his sailing adventures throughout the nation.

4. *Professional leaders must be highly competent and totally committed.*   Competency was not an issue, and anyone who has the nerve to sail alone around the world in a small vessel is totally committed to this sort of project.

5. *Campaign needs must be specific, attractive, and timely.*   Roth intended to make a second bid to show that he, with the benefit of United States technology, could compete with the best of foreign sailors. Roth had 11 months to raise his funds before the start of the race.

6. *Results must be measurable.*   A weekly schedule showing expected refit progress was included in the appendix.

The next portion of a proposal is the overview, a description of the project mentioned in the introduction. (The examples are excerpted.)

Department of Audiovisual Resources

One method that has proven indispensable to modern education is the use of audiovisual aids. Textbooks, lectures and laboratories must be supplemented with instructional films, videotapes, slides, printed materials, medical illustrations, and photographs.

The Department of Audiovisual Resources will house a complete communications center . . . [The overview continues by describing proposed film and television production facilities, and programming, medical art, illustration, and additional services. These subjects were covered in six and one-half pages.]

Again, the sailing competition.

Overview

The Race

With the experience of having completed an earlier BOC Challenge in the same vessel and with an intimate knowledge of the earth's wind systems, Mr. Roth knows how to improve and oversee an American challenge. He plans to recruit the best sailmakers, riggers, shipwrights, mechanics, plus other experts to make American Flag as competitive as possible. With the proper yacht and suitable support, Mr. Roth projects an elapsed time of 150 sailing days for the four legs of the race. This would be a new record. [The overview continues with additional technical information concerning new equipment and such.]

(Continued)

The Educational Program

During the race Mr. Roth will participate in an educational program called the Student Ocean Challenge. The program, designed for children from grades three to twelve, tracks the racers as they progress around the world. Students experience the excitement of the adventure as they learn about computer technology, history, geography, language arts, mathematics, and science.

Previously, the Student Ocean Challenge reached more than 300 schools and 20,000 children in the United States, Canada, Europe, South Africa, Australia, and Brazil. [Continued description of the program]

Having completed the overview, there are two ways to list a budget in a proposal:

1. The organization's entire summary of needs can be reproduced. The sailboat competitor chose this option since the total campaign was devoted to a single enterprise.

2. Specific project costs relating to the subject of the proposal can be broken out from the organization's total summary of needs. The medical center reproduced only that portion of its summary that pertained to funding the new audiovisual department.

The last part of a proposal is the solicitation. Get right to the point. Avoid flowery language such as, "How noble and uplifting it would be if your foundation were to become a part of our organization family by funding the . . ."

Again, the medical center.

Proposal

The University Medical Center invites the ABCD Foundation to consider a gift of $2.5 million, payable over a period of five years, for the establishment of the Department of Audiovisual Resources. Such a grant would mark the turning point in the development of audiovisual aids for medical education.

. . . and the sailboat competitor:

The Proposal

We believe that the refitting and equipping of the racing yacht American Flag for the upcoming world-class BOC Challenge race benefits all those dedicated to international sporting competitions. In keeping with your foundation's aim to foster goodwill among international communities, we ask that you consider a grant of $28,000 to purchase navigational equipment for the Spirit of America project.

The final segment of a proposal is the appendix. Include documents that support your organization and project. For the sailing race we included plans of the yacht, a schedule of refitting, Hal Roth's résumé, and a copy of the Oceanus Institute's Internal Revenue Service statement declaring that the organization was tax exempt. *That statement is essential for any group that is totally or comparatively unknown.*

What to Do Once You've Received a Grant

1. Make certain you know how the foundation would like its name used in publications such as brochures or press releases, e.g., "The Alpha Symphony Orchestra Annual Festival Concert is sponsored by a grant from the Bravo Foundation."

2. A foundation may ask that you submit a report so it can check on how its grant is being put to use. Be sure reports are filled out properly and sent in on time.

3. Grants are often renewable. After the original grant period is up, write a short, straightforward letter to the foundation explaining why you need additional funding. Again, request a specific contribution: "Will the BCD Foundation consider renewing its $125,000 grant to help save seals from extinction?"

Make Your Proposal Do Double Duty

A proposal is an extremely convincing solicitation aid when approaching individual and corporate prospects.

- It shows potential supporters you consider them important enough to have prepared a formal gift request.

- It allows prospects to keep the details of your request on hand and share it with others who play an important role in gift decisions, such as a spouse or corporate committee.

- It incorporates proper business procedures. Many executives deal with highly structured, written proposals every day. They, like foundations, often need a board or committee decision before approving your request.

When you adapt proposals for known individual and corporate supporters, limit or eliminate background information and addendum.

Inquiry Letters

Some foundations require a query before seeing a full proposal. Make your letters brief and concise—one or two pages are sufficient. Interest the foundation in your project and attempt to arrange a personal appointment with a staff person or trustee.

Address the letter to the contact suggested in *The Foundation Directory* (see page 52) or similar reference guide. If you can't find a name, address it to "Principal Officer."

Dear _____,

Since your foundation concerns itself with combating drug abuse, we ask that you consider funding a drug education program to be undertaken by this organization. The year-long program will cost $500,000.

The lead paragraph aligns the foundation's interest (combating drugs) with the organization's project (drug education), and states the cost. Following paragraphs include:

- A short description of the project
- A brief description of your organization's qualifications to take on the project
- Brief qualifications of the people who will be in charge
- The amount of money you are requesting

The closing might be:

I would like very much to arrange a personal visit with you to discuss our complete proposal. Any additional information you may require will be furnished at once.

Sincerely Yours,

J. W. Fiske

Executive Director

Have the chief executive sign the letter, and enclose a campaign brochure. If you don't get an answer after waiting a reasonable time, phone the foundation representative and ask about your request. It gives you a good reason to start up a conversation about your organization and project. If your inquiry is turned down, thank the foundation for its courtesy and mention that you will submit additional requests in the future.

A closing reminder: you can't create proposals that are all things to all prospects. Concentrate on designing them to be attractive to foundations, individuals, and corporations who share your organization's values and interests.

PART 4

Running a Profitable Small Gifts Drive

10

Understanding Small Gifts, Givers, and Approaches

Stop Baking and Start Fundraising

Organizations who run entire small gift drives based solely on reward-offering occasions such as bake sales, raffles, and auctions are selling themselves short. One frustrated woman told me recently, "I am sick of selling ice cream to fund our local little league team. Surely there must be better ways of raising money."

A high school, short on funds for sports programs, raised $4000 by having students make and deliver pizza—a wonderful gesture. But the school could have easily doubled that amount of money in the same period. Although fine for community relations, these popular fundraising chestnuts produce comparatively little income compared to those that follow. Save them for the final wrap-up of a full-blown drive.

Who Are Small Gift Prospects?

It's Saturday, you're relaxing at home when the doorbell rings. You open the door and a man and woman introduce themselves. They would like you to donate money to the local cultural arts building-fund campaign.

Later, you the tune the radio to a public broadcasting station. The announcer is asking for gifts to support the station's programming.

That afternoon, you find a letter in your mailbox: a national health organization asks that you make a gift to its yearly appeal.

In each of these cases, you were considered a small gift or mass appeal prospect, one of a large number of persons who uses an organization's services, supports its mission, or both. Unlike many upper-level givers, small gift contributors don't receive rewards for their donations, such as public recognition, significant named gifts, or key leadership posts. They are most often motivated by total belief in an organization's principles. People with comparatively small means often sacrifice personal pleasures to make a $500, $100, $50, or even a $10 gift to a campaign. In that sense, these donors can be greater believers in your purpose than those who give you far larger gifts.

Another reason not to ignore small givers is their future potential: with an upswing in income, many of these persons will move into higher gift ranges.

Small Gifts in the Order of Things

Defining what amount of money constitutes a small donation is relative and arbitrary. It depends on the size of the goal and the giving potential of a constituency. More importantly, the small gift appeal concentrates on the largest group of prospects who contribute the smallest amounts of money. Let's look at the second rule of thumb from "Expecting the Most from the Least," first encountered in Part 1.

2. Approximately 80 to 90 percent of incoming funds are donated by 10 to 20 percent of a membership or constituency.

Put the opposite way, approximately 10 to 20 percent of your goal will be donated in small gifts from 80 to 90 percent of your supporters. For example:

Overall goal	Total membership	Small gift prospects	Anticipated small gift income
$1,500,000	1500	1200 to 1350	$150k to $300k
100,000	1000	800 to 900	10k to $20k
50,000	500	400 to 450	5k to $10k

Earlier I suggested it would be best for a campaigner to handle no more than five prospects. Using that figure, look at the number of workers needed for several drives:

Total membership	Small gifts prospects	Number of workers needed
1500	1200 to 1350	240 to 270
1000	800 to 900	160 to 180
500	400 to 450	80 to 90

Based on five cards per solicitor, 16 to 18 percent of these memberships would have to be recruited as small gift workers. These are unlikely percentages for many organizations. So it is not unrealistic in small gift appeals for volunteers to handle more assignments than their major or intermediate gift counterparts—and do so effectively. Small contributions take less time to get than larger donations.

Choosing an Approach

The more personal the solicitation, the more gift income is received. Let's compare options:

Visits by Appointment	Most Personal
Membership–Constituent Canvassing	Personal
Nonaffiliated Prospect Canvassing[1]	Personal
By Phone	Semipersonal
By Mail	Least Personal

The way in which you select to solicit small gift prospects depends on the:

1. Number of people to be seen. If possible, see everyone by appointment or canvassing.

2. Availability of workers. If campaigners are scarce, you must solicit by telephone or mail.

3. Potential giving level of the prospect. The highest-evaluated potential givers, or those with the best prior giving records, should be seen personally.

4. Prospect's location. If potential donors don't reside in your area, you cannot visit them. However, an option commonly used by alumni campaigners is to organize local chapters and enlist volunteers to visit each graduate.

Developing a Coverage Plan

Take another look at the divisional pyramid from Chap. 3:

---

[1] There are essential differences between membership–constituent and nonaffiliated prospect canvassing. The former is limited to visiting friends of an organization. Solicitors have an excellent chance of being welcomed, fully presenting the campaign case, and obtaining generous gifts. Soliciting nonaffiliated prospective donors involves campaigners ringing doorbells at the beginning of a street and continuing that process from block to block. Depending on the nature and visibility of the cause, the chances of being welcomed are fair to poor. As well, workers may not be given a chance to tell their full story. Without a proper presentation, no impetus exists for the prospect to make more than a token contribution, if any at all.

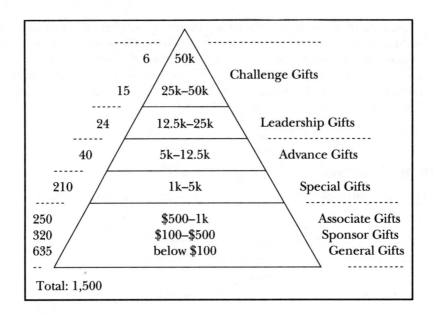

6	50k	Challenge Gifts
15	25k–50k	
24	12.5k–25k	Leadership Gifts
40	5k–12.5k	Advance Gifts
210	1k–5k	Special Gifts
250	$500–1k	Associate Gifts
320	$100–$500	Sponsor Gifts
635	below $100	General Gifts

Total: 1,500

In the example, 1205 prospects, roughly 80 percent of the 1500 person membership, are assigned to three small gift divisions. Let's assume they are made up of members, constituents, and nonaffiliated persons. These who contribute are forecast to donate individual gifts of less than $1000.

Using a team approach, the example organization enlists 240 small gift campaigners to solicit these prospects, each worker finds a teammate, then each pair solicits 10 prospects. But what happens if the same organization only rounds up 90 workers. How could they most effectively be used?

1. As many as possible of the 250 prospects in the $500–$999 gift range should be solicited by personal appointment as are upper-level potential donors: they have the largest giving potential of the three divisions.

2. The 320 prospects in the $100–$499 group could be canvassed by a single worker instead of a pair.

3. The 635 prospect General Gift Division (below $100) has the most prospects and will contribute the least income. They would be approached through a combination of canvassing, telephone, and mail.

As an illustration, I've assigned the 90 workers to the above three divisions to show you one way they might be used.

Division and Logistics	**Coverage Plan**
Associate—$500–$999—250 prospects, 20 workers.	The 10 most experienced workers will each make appointments to visit 10 of the highest-evaluated prospects. An additional 10 workers will canvass the remaining 150 prospects, each seeing 15 of these people.

Sponsor—$100–$499—320 prospects, 20 workers.	The highest-evaluated 200 persons to be canvassed, 12 prospects per worker. The remaining 80 lowest-evaluated prospects slotted for solicitation by phone.
General—below $100—635 prospects, 40 workers.	Three hundred prospects to be seen via a door-to-door canvas by 20 workers each seeing 15 prospects.
Phonathon and mail—10 workers.	Remaining 335 prospects assigned to phonathons. Those who cannot be reached by phone will be solicited by mail.

Even when you have a shortage of workers, see as many prospects as possible personally. Suit coverage plans to the strengths and limitations of your small gift volunteer force.

11
Knocking on Doors— How Canvassing Pays Off

Getting Started

Know Your Prospects

Evaluate as many prospects as possible using past giving as a guide. It's a waste of potential gift income not to find out which supporters can give you larger donations. Assuredly, the information won't be volunteered.

A donor who had been contributing $50 a year to an organization came into an inheritance. When a campaigner discovered the man's good fortune, he evaluated the donor at $2500 and later received a $1000 gift. The donor was asked why he had not made a similar contribution earlier. He replied: "Nobody asked me to." Make sense?

It's often impossible to evaluate every prospect. Yet to be effective, volunteers need definite gifts to request when they solicit. An alternative exists for past donors and other known prospects who are not evaluated: *assume* they can make a donation at the top of the giving range in which they are placed, and solicit them accordingly. For instance, a prospect in the $500 to $999 division would be asked for $1000, in the $100 to $499 range the solicitor would request a gift of $500, and so forth.

Recruit a Workforce

Small gift chairs are responsible for enlisting an adequate number of workers for the various divisions or categories to which they are assigned. Often, that's a tough job because volunteers get little glory for their efforts. When major gift campaigners report outstanding contributions everyone applauds and spreads the word. A small gifts worker brings in a pile of $100 donations and the person receives a well-meant thank you and a request to take another handful of prospects.

To share responsibilities in large campaigns, intermediary leadership positions are created between small gifts chairs and workers. For example:

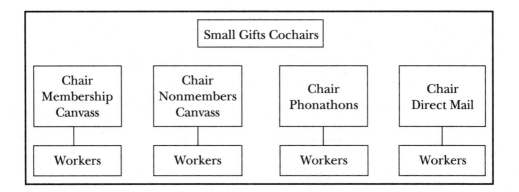

Design an Area Chart

Designate areas of neighborhoods or communities in ways that make maximum use of a canvasser's time and energies. Enable them to visit the most people in the shortest time possible. Here's an example:

Membership–Constituent Canvassing

Sector 1
    Border Creek—various homes
    between 2d Street and Avenue D.

Sector 2
    #101, 405, 708, 1015, 1250 E Street.

Nonaffiliated Canvassing

Sector 1
    Border Creek—homes from
    4th to 10th Streets, and Avenue E.

Sector 2
    All of zip code 12345.

Marketing

Make the small gifts phase the most publicized portion of your drive. Be sure to promote an upbeat, "join the bandwagon" attitude among potential donors. Use newsletters, posters, public service announcements, and other marketing tools to let prospects know the small gifts drive is about to take place.

Avoid cold calling by sending a brief letter and brochure announcing the campaign to prospects shortly before they are solicited. The letter should contain the following information:

- A description of the project and who will benefit from its being funded—the case statement.

- The campaign goal and a statement saying that it is within reach if each prospect does his or her part.

- Rewards that the prospect will receive by making a contribution. "You will allow disabled people the chance to show that physical handicaps have nothing to do with their pride as human beings."

- Types of giving: share plans, associations, clubs, challenge gifts, and so forth.

- A request to welcome campaign workers when they arrive.

Materials You'll Need for Orientation and Assignment Meetings

1. Prospect file cards or pledge cards (for a capital campaign) with pertinent information filled in for each prospect.

2. Alphabetically arranged prospect listings by category or division.

Prospect Listing by Category or Division						
			Category or Division: Patrons			
Name	Address	Phone	Evaluation	Assigned to	Gift	Named Facility
Arned	1 Oak Ln.	123-4567	$400			
Bass	25 Elm St.	123-3456	$500			
Carr	34 Bank St.	123-5678	$300			

3. Worker assignment forms.

Worker Assignment Sheet

Worker's Name:_____   Chair:_____

Category or Division:_____   Phone:_____

Phone:_____

Name	Address	Phone	Evaluation	Gift	Named Facility	Remarks

4. Orientation meeting notices. Send a letter or save-the-date note to workers announcing training and assignment sessions, like in this illustration:

Post This Notice

Attach this meeting announcement to the refrigerator, put it by the coffee pot, hang it on the mantelpiece . . . just don't misplace it.

On April 8th, the Organization Campaign will hold an Associate and Sponsor's Division Worker Rally beginning at 11:00 A.M. in our lecture hall. There you will be taught the best ways to ask for contributions, receive assignments, and begin soliciting. By the end of the afternoon we will have talked to hundreds of potential contributors and received many outstanding contributions.

Through your efforts we will soon reach our goal.

We look forward to working with you on the 8th. Thank you again for joining our team.

Dave Buff   Anita Brown
Associate Gifts Chair   Patron Gifts Chair

P.S. Refreshments will be served.

If you ever attended a meeting planned for 100 people and only a third of them showed up, you know how depressing that can be. Don't depend only on written notices. Phone each worker shortly after you send the meeting announcement to make sure the date is reserved.

5. Audiovisual equipment.

6. A folder for each worker containing:

A Campaign brochure

Several blank pledge cards for a capital campaign or gift receipt forms

A list of named gift opportunities

A copy of solicitation methods that the trainer will discuss

A list of objections that your organization may encounter, and responses for each

A "Guidelines for Giving" list (unrestricted, challenge grant, etc.)

A copy of the letter sent to prospects

Overcoming the Perils of Soliciting

Canvassing is often rough going, even when friends of an organization are visited. You take a deep breath, ring the doorbell, and wait. Maybe you've arrived right in the middle of an argument. Perhaps the prospects just had a financial setback. The door opens and you get an icy stare or a verbal dart. It takes a mighty person not to be put off by such reactions. So what makes thousands upon thousands of volunteers successfully solicit donations in this way every year? They are charged up, turned on, totally committed to their projects. Equally important, these volunteers *know that they are not alone, but part of a cadre of solicitors* combing the neighborhoods at the same time. Canvassers must be among your highest-motivated campaigners. They will reach that plane immediately following a properly run orientation session, and that's when you ask small gifts workers to begin soliciting.

Short-sighted groups take the easy way out and mail training material and prospect assignments to volunteers. Nothing could be more unproductive. Workers scan the material, ring a few doorbells, get a few turndowns, and then give up. Your small gift coverage is kaput.

Membership and Constituent Canvassing

Visiting a Small Gifts Orientation and Distribution Rally

It's 11:00 A.M. on a weekend. Into a large, open meeting room stream 60 volunteers, members of an environmental activist's organization. They had a written notice and phone follow-up to make sure of their attendance. Two long tables, each for a separate division, are placed along one side of the room. Prospect listings are laid out in alphabetical order by sectors on the tables. The workers have coffee, are asked to be seated, and the program begins. [As with upper-level gift solicitation training, my comments are in brackets.]

I. Welcome & Statement of Purpose. . . . Campaign or small gifts chair

CHAIR: Welcome, and thank you for attending this important event. It will be a long day, but a fruitful one. After the training session you will be visiting many of our friends to discuss this year's plans and ask their support. Yours is one of the finest campaign teams we've ever put together. Now, let me bring you up to date on the drive . . .

II. Campaign Progress Report. . . . Campaign or small gifts chair

CHAIR: During the past six months we have received exceptional support from private individuals, corporate leaders, and three area foundations. I am pleased to tell you that as of today we have received gifts and pledges totaling $874,000 toward our goal of $900,000. The drive is 92 percent complete. I am grateful to our donors and to the dedicated campaigners who have led the way. Now it's up to each of you to help raise the remaining 8 percent of the money needed to balance a bare-bones budget.

[In opening remarks, make it clear that workers are being counted on to make the drive successful. Remember, small gift volunteers will believe they can conclude a drive only if the total goal is within reach. If, for instance, an organization reported that it raised 40 or 50 percent of its gift income, the workers would realize that they could never bring in the remaining funds.]

CHAIR (*continues*): During the early stages of the drive, we produced a slide show that examines our organization's background and summarizes current needs. I know you'll enjoy watching it.

III. Slide Presentation [If no presentation exists, describe the latest organizational accomplishments and campaign needs. Use as many exciting visuals as possible.]

IV. Introduce Trainer. . . . Campaign chair

V. Solicitation Training

TRAINER: Solicitation is like selling. It's not easy and it's not glamorous. But you represent an organization whose mission is to improve the environment, and therefore the health and physical beauty of the community. Inviting a person or a family to support those purposes financially gives them and future generations the opportunity to have safe and attractive surroundings in which to exist. You'll find most people gracious, and interested in our project. If they aren't, don't get hot under the collar. Say thank you and go on to the next prospect.

Let's examine the methods that will help you obtain the largest possible gifts from your prospects. May I have the first slide, please.

[The text for each slide is superimposed over striking environmental photographs depicting both natural beauty and awesome destruction caused by people's abuse.]

Start With Your Contribution
See Prospects in Person
Figure Out the Prospect's Interests

TRAINER (*continues*): Most of you have already made personal gifts to the campaign. I urge those of you who haven't to do so following the meeting. Your donation shows a personal financial commitment to protecting the environment. It's unfair to expect other people to contribute when you have not. Your gift will motivate prospects by setting an example for them. We'll see how this works shortly.

Donors respond more generously to people they see face-to-face than they do to telephone or mail solicitations. Take the time to see each prospect.

People naturally give money to projects that interest them the most. For example, some folks are most concerned about ecological restoration. Others care more about wildlife. Another group has polluting the world's oceans uppermost in its mind. From the moment you meet your prospects, find out what most appeals to them about the organization. Then pattern the solicitation around that concern. You wouldn't want to ask me to donate to a forestry project if I am primarily interested in preserving waterways.

Mention Campaign Progress
Present The Case Thoroughly
Give Your Personal Viewpoint
State Your Gift

Few want to give money for a campaign they think is barely supported. Let your prospects know that 92 percent of the goal has been reached, and that community involvement has been outstanding.

Don't assume prospects know all there is about the organization and campaign. Present the case—why the campaign is taking place, what the result will be, and the people who will benefit from a goal-reaching effort. The campaign brochure contains this information, but it's up to you to make the campaign come alive by engaging in discussion with prospects and persuading them to make a first-rate gift. If a brochure could do that, we wouldn't be here today.

Tell each prospect how *you* feel about the organization, how you, your family, or friends have made use of its services. This will naturally lead you to mention your contribution, which will serve as a guideline for potential donors to emulate. Next slide please.

Request a Specific Gift Aimed at Maximum Giving
Be Prepared to Overcome Objections
Close the Solicitation
Be Ready to Offer Alternatives

The quickest and easiest way to get donations is to ask prospects what *they* want to give instead of requesting a specific gift. It's the difference between the salesperson who sells a product to a customer and the one who takes orders for one. Merely asking for a contribution guarantees a minimal amount of money—it's human nature. So you won't have to do that, one of our campaign committees has evaluated many prospects and recommended contributions for each of them based on their ability to give. These suggested figures appear on the pledge cards you will receive. That's the amount you first request. If prospects were unfamiliar, gift recommendations were based on either upgraded past donations or an amount equal to the highest gift in the giving range to which the prospect is assigned. Let's say the committee's best information was that I could give between $100 and $500. You would first ask for a $500 contribution.

Once you've asked for a donation, prospects may criticize the organization, leadership, staff, or programs. They might mention other reasons why they can't make the gift you suggested. These are called objections. Don't ignore or get into an argument about objections. Instead, be prepared to discuss them.

WORKER: Why do objections come out at this point?

TRAINER: Because prospects rationalize why they don't want to contribute the amount of money for which they were just asked. This happens often during the closing.

WORKER: But I don't want to hassle with people. We represent a cause that speaks for itself.

TRAINER: It will, but to meet our goal we must get the best possible donations from prospects. Objections stand in the way of that happening. The ability to reverse an objection is the difference between getting token support and a consequential gift. Take a look at the next slide.

TYPICAL OBJECTIONS:
I Have Other Priorities
Let the Government Deal with the Environment
I Don't Like Some Organization Policies

These are several objections you're likely to hear. If you have positive responses to these comments in mind *before* you see a prospect, you will easily dispense with them. Then rerequest the evaluated gift.

WORKER 2: What if the prospect still doesn't want to make the contribution I ask for?

TRAINER: You offer alternatives. If you were selling a line of products, you would first try to interest a customer in the most expensive and appealing item in your line. If that didn't work, you would try to sell the next most costly item. It's the same with fundraising. For example, if your prospect can't or won't give you $500, maybe the person will give you $300 or $200. Be in charge and be persistent without being insulting.

WORKER 3: Sounds like bargaining to me.

TRAINER: It is. Some people call it negotiating. It's better to negotiate than accept a token contribution.

Now I'd like you to watch a training video that shows the solicitation methods we've been discussing. (*Fade up on exterior of a small suburban house and surroundings. It is a weekend day—a neighbor is mowing the grass, people stroll by in leisure clothing. The home is that of Bill and Judy Allen. Bill is outside trimming a hedge. Tony and Peggy, two campaign workers, enter the picture. The camera zooms in as they approach Bill.*)

TONY: Mr. Allen?

BILL: Yes. Hi.

TONY: Hi. We're from the environmental activist's organization. I'm sure you heard that we'd be out seeing members today to discuss our annual campaign.

BILL: I remember reading something about it. But I have to finish trimming these hedges. I'm way behind schedule.

PEGGY: You sound just like my husband. He never seems to catch up on his outdoor work either. Aren't you pretty active with the organization? I'm Peggy Lucas.

BILL: Hi, Peggy. Well, not as active as I should be. But I served on the education committee some time back. I guess I can take a few minutes off. Good excuse anyway. Come on in. (*Cut to interior of living room. The trio enters. Bill looks up the stairway and calls . . .*)

BILL: Judy, we have visitors. Come on down. (*To campaigners*) You think I'm busy with outdoor work. I can't get Judy away from her aerobic exercises. (*Judy enters. Introductions take place.*)

TONY: You're an aerobics buff?

JUDY: Yes, I teach it at the community college. (*They all sit.*)

[Our campaigners have learned that their prospects have at least two interests relating to the campaign—environmental education and physical fitness.]

PEGGY: We won't take much of your time. Let me go over the thrust of our drive. To continue turning around the damage done to our bay, we must make a stronger effort to stop industries north of us from pouring pollutants into its waters. To many of them, the bay is a sewer. Here is one of the most magnificent bodies of water in the nation, and the marine life is dying instead of reproducing. The fishing industry is crippled. Without a massive and continuing educational program to keep citizens alerted to these and other environmental problems, and to get them to actively support us, nothing will change. If we can fund these programs, it will help all who live in and visit this area for a long time to come.

TONY: Our family has a small boat. The other weekend my young son and I took a ride across the bay to a creek I've known since I was a kid. I told him that not long ago the water was so clear you could see fish swimming near the bottom. My boy said to me, "I don't even want to put my hands in that dirty stuff." Then he asked if the water would ever be clean again. I told him that if enough people got together to stop the pollution, when he grew up he could fish, swim, and watch the wildlife along the banks as I did when I was his age.

BILL: We have a major problem, no doubt about it. (*He and Judy page through the brochure they received in the mail.*)

PEGGY: Bill and Judy, many members of the community are backing our organization. So far we have $875,000 toward our $950,000 goal. I think that's fantastic. I feel so strongly about this campaign that my husband and I made a $500 gift.

TONY: I have done the same. We would like you and Judy to consider a $400 contribution to support our education program.

BILL: I think the plan *sounds* good, but I don't have much faith in the president of the organization. I think he's full of hot air, and I'm not sure he won't buckle under to the industries that are at fault.

[The prospect has voiced an objection at a crucial time. If not handled properly, the requested gift will be out of the question.]

TONY: Bill, you have a right to your opinion, but the plan you agree with comes from recommendations of a large committee and is approved by the board of directors. Even if you're right, the president can't ignore the wishes of those people.

BILL: Well, you have a point there.

PEGGY: Won't you think about donating $400?

BILL: I'm afraid you've overestimated our finances. Last year we gave a $100. We still have a student loan to pay off, among other bills. But we obviously care about the bay and will give you the same gift as last year.

JUDY: I agree with Bill. And I have some other charitable priorities—in the physical fitness area.

PEGGY: Judy, I'm also a donor to other organizations. The way I see it, physical fitness and the environment go hand-in-hand. Your interests in physical well-being are completely aligned with our interests in a healthy environment.

JUDY: Well, let us think it over. We'll get back to you.

TONY: I know you will. But today many of us are seeing hundreds of supporters to complete the campaign. While all the details of our drive are fresh in your minds, we would really appreciate you coming to a decision before we go.

BILL: Well, okay. Give us a minute to talk about it.

PEGGY: Of course. We'll wait outside. (*Peggy and Tony stand and move to front door. Cut to exterior as they walk out onto porch.*)

[Tony and Peggy have countered objections, and asked for a specific gift for a definite project. Now they are pushing for an acceptable close while the campaign is foremost in their prospect's minds.]

(*Judy and Bill enter*)

BILL: Judy and I have agreed to donate $100. Perhaps we can do something better later on.

PEGGY: You are both concerned people. I know you understand that the moment we let down our efforts, we will be faced with worse problems than we already have. It will soon be impossible to catch up. I realize it is more than you want to contribute, but could you see your way clear to donating $300 to support our educational program? Our members must lead the way.

BILL: It's hard to argue with your point of view. Look, if Judy agrees, the best we can do is double last year's donation—$200. (*Judy nods affirmatively.*)

TONY: That's wonderful. Thank you very much.

PEGGY: Thank you. (*Camera pulls back as Tony fills out a gift receipt card and the scene fades out.*)

TRAINER: By not accepting the Allen's first offer, Peggy could upgrade the gift. Those of you who have solicited larger gifts will have noticed that our campaign team didn't use the technique of not accepting the gift, asking the prospect to continue thinking about the request, and planning another visit in a short time. That method of upgrading donations is not particularly effective in canvassing small gift contributors.

The solicitation techniques you just learned won't come to you all at once during a solicitation. Try these methods on several prospects you know are highly supportive first. After you gain experience, your presentation, gift request, the ability to counter objections and negotiate the close, will come a lot easier.

Remember to:

Discover which part of your project would most interest a prospect.

Present the campaign case thoroughly.

Tell the prospect a personal story about how the organization has helped you or others.

Have answers to common objections firmly in mind.

Request a maximum gift to begin.

Solicit with enthusiasm; it's catching.

That concludes the scripted portion of the example small gifts worker training program. Solicitation is best taught by demonstration. If you don't have an audiovisual presentation, following training, have the trainer play the prospect and one of your experienced small gift campaign teams play the solicitors. (See "Role Playing" on page 131.) Unlike upper-level solicitors, it is usually impossible for a large group of small gift workers to each have a chance to rehearse their presentations.

Assigning Prospects to Large Numbers of Workers

Before solicitation takes place, be certain that each prospect is sent a letter outlining the campaign and mentioning that a representative of the organization will soon be asking for support. During the assignment portion of the meeting go over the letter with volunteers so they are familiar with its contents.

Place alphabetically arranged prospect listings on tables or, with large groups, tape them to a wall. If you have a sector chart, explain it to the campaigners. Then . . .

1. Ask workers to form into teams of two (if the manpower exists).

2. Tell volunteers who want to solicit people they know to find their names on the prospect listings and write their own name next to the potential donor in the "Assigned to" column. For example:

				Prospect Listing by Category or Division		
				Category or Division: Sponsor		
Name	Address	Phone	Evaluation	Assigned to	Gift	Named Facility
Mills	6 Jan St.	123-7698	$500	P. Edles		
Monte	3 Sea Dr.	123-6352	$350	P. Edles		

3. Inform those who select strangers to choose them from a convenient area in which to work.

4. Give one of the team the prospect's gift or pledge card once the assignment is recorded.

5. Urge volunteers to report results after completing their visits.

The trainer and leadership should always be available to answer questions and keep workers motivated.

You may suspect that assigning numerous prospects to many workers is like a scene out of the *Keystone Cops,* one of bedlam and gross disorder. It isn't. There have often been times when we literally "papered" the walls with prospect listings. Somehow the workers chose names and received their gift or pledge cards with a minimum of confusion. Trust a prepared staff and the group spirit to overcome logistical obstacles.

A small gifts worker rally requires tremendous organization and a maximum amount of staff time, but volunteers will be well trained, fired up, and at their best.

Nonaffiliated Prospect Canvassing

First, some assumptions. Getting contributions from people who may only have a vague idea of what your organization and campaign is all about is the most difficult form of personal solicitation. In a nonmembership–constituent appeal:

- Potential donors are often not up-to-date with a group's services, do not take advantage of programming, and therefore are not particularly motivated to make donations.

- Campaigners will be given a brief time to explain the drive.

Getting in the Door

Since there is often no relationship between prospect and solicitor, the first impression a volunteer makes on a potential contributor is all-important. Don't use the approach this campaigner took.

A man I know lives in an apartment in a two-story house. One evening the doorbell rang. When the man answered, a woman announced that she was fundraising for a local citizens action group.

"I must see the people in both apartments right away," she said haughtily.

"Why?" responded my friend.

"Look," the woman said, "I've got very important things to discuss and I want to do that with everyone from this house at the same time."

"Well," said my friend, "the people downstairs are out of town, but let me tell you something. If your organization expects any cooperation from this home, send someone else. You have a rotten attitude!" With that he closed the door in the woman's face.

I think I know what that solicitor was *trying* to do—show that her organization's business was urgent and no time would be wasted in getting to the point of her call. However, because of her aggressive personality, it didn't come off.

To get unfamiliar prospects to listen, you must be especially personable and believable. Get their attention by looking them straight in the eye, saying who you are, and stating why you are excited about calling on them. "Hello, I'm George Bell from Philanthropy America and this year we are going to put more than a dent in illiteracy in the United States. I want to tell you about the problem and what can be done to relieve it."

Make sure to carry organizational identification so prospects know that you represent a reputable nonprofit group: an ID card, a piece of campaign literature, or even a copy of the organization's IRS statement that assigns it 501(c)(3) status.

The Worker Rally

Organize the orientation and distribution of assignments meeting the same way the member and constituents meeting is organized:

    I. Statement of Purpose
   II. Campaign Update
  III. Presentation of Needs and Goals
  IV. Solicitation Training
   V. Prospect Assignments

If you are canvassing for a capital appeal, use pledge cards but be aware that mostly you will receive a one-time cash gift from nonaffiliated prospects. If that's the case, fill out the pledge card for the record and print your name on the signature line.

Because prospects are not likely evaluated, have share plans, clubs, or associations formed as part of your guidelines for giving. These options enable you to request specific amounts of money instead of just asking for a gift, as in the following example:

> TRAINER: Your prospects are not people who you know as friends of the organization. Many of them have no giving history. So you won't find an evaluation noted on the gift cards. That doesn't mean that these people won't be sympathetic to what you did in the past and want to get done in the future.
>
> Here's one way to ask for a donation: "I'm from our Citizens Action Group. Could you give something to our campaign this year?" That leaves the option to the prospect. And it's a safe bet you'll return with a token donation at best. We've come up with a more profitable alternative. Your organization has been in business 20 years. We've formed the "Decade Plus One Association." To become a member, a person must donate $20 for the past decade and the same amount for the present decade, a total of $40. Each member will receive a special quarterly newsletter. By asking prospects to join the association, something is given in return for their contributions. Let's look at a short film which illustrates how this technique works.
>
> [Again, if no presentation exists, have your most experienced volunteers role-play a sample solicitation.]
>
> (*Fade up on exterior of house. A woman approaches the door and rings the bell. She wears a large neighborhood council button. The door opens.*)
>
> PROSPECT: May I help you?
>
> LINDA: Hello. I'm Linda from our Neighborhood Council and we're . . .
>
> PROSPECT: Oh yes. (*Smiling*) I gave at the office.
>
> LINDA: (*Returns the smile*) Well, if you did we didn't receive your gift because we don't call on offices. Look, you're probably busy but I just want to take a few minutes of your time. In the past 10 years our Council made many positive changes in the community. We've been able to landscape our parks and . . .
>
> PROSPECT: Well, I don't deny all you're saying. I'll be happy to give you a couple of bucks.
>
> LINDA: Thank you. I appreciate that. But you know, we exist because of the generosity of people in our neighborhood. This brochure tells you more about the organization. (*Hands the prospect a brochure.*) As I've said, the council has been in business for 20 years. To celebrate, we've formed a "Decade Plus One Associa-

tion." Today we are seeing everyone in this part of town and asking them to become members. Each member will receive a confidential newsletter four times a year. Membership is $40. It would mean a lot to everyone.

PROSPECT: A few bucks is one thing, but I'm out of town about four months a year. I've never been to one of your meetings. I'm not much of a joiner. You're asking for too much money.

LINDA: I'm not asking for myself, but for all our neighbors. Even though you aren't here all the time, your donation will help many other people, especially those who can't afford to make a donation.

PROSPECT: I'll tell you what I'll do. I'll give you $20 for one decade, and we'll worry about a second gift the next time around. Is that a deal?

LINDA: (*Smiling*) Well, let me ask you to think about a better deal. You say you're here three-quarters of the time. That would be $30.

PROSPECT: (*Laughs*) All right. If you think about it, send me a membership form.

LINDA: I'd be happy to. For the whole council, thank you.

PROSPECT: I'll get you a check. (*He exits*) (*Linda takes a gift card out of her purse and fills it out. The prospect returns with a check.*)

PROSPECT: (*Now a donor*): Here you go.

LINDA: (*Taking check*) Thanks again and here's your receipt. (*They shake hands as scene fades.*)

If Linda had left the gift up to the prospect, she would have received one or two dollars. The association concept allowed her to ask for a specific gift that offered the prospect a membership for his contribution.

There are several reasons why your organization may not be able to canvass small gift prospects. If that's the case, the next best way is to solicit them by phone.

12

Telephone Appeals: Dialing for Dollars

The Pitfalls of Soliciting by Phone

When it comes to answering phones, I don't think I'm any different from most people. If a stranger who sounds anything like a salesperson is on the other end of the line, my initial reaction is to be wary. I suspect that my privacy is about to be invaded. So, the initial difficulty organization phone solicitors have is to keep prospects from hanging up before their presentation can be made. Having gotten past that hurdle, the remaining major problems are:

- The voice is the only tool at the worker's disposal. Eye contact and other useful body language is obviously out of the question. Aids such as audiovisual presentations, plans, and photographs cannot be used to support your case and gift request.

- Because solicitor and prospect are not face-to-face, it's far easier to turn down a gift request.

- It is difficult to judge a prospect's real reaction as the solicitation progresses since the person can't be seen.

- A prospect's attention easily wanders because of distractions. For example, in the midst of a personal visit by a campaigner it would be rude for a prospect to idly stare out a window watching children play. A phone solicitor wouldn't know the difference.

- Prospects invent many polite reasons why they must hang up the phone, usually ending the solicitation at a critical time: "Sorry, someone seems to be leaning on the doorbell."

Phonathons are immensely successful ways to produce small gift income once these dangers can be overcome by proper planning and using talented, trained volunteers.

First Steps

How Not to Get a Quick Disconnect

1. *Don't read from a script; use an outline.*   Much as scripting is used by telemarketers, unless you're an accomplished actor, reading a presentation won't come across as believable. I recently received a solicitation call from a nonprofit agency whose volunteer was friendly and natural as he introduced himself. But as soon as he began his talk, I knew he was reading from a narration.

   "Wait a minute," I said, not unkindly. "Please don't read to me. It sounds phoney. Just tell me the story in your words."

   "Absolutely," he said happily. With that, the man proceeded to read from his script again. I was bored to death by his presentation.

2. *Be aware of your vocal delivery.*   For instance, nothing is worse than a monotone-voiced solicitor:

   Hello. How-are-you. I—am-Barb. I—am—calling—for—the—friends-of-pets-fund. I know-that you know-that we are holding a campaign. You don't? Well, we are. Now-I-would-like-to-tell-you-about-our-fund . . .

   Another lifeless presentation. Why would anyone care why Barb was calling? Speak to prospects with vitality as if they were friends in the same room with you. That may not be as easy as it sounds. Many people have special voices for the telephone, unexpressive of their real warmth and sincerity. I know a man who forces his voice down half an octave when he's doing business over the phone. He comes across as a person trying to sound authoritative—I wouldn't give him a dime. Record your presentation and study the playback, or find out how someone close to you reacts. (Many people don't approve of their recorded voice, even when it's quite presentable.) If you find yourself sounding unnatural, practice until you come across as conversational and enthusiastic.

3. *Speak to prospects personally.*   A volunteer representing a national health agency agreed to solicit her business colleagues by phone. Being a busy corporate manager, instead of calling each prospect individually, she selected a quicker method. Taking advantage of her company's voice mail system, she left the same solicitation message for all her colleague-prospects with a single call. When her coemployees phoned for messages that day, among them they heard her plea for funds. My wife, who told me this story, was disgruntled by the call. She thought that if the solicitor couldn't take the time to call each colleague individually, she couldn't be taking the cause she represented very seriously. Apparently my wife wasn't the only person who reacted similarly. The worker raised very little money

because apparently most of the people with whom she left the electronic message zapped it before it was completed.

Who and When to Call

Prospects fall into the same two categories as in canvassing:

- Members and constituents, people who already support your organization in one way or another
- Unaffiliated persons, most of them presently nonsupportive

If there's a choice, contact prospects during weekends because you can double or triple the coverage. Plan on two shifts of phoners who begin at 11:00 A.M. and end at 5:30 P.M. When phoning at night, make calls between 7:00 P.M. and 9:00 P.M.

Determining How Many Phonathons and Workers You'll Need

During a typical week night, expect to complete about 25 calls per worker during a two and a half hour period. Here's an example:
An organization places 1500 prospects in the phonathon portion of its campaign.

- Sixty phoners are recruited.
- Twelve phone lines are available each night.
- Using 12 workers per night, with each person making 25 calls per session, the prospects will have been phoned at least once in 5 nights.
- Allowing an additional two sessions for callbacks and pledge completions, the 60 workers will complete the phonathon drive in 7 nights.

If the same number of workers phoned on a weekend for six and a half hours each day, they would make the initial calls in two sessions. A few night-time follow-ups during the week and phone solicitation would be finished.

The Role of Phonathon Leadership

Phonathon chairs play the same role as do other leaders, enlisting and motivating workers, making strategy decisions, and serving on the campaign cabinet. Yet they have a distinct advantage over their counterparts. Being present during their worker's solicitations, they can observe and judge a worker's effectiveness and offer necessary advice on the spot.

The importance of recruiting dynamic phonathon leaders cannot be overemphasized. When workers begin making calls, the chair or captain must continually motivate each campaigner to do his or her best work. Phonathon heads should be a combination of coach, cheerleader, and scorekeeper, continually whooping it up for your team.

If many phone solicitations are necessary, have the chair enlist other experienced phone workers to serve as weekend or nightly captains. These people also are expected to aid the chair in signing up workers.

Enlisting Workers

Not being in the same room with a prospect takes away the anxiety that many volunteers feel about soliciting. Often, people who won't see potential donors face-to-face make highly capable phoners. Callers also run the gamut of organization members. It's common for trustees and those from other upper-level gift categories or divisions to spend time phoning prospects. So long as a person makes a contribution, he or she can qualify for telephone duty.

Where to Hold Phonathons

The most efficient place is your organization's site—records, supplies, and other support material are readily available. If need be, have the phone company install extra lines for the run of the phone campaign. Sometimes, using your facility is impractical. Attempt to get the local telephone company, a stock brokerage, market research company, or any place where a business needs many phones to donate space and lines for the run of your phonathons. Many businesses see this practice as a public service. You will be asked to report and pay for long-distance calls and leave the facilities tidy.

Motivating Workers

Volunteers will be more productive if they telephone from the same room. A camaraderie and friendly sense of competition will influence them to make more calls and solicit more forcefully, and the chair or captain can monitor solicitations and be immediately available for consultation.

Let's say one of your phoners, Jeff, is seated alone in a private office. He runs into a series of difficult prospects. Discouraged, Jeff puts down the phone, shuffles papers, and wonders what he's doing wrong. He doesn't want to admit that things are going badly. Pretty soon Jeff is not only behind on his calls, he's getting nowhere with the ones he completes. On the other hand, if Jeff is seated with his coworkers, he sees that others have problems from time to time and realizes that many people are not easy prospects. When he gets discouraged, others in the group pick up his spirits. The phonathon captain helps sharpen Jeff's soliciting techniques; the net result is a confident volunteer and additional gift income.

Promote friendly competition among your workers by presenting awards each session for the most dollars brought in, the greatest number of pledges, or the most phone calls made.

Visit to a Phonathon Orientation Meeting

In the center of a room are six tables organized in a rectangle. On each table are phones, pens, and scratch paper. A refreshment area is set up in a corner of the room along with a stand containing alphabetically arranged prospect pledge cards.

Forty-five minutes before calls are scheduled to begin, the chair brings the group up-to-date on campaign needs and progress. Then the trainer is introduced. Each worker is handed a booklet containing solicitation methods and information on how to complete necessary paperwork. It will be used as a guideline during training. (Use the example booklet that appears segmented on this and the following pages as a sample for your organization.)

**THE COMMUNITY CENTER PHONATHON CAMPAIGN
SUGGESTIONS FOR TELEPHONING**

This booklet outlines various parts of the solicitation process. It is not a script. *You will be most effective if you tell prospects about our campaign in your words.* Attempt to complete about 25 calls during this session. A steady pace will be necessary, but you shouldn't feel rushed.

Opening

Begin the solicitation by telling potential donors who you are and that you are calling for the community center building campaign. As quickly as possible move on to the purpose of the call. For example:

Example only: "Hi, this is _____. I'm calling for the Community Center Building Fund Campaign along with many other volunteers. We are calling hundreds of our members to discuss funding the proposed new facility."

TRAINER: Fundraising by telephone is a very effective way of soliciting small gifts, but often very poorly handled. When a prospect first picks up the phone, he or she will not be sure if they want to hear you out. Two things will capture that person's interest: mentioning the urgency of the campaign, and the tone and sound of your voice. If you were seeing a potential donor in person, you would greet them with a smile. Make that smile come through the phone lines. Here's how. When your prospect answers the phone—smile. *I mean it. Literally smile just before you speak.* You'll be amazed how warm that makes the sound of your voice. Even if a prospect asks you nastily, "Whadda ya want?" if you sound friendly, you will cut through that cold greeting and get the listener to let you go on.

Don't get caught up in small talk. After introducing yourself, tell prospects they are part of a large group who will be asked to participate in this campaign. Don, try an opening for us.

DON: Hi, Mr. Smith. This is Don James. I hope you're having a nice day. I'm calling from the Community Center campaign headquarters and I'm one of many volunteers contacting our members to talk about the building campaign.

TRAINER: That was good, but let me pick on one point. Your line about hope you're having a nice day is unnecessary. First, because of overuse, the words are meaningless. More important, it gives your prospect a perfect opportunity to tell you why his day is turning out horribly. Unless you know the person, get right to the reason you are calling.

Let's return to the booklet.

Presentation

Example only: "I hope you've had a chance to look over the material we sent you recently. We are holding this appeal to . . ." [When you prepare a workers' booklet, state your campaign case here.]

TRAINER: As you begin stating the case, some prospects may tell you that they are familiar with the campaign material recently sent them. Take nothing for granted. Review highlights of the case anyway. As important, tell them why you are involved. Relate to your prospects on a personal level. As you begin talking about the campaign, a potential donor may interrupt to ask a question or offer an opinion. Encourage discussion, it further involves people. If you can't answer a question, ask one of us to help you.

The next part of a solicitation is to ask for a contribution. Jane, how would you do that?

JANE: I'd say something like, I'm glad you're as enthusiastic as I am about our project. What would you like to contribute tonight?

TRAINER: That's a common way to ask for a donation, but it will guarantee the smallest possible gift. You must take the lead and ask for a specific amount of money. Plan on asking each prospect to make a contribution for membership in one of our campaign clubs.

[Capital campaigns and some annual appeals stress making donations for items contained in named gift listings. When no such listing exists, ask prospects to donate to an item in the "summary of needs," a share plan, or a special club or association, the same technique used in canvassing. For example, a contribution of $200 entitles a person to share in the project being offered for funding. Or the prospect might be requested to give $350 to become a member of a "Patron's Club." Recall, these are the giving ideas that allow solicitors to ask for definite amounts of money and donors to be rewarded for their support. Don't overlook the proven drawing power of these techniques.]

Seeking the Gift

Example only: "Our brochure lists the clubs we've formed to thank donors for their gifts. We've already gotten a tremendous response to this plan. We would like your family's name to be inscribed on a plaque in the new facility as a member of our patron's club. That requires a gift of $150 a year for five years—$500. Could you consider donating that amount?" [Substitute a description of your share plan, clubs, or associations.

TRAINER: When you ask for a specific amount of money, prospects become most vocal about criticizing the organization or project, or tell you why they can't donate the amount requested. These are called objections and are listed in your booklet.

Objections and How to Deal with Them

[List the common objections that might be brought up to your organization and what can be said to counteract them here.]

Closing the Gift

Once you've countered objections, continue selling the club concept and you'll stand a good chance of getting the requested contribution. But let's say you are unable to get a $200 commitment from a prospect to join a club. Mention that many people have been making one-time gifts of $150. Again, give the prospect a point of reference by bringing up specific dollar amounts.

When you receive a pledge, express your appreciation. Then tell the prospect:

1. You will report the gift to the campaign office.

2. You will send the person a gift acknowledgment, a pledge card showing the gift, and a return envelope. The donor should then mail back his or her donation or indicate a payment schedule.

3. A formal gift acknowledgment letter will be sent from the campaign office after the actual gift or pledge has been received.

TRAINER: Each time you make a call, four possibilities exist:
   1. Your prospect makes a pledge.

2. The prospect agrees to contribute, but doesn't know how much the gift will be. That's called an unspecified pledge. Do everything to discourage this response. Faced with a pledge card on which no gift is indicated, prospects often make small contributions. Get firm commitments.

3. Your prospect refuses to donate.

4. Your prospect was unreachable.

Each situation calls for a different written response and record-keeping procedure, as shown in your booklet.

WHAT TO DO FOLLOWING THE CALLS

1. When You Receive a Pledge

  a. Note the amount on the left panel of the pledge card (detach the right panel) and sign *your* name on the signature line followed by the words "Phonathon gift" and the date, as in the following example:

> **THE COMMUNITY CENTER CAMPAIGN**
> Campaign Headquarters – 1234 G Street
> _____
>
> No.   Name & Address
>   Mr. & Mrs. H. Helper
>   546 Donor Lane
>
>   In consideration of the gift of others, I/we promise
> to pay to the Community Center the sum of
> _____*Fifty*_____ Dollars $___*50*____
> X___*Bill Jones Phonathon gift*___ Date: _*5/19/92*_
>   (Signature)

  b. Fill out the acknowledgment section of the donor return envelope (top portion) as in the following example by adding a salutation, noting the amount, and signing your name. Personalize the envelope by handwriting a note. Leave the bottom portion blank.

Dear Mr. & Mrs. Helper,

I enjoyed talking with you about our new facilities and am most grateful for your $___50___ pledge. Your support is greatly appreciated.

This return envelope is provided for your convenience.

Enjoyed our conversation   *Bill Jones*

-------------------------------------- fold --------------------------------------

Please complete
the information
requested to
help us in properly
recording your gift.

Amount enclosed $_____

Balance payable as follows:

_____

_____
(Print name)

_____
(Street address)

_____
(City, State, Zip)

Make checks payable to the Community Center Campaign. All gifts are tax deductible for income tax purposes.

c. For our records, turn the envelope over and sign your name in the lower left hand corner below the printed return address, as in the example following.

NO POSTAGE
STAMP NECESSARY
IF MAILED IN...

Business Reply Envelope

The Community Center Campaign
1234 G Street

Bill Jones

d. Address the second envelope (with "THANKS!" printed in the lower left) to the donor and place the donor envelope (acknowledgment message facing) inside. Do not seal the envelope.

The Community Center Campaign
1234 G Street

Mr. & Mrs. H. Helper
546 Donor Lane

THANKS!

e. Using a paper clip, attach the donor envelope and the "Thanks" envelope, and place them aside for pickup by the chair or captain.

2. Unspecified Pledges

a. When a prospect tells you that he or she will make a gift or pledge but is unsure of the amount, mark the word "Unspecified" on the pledge card, sign your name on the signature line and enter the date.

THE COMMUNITY CENTER CAMPAIGN
Campaign Headquarters – 1234 G Street

No.   Name & Address
               Mr. & Mrs. H. Helper
               546 Donor Lane

In consideration of the gift of others and the I/we promise to pay to the Community Center, the sum of _____*Unspecified*_____ Dollars $_____
X_____*Bill Jones*_____ Date: *5/19/92*
        (Signature)

---

b. Fill out the acknowledgment section of the donor return envelope as seen on the next page. Add the salutation as you did when you received a pledge, but this time note the word "Unspecified" in the space reserved for the dollar amount and sign your name.

Dear Mr. & Mrs. Helper,

I enjoyed talking with you about our new facilities and am most grateful for your $ *Unspecified* pledge. Your support is greatly appreciated.
This return envelope is provided for your convenience.

Bill Jones

------------------------------------- fold -------------------------------------

Please complete
the information
requested to
help us in properly
recording your gift.

Amount enclosed $_____

Balance payable as follows:

_____

_____
(Print name)

_____
(Street address)

_____
(City, State, Zip)

Make checks payable to the Community Center Campaign. All gifts are tax deductible for income tax purposes.

c. Flip over the envelope and write your name in the lower left corner.

NO POSTAGE
STAMP NECESSARY
IF MAILED IN...

Business Reply Envelope

The Community Center Campaign
1234 G Street

Bill Jones

d. Address a "THANKS!" envelope to the donor and place the donor return envelope inside with the acknowledgment facing out. Do not seal.

The Community Center Campaign
1234 G Street

THANKS!

e. Attach the two envelopes with a paper clip and place them aside for pickup.

3. Refusals

a. Write "Refused" in the space reserved for pledge amount on the donor return envelope and, in a few words, show the reason. Print the name of the prospect, print your name, and place the envelope aside for pickup.

I enjoyed talking with you about our new facilities and am most grateful for your $ *Refused* pledge. Your support is greatly appreciated.
This return envelope is provided for your convenience.

_____ *B. Jones*

Unemployed

-- fold --

Please complete
the information
requested to
help us in properly
recording your gift.

Amount enclosed $_____

Balance payable as follows:

_____

_____
(Print name)

_____
(Street address)

_____
(City, State, Zip)

Make checks payable to the Community Center Campaign. All gifts are tax deductible for income tax purposes.

4. **Cannot Be Reached**

   a. If after trying several times, a prospect cannot be reached, mark "not reached" on the top section of the donor return envelope, show the date, print the prospect's name and your name. Place card aside for pickup.

   I enjoyed talking with you about our new facilities and am most grateful for your $_____ pledge. Your support is greatly appreciated.
   This return envelope is provided for your convenience.

   _____ *Bill Jones—5/19/92*

   Larry Brown
   Not Reached

- fold -

Please complete
the information
requested to
help us in properly
recording your gift.

Amount enclosed $_____

Balance payable as follows:

_____

_____
(Print name)

_____
(Street address)

_____
(City, State, Zip)

Make checks payable to the Community Center Campaign. All gifts are tax deductible for income tax purposes.

TRAINER: Avoid a logistical nightmare by paying close attention to paperwork, and the operation will be smooth and efficient.

Prospects who can't be reached during the phonathons will be solicited by mail.

I know some of you are anxious about soliciting. After a few calls, you will feel more confident and begin to enjoy the challenge of persuading prospects to make their best contributions. When you run into people who are vehemently negative, they are not going to be convinced that you are right and they are wrong. Arguing serves no useful purpose. If they feel that strongly about running down the organization, let them blow off steam, thank them for speaking to you, and go to the next call.

To recap, I want to play an audiocassette for you. It contains highlights of a phone solicitation produced for our training meetings. Listen carefully: there are a few things we haven't touched on so far. (*Plays tape.*) (*Phone rings and is picked up.*)

PROSPECT: Hello.

PHONER: This is Jane Burke from the Community Center Building Fund Campaign.

PROSPECT: How y'all doing?

PHONER: Fine, thanks. I'm part of a group of volunteers who are calling hundreds of people today to seek their support. We hope to make this the most successful campaign in our history.

PROSPECT: After me again I see. Put me down for the same as last year.

PHONER: (*Cheerfully*) I appreciate that, but here I am, raring to go, and you won't even listen to my presentation. Did you get a chance to look at the brochure we sent you?

PROSPECT: Well, I went through it quickly.

PHONER: You probably noticed that this drive is different from last year's. It's a capital campaign for a new facilities. Let me highlight the project for you. [Phoner presents the campaign case.] You and the other people we are calling today can insure that we reach our goal.

[This illustration is for a capital campaign. If it were for an annual drive, the phone solicitor's retort would be words to the effect of: "Because of you and other supporters, we successfully funded a variety of important programs last year. But this is a new year, and we must continue the work. In great part, fundraising keeps us in business."]

PROSPECT: Seems to me you could get a lot done for less money.

PHONER: I wish we could, but we're short on space. The goal is based on two factors. Expansion is the only way to meet increased demand for services. Second, our facilities committee has spent months cutting every possible cost. What's left is a bare-bones budget.

Last year you were kind enough to give us $50. Because of our large goal, we are asking supporters to make a long-term pledge instead of a single gift. This is a special, one-time-only campaign. I would like you to join me in becoming a member of our Team Player's Club. The club is made up of people who pledge $100 a year for five years, $500.

PROSPECT: Do you still expect me to make a contribution for this year's annual campaign?

PHONER: Yearly donations are what keeps the doors open. I'm asking you to make this pledge over and above the annual drive.

PROSPECT: I'd like to give what you ask, but I can't. However, I would like to make a one-time contribution to the capital campaign this year of a $100.

PHONER: I appreciate that. You realize that I am asking for the long-term pledge because of the enormity of our drive.

PROSPECT: (*Firmly*) Yes, I do. But $100 is all I want to give for the moment.

PHONER: I would be happy to accept your $100 gift. And I thank you very much for it. Could I ask you something? Would you object if I or another campaign worker gave you a ring next year to see if you might be willing to give a second $100 to the capital campaign?

PROSPECT: No, that would be all right.

That concludes the phonathon training session. If you don't have an audio presentation, role play a telephone solicitation.

The final portion of the tape depicted two common scenarios encountered by solicitors working at all giving levels. If your organization is conducting both annual and capital funding efforts, don't attempt to get one gift at the price of another. Be straightforward and tell the prospect that the annual drive must be supported at the same time as the capital campaign.

Next, the prospect offers to make a gift, but not a pledge. Continue trying to get a pledge, but in doing so don't lose a supporter by being too aggressive. Once you feel a pledge will not be imminent, graciously accept a one-time gift and leave the possibility open for a future solicitation. Make certain the staff records that information on the prospect's master record and in a future or tickler file.

How to Assign Prospects and Follow Through

1. Stack alphabetically arranged pledge cards from left to right in sets of 25.

2. Ask workers to start by choosing 25 cards each. They can either pick a set at random or select prospects familiar to them. (Obviously, selecting known potential donors can reduce the number of cards in various sets. It matters not.)

3. Announce the prizes that will be awarded following the session. For instance, "To the person who brings in the most money today we have two front row seats to the symphony donated by one of our board members."

4. Post solicitation results on a blackboard, flip-chart, or similar device at intervals during the session.

5. Remind volunteers to ask for help when they have a problem.

6. Make workers take a break when you see them tiring.

7. Have each worker fill out the following telephone call report form. Explain this is for both the campaigners records and the chair's or captain's report on the session.

Telephone Call Report
Date:_____

Caller:_____   No. of Outgoing Calls:_____

Area Code	Number	Person Called	Check if Long Distance
1.			
2.			

Using the workers' telephone call reports, the chair or captain should complete the following report after each phonathon. This form, pledge cards, and envelopes must be taken to the campaign office as soon as is practical.

PHONATHON REPORT

Date:_____   Person Making Report:_____

Date promotion material mailed to prospects:_____

Volunteers Needed   _____   Phonathon Prospects _____

Volunteers Enlisted   _____

Volunteers Attending _____

Calls Attempted   _____   Average per volunteer _____

Calls Completed   _____   Average per volunteer _____

Pledges   _____   Totaling $_____

Unspecified   _____

Refusals   _____

Unable to Reach   _____

Number of prospects to be
  followed up in future sessions _____

Office Procedures Following
a Phonathon

1. Post pledges, unspecified gifts, and refusals onto the master prospect list.

2. Post the date that pledge cards were mailed to prospects.

3. Place pledge cards into the "THANKS!" envelopes. (The acknowledgment envelope should already have been put inside.) Seal and stamp.

4. Mail gift or pledge cards as soon as possible.

Following Up If a Gift Doesn't Arrive

If a pledge payment doesn't arrive after a reasonable time, make follow-up phone calls to those not responding to ask for their donations. A less effective alternative is to send a letter signed by the phonathon chair or solicitor. Something to the effect of:

> Dear Mr. Central,
>   Thank you again for your pledge of $100 to our campaign. When we receive the few remaining contributions promised us, our campaign will be a total success. Then we can provide . . . [reiterate the case.]
>   Please mail your donation as soon as possible. We are counting on you as one of the supporters who will make our dream a reality.
>
>   Gratefully,

If there is no response, make a second phone call to the prospect. Find out the reason why the person has not made good the pledge, and see if you can resolve the problem. Perhaps you might have to wait until the donor is in a better financial position. If you choose to send a second reminder, have it signed by the campaign chair(s). After that I leave pledge collection to your good judgment. For a very small contribution, don't spend more money attempting to recover the gift then it's worth.

> Dear Mr. and Mrs. Central,
>   The people we contacted in our phonathons mean a great deal to our organization. Without their gifts we cannot fully provide badly needed services.
>   Our campaign closing date will soon be upon us. Again we ask that you mail your gift of $100 to help assure our project begins on schedule.
>   Thank you.
>
>   Sara Blass   Joe Glen
>   General Campaign Cochairs

Thank Your Volunteers

When your phonathon campaign is completed, let workers know the results of their efforts by sending them a short report:

The Community Center
Building Fund Campaign

TO: Phonathon Workers
FROM: Sara Blass, Joe Glen, Campaign Co-Chairs
       Paul Red, Ginny Greene, Phonathon Co-Chairs
SUBJECT: Phonathon Completion Report

Because of your efforts our phonathons have gotten startling results.
Each of you has a right to be very proud of the time, effort, and
dedication you have given our campaign.

Volunteers Enlisted _____   Average per volunteer _____
Calls Attempted _____   Average per volunteer _____
Calls Completed _____   Totaling $_____
Pledges _____   Totaling $_____
Unspecified _____
Refusals _____
Unable to Reach _____   (Will be solicited by direct mail.)

Grand Total $_____

Phonathon Checklist

The following support materials are needed for each phonathon:

- A letter announcing phonathon dates and a campaign brochure sent to prospects before they are called

- "Guidelines for Giving," e.g., restricted, unrestricted, share plan, clubs, associations, matching grants

- Pledge cards filled out for each prospect (even if it's not a capital campaign, you can only receive a pledge of support over the phone)

- "Suggestions for Telephoning" training booklet

- Acknowledgement, return, and mailing envelopes

- A device of some sort for holding sets of pledge cards

- "Telephone Call Report" forms

- "Phonathon Report" forms

- Pens (not pencils) and scratch paper

- Refreshments

Key Factors to Remember

1. Make sure phonathon leaders are experienced fundraisers.

2. Choose a site with enough telephone lines convenient to the majority of workers.

3. Have volunteers phone from the same room.

4. Don't use scripts. Urge campaigners to create a thought flow based on their "Suggestions for Telephoning" booklet.

5. Gain the prospect's trust immediately. Open with a smile. Tell the potential donor who you are, the organization you represent, and why you're calling.

6. Point out how successful your campaign is and that the prospect's contribution will play a part in helping reach its goal.

7. During presentations, emphasize the people who will profit from a successful drive.

8. Encourage discussion to involve prospects.

9. Ask for a predetermined gift for a definite reason, as stated in your "Guidelines for Giving" list.

10. Stay ahead of the prospect. Be prepared to counter objections by forecasting what they might be *before* you solicit.

11. Avoid unspecified gifts.

12. Be sure workers understand how to fill out forms. Each campaigner must pay strict attention to properly filling out pledge cards and envelopes. The more quickly campaign office personnel can mail pledge cards to prospects, the fewer problems with pledge collection.

13. Mail pledge cards to prospects at once.

14. Send donors formal acknowledgment letters immediately after donations are received.

The greatest test of any solicitor comes during the closing. You need to be in charge, to be aggressive without being overbearing. If your first gift request is turned down, don't be deterred. Suggest lesser amounts based on your organization's gift requirements. Many people will upgrade the contributions they first had in mind when you use this proven technique.

The last method of solicitation challenges not only your design and writing skills, but also your long-term patience. In many ways, mail campaigns are in a different world from other methods of requesting contributions.

13

Word Power: The Small Gift Alternative

Gaining a Perspective

A mailing is often the most practical way to reach many small gift prospects. Sending letters also is a simple way to campaign. There is no need to recruit, train, and motivate a large workforce—a few talented souls can run the entire operation. That's not to say all one must do is write a letter, post it, and wait for the returns.

My major complaint with a mail campaign is that it's one-sided. No allowance exists for a campaign worker to motivate prospects personally. The most enthusiastic letter simply cannot match the give and take between a skilled solicitor and an open-minded potential supporter. Lacking aggressive salesmanship, only minimum gifts can be expected, no matter how well-written the solicitation letter and enclosures may be.

Here's another angle to ponder. Assume that I'm a small gift prospect with some interest in your endeavors. There's a good chance that I'll donate generously to your appeal if you knock on my door or phone because your enthusiasm and presentation will be hard to resist. And how many other organizations will solicit me in these ways? Very few. But send me a solicitation letter and you place your request in the midst of enormous competition for my same gift dollar. And because it's a letter, I have little problem withstanding its impersonal nature. If your organization is not among my very favorites, you won't receive a contribution of any consequence.

You see, although I think highly of your project, I have a desk piled high with fundraising letters, from the best-known national charities to all sorts of noteworthy regional and local groups. I am saturated with mail appeals. After sorting through them and making my top-ranked selections, I find my charitable budget is about depleted. But I still care about your cause—here's five bucks to show you my heart's in the right place.

With these factors as a downside, letter solicitations can produce highly profitable small gift income for organizations that plan and carry out meticulous programs. If you're serious about getting involved in fundraising by mail, there are six elements to understand right off the bat:

1. Mail solicitation is an ongoing component of annual giving programs. In capital campaigning, letter writing is a tool for wrapping up an appeal.

2. Properly run mail appeals focus equally on retaining and upgrading present small gift contributors while discovering and cultivating new prospects to make up for donors lost to attrition and to enlarge the donor pool. Present givers won't always be an available source of funding.

3. Donors don't come free any more than customers do for a commercially run, direct-mail operation. To obtain a new contributor, plan to spend from $1.25 to $1.50 for each initial dollar raised from that person.

4. Mail programs are long-term propositions—instant financial rewards are a rarity.

5. Be clear whom you designate as a donor and whom you label a prospect. Donors are people currently contributing to your campaign. Someone who gave you a gift two years ago or a person who once contributed a painting to your auction are prospects, not donors. Get used to thinking of three distinct groups: current donors, past donor prospects, and other prospects.

6. Some prospects have more interest in and knowledge about an organization than others. Cultivated potential donors are first approached because they represent the highest rate of return. For instance, a past donor prospect is a better bet to send you a new donation than someone who once came to a special event that you held. The person who came to the special event is more likely to fund you than someone who never heard of your group.

In planning a mail campaign, don't lose sight of the fundraising requirements first mentioned in Part 1. Three of them most apply to seeking contributions by letter. Make sure your project has:

- Compelling goals
- High visibility
- Specific, attractive, timely needs

Since the highest percentage of return comes from current contributors, they are the first group to target. If a goal is reachable by only contacting these people, expenses will be the least and your problems will be solved. If that's not realistic, additional prospects who might fund your project would need to be reached. That's fine so long as you realize that their percentage of return will be far less than supporters. For instance, you send a letter to current donors and perhaps 50 percent of them respond with gifts. A letter sent to brand new prospects typically yields responses of one-half to one percent. Until you've won over a new potential giver, don't expect many contributions.

Begin by placing prospects into categories and rank them from the most to the least supportive. Here's a typical example for a membership organization:

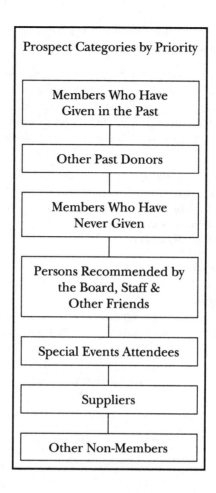

Prospects are classified in this manner so each group's response can be tracked. Then more attention is paid to categories that are most inclined to help fund a project. In our example, the fourth prospect group is people recommended by trusted supporters. Another organization may find its special events attendees more cultivated and therefore a higher-priority group to receive mailings. One client who provides services to university students ranks its direct mail prospects as: parents of undergraduates, undergraduate students, alumni, graduate students, parents of graduate students, and unaffiliated prospects. By analyzing your donor and prospect base, categories will fall into place.

Set Goals for Dollars and Donors

A campaign's professional staff and governing body is responsible for arriving at two direct mail goals: the contributions needed to fund or complete the funding of a project, and the number of new donors necessary to reach that goal. There are two ways to set goals, depending on the type of appeal put into operation:

1. If a capital campaign has been successfully run to this point, the goal will be near because of personal and phone solicitations. Assume an organization seeks $500,000 and has obtained 98 percent of its funding. It still needs to raise $10,000. The group has 1000 highly supportive members who will receive fundraising letters. If 40 percent of these people make an average gift of $25, the goal is reached.

2. Organizations conducting yearly appeals set dollar and donor goals based on past giving, upcoming funding requirements, and attrition. Imagine a group loses about 10 percent of its mail donors yearly. It will need to replace that 10 percent and add, let's say, another 5 percent to its mailing list to meet an increased dollar goal for its next drive.

Keep a proper mindset when you start up or expand a mail program. The first mailings to new prospects are to raise awareness. Consider profit a future objective, not an immediate expectation.

Direct mail campaigns obviously must be sensitive to cost factors. You don't want to end up losing money, but this can happen initially. For example, you have 5000 new prospects. This means producing and paying postage for as many letters, enclosures, and mailing and return envelopes. Let's assume you get a one percent return on the mailing. This is how first results would look:

Total Mailing	Cost Per Prospect	Total Expenditures	Number of Responses	Average Gift	Total Income
5000	$.45	$2250	50	$25.00	$1250

One thousand dollars is lost on the mailing. But wait a minute, there are other factors to consider:

- Will a significant number of the same prospects who didn't respond to the mailing donate money if you send them a second, third, or fourth fundraising letter? You can bet on it!

- Were some people who received the letter motivated to care about the reasons why you are campaigning? It's fair to expect so. Because a prospect didn't give doesn't mean he or she didn't learn anything about an organization or agree with its campaign premises.

- Will a percentage of those who did respond to your letter continue to contribute, and will they raise their contributions in the future? Absolutely!

These optimistic answers are realistic only if a full-scale mail campaign is run over an extended period.

You must keep up with the competition. As discussed in Chap. 3, take advantage of computer-driven fundraising management systems especially designed to track direct mail donors and prospects, forecast gift potential, and recommend the best ways to generate income over projected periods. (See page 84.)

You might want to investigate companies that aid nonprofits in running annual mail appeals. Several of these firms are listed at the back of *Fund Raising Management,* whose address appears in "Recommended Reading." Also, check your phone directory. Get in touch with company representatives and find out the services they offer, the fee structures, and clients who have used their services. Then check them out.

Finding Prospects

Send mail packages to the most people you can afford: the more mailings, the more contributions. Just remember that these returns will come in small, not large percentages of increase.

A membership organization knows who its prime group of mail prospects are: people who were not contacted in person or by phone during a drive. If you have no prospects, or need to broaden the prospect pool, consider exchanging or renting names of people who might be interested in your organization's point of view.

Trade a List for a List

Exchanging membership or donor lists with other nonprofits is one way to find new prospects. Contact the group whose list you would like and find out its policy about name swapping. Don't be concerned that by exchanging lists you will lose contributors to the other organization. That's most unlikely. The trading organization will allow you to use its list one time, and trust you not to make copies. You will, of course, require the same arrangement—in writing.

Try Your Hand at Renting Names

Using list rentals in the commercial world is big business. In fundraising, the same procedure is more risky and often less lucrative. However, it is still a valid way to develop new donors. List rentals are potentially profitable if the people contacted have a definite interest in your projects, if lists are used properly, and if the mail package is smashing.

Take a trip to your library's business section and find *Direct Mail Lists & Data,* a publication of *Standard Rates and Data.* This volume serves both commercial direct-response marketing people and nonprofit organization fundraisers. Its lists are classified by businesses (which includes professions) and consumers. As an example, for the sailor who mounted a campaign to fund his entry into an international race, we looked up "Boating" in the business classification. Among the many available rental lists focusing on the marine industry are subscribers to national magazines devoted to sailing. One of these publications specialized in yacht racing. It pinpointed readers who were likely to be interested in the sailor's project.

It's not necessary to rent an entire list, nor should you until you've tested a sampling. The minimum number of names to rent is usually 5000; costs range between $50 and $75 per 1000. By choosing options (at an additional expense) such as state, region, or zip-code breakdowns, the list can be pared to meet your requirements.

This is what each list furnishes:

- The name, address, and phone number of the firm that manages the list for the owner, and the name of the person to contact—the list manager.

- A description of the list and how many names it contains.

- The cost per thousand.

- The list source: where it came from.

- Costs for breakdowns of the total list. For example, a listing of 25,000 members of an association might cost $55 per thousand. A listing of 7500 members who joined during the last six months could cost $65 per thousand. If you would want the latter list broken down into certain states or zip codes, there is an additional cost per 1000 for each request.

- Addressing methods: pressure sensitive labels, magnetic tape, and so forth.

- How long it will take to receive your order.

- Restrictions. A sample of your mailing package is expected for approval, and prepayment is not an unusual request.

- Letter shop services. For a (stiff) fee you can have mail packages printed and posted by many of the firms that rent lists.

- How recently the list was updated.

Getting the Most Out of a Rental List

Become thoroughly familiar with *Direct Mail Lists & Data*. If you decide to rent names, choose between dealing directly with list managers and engaging professionals called "List Brokers" to represent your organization. These agents will recommend names that might be profitable and take care of ordering the lists you chose. Brokers are paid a commission, usually 20 percent, by list owners. *Direct Mail Lists & Data* furnishes the commission structure for each list.

A way to conserve money is to track down your own lists and deal with list managers directly. Then your organization can receive and deduct the 20 percent commission from rental expenses. Appoint a staff person or volunteer as the organization representative for list rentals—your in-house list broker. Some managers will challenge this scheme, but be firm. Tell the person you are the agent of record for your organization, and that your group expects to use the list often if it pays off.

If you decide to use a broker, *Direct Mail Lists & Data* furnishes companies that have paid to be included in its brokerage section. Other firms may be in your telephone book under "Mailing Lists," or find them in the back of *Fund Raising Management*, whose address appears in "Recommended Reading." Be certain the broker explains the *total* charges for a particular list rental. Besides fees for renting names and special breakdowns, there may be additional charges for handling and mailing. That's why it's important to have a working knowledge of *Direct Mail Lists & Data*. Make sure you know when the list was last updated. Sending letters to an ancient list of subscribers is a waste of money.

Test Mailings and Prospect Sampling

Imagine you've discovered a list of 30,000 names and want to find out how this group of prospects reacts to your project. Begin by renting the minimum number of names—5000. That becomes your test mailing. If results are dismal, you haven't spent a fortune to find that you're soliciting a nonsupportive group. If the response is promising, try another 5000. If you continue to be pleased, keep rolling over 5000 names until the list is completed.

When you order names from a list, exercise control over the sampling. For instance, an alphabetical listing that begins at "A" and runs consecutively to the 5000th name may not represent the demographics of those on the entire list. And who's to say that when you order an initial list that some dishonest broker or manager won't stack the deck—give you names that he or she knows are more likely to respond than others. Then you'll be induced to rent the remainder of the list. It's not a practice that's likely to happen, but why take a chance? The way knowledgeable commercial and nonprofit professionals order lists is by "nth" names. In other words, "I would like to have every 10th name of a 50,000 name mailing list." That's 5000 names. Or, "Please give me every 15th name of your 25,000 total list, 5000 names." By ordering "nth" names you receive a full cross section of each listing.

Projecting accurate returns from rental lists is impossible. I recently spoke to an executive who has spent his entire career in the commercial and nonprofit direct-mail business, an expert in the field. "What do you think my return on a $2150 investment for 5000 rental names would be?" I asked him.

"I have no idea," the expert answered. "If you placed a new display ad in a newspaper or magazine, or on television, could you project how many orders you would get for the product?"

"Not that I know of," I offered.

"It's the same with rental lists," the expert told me. "I've seen all kinds of returns for test mailings, but none of them were adequately forecast in advance."

Knowing this, you still need a starting point. Remember, these are new, completely uncultivated prospects. Probably, the return will be between one and one-half percent.

Let's look at why counting on a list rental as a sole source of mail campaign income can be a risky business, beginning with the initial cost:

List Rental @ $55 per 1000,

5000 names less 20% commission	$ 220
Postage @ 19.8 cents per unit (bulk rate)	990
Paper & printing of letter	140
Printed mailing & return envelopes (in-house)	200
Campaign piece	225
Total	$1,775

The example mailing costs $0.35 per person. If you chose the right list and sent a compelling package, a portion of the investment will be returned as donations. Let's say that one-half percent, 25 people, respond with an average gift of $25. That's $625. You're out $1150. Do you send a second mailing to these same people? Without fail. They are not "other" prospects anymore; they're current donors. A few months later when you mail another letter to those contributors, many will repeat their gifts. And since you are now concentrating on addressing 25 believers instead of 5000 unknowns, the second mailing will cost hardly anything.

Postage @ 29 cents	$7.25
Paper and printing of letter (in-house)	.75
Mailing and return envelopes	1.00
	9.00

Assume 60 percent of the 25 people make the same contribution a second time—that's $375. Your organization is now $784 in the red. Given the same mailing expense and the same number of donors repeating their gifts, after the fourth mailing you are $102 in the hole, a year has gone by, and the drive is concluded. You see, soliciting complete strangers by mail, prospects totally unaware that they will be contacted, is far more difficult than canvassing or phoning unaffiliated potential donors. There, the campaigner's presence (even if it's only a vocal one) and sales ability can capture and influence prospects in a way that is impossible to do by letter. Remember though, the up side—and it's a strong one—is that you have uncovered 25 new donors to continue cultivating. Some will eventually make larger and larger donations.

Keep in mind that the above scenario is an example of what can happen with list rentals, not what must happen. Again, success depends on the importance of the project, prospect motivation, and the power of the mailing package.

In any case, when you consider renting names, think of the old carnival barker's legendary words, "You pays yer money and ya takes yer choice." Because of the risk, use this means of identifying prospects as a last option.

Planning Effective Multimailings to Turn a Profit

In a capital campaign, recall that solicitation letters are used as wrap-ups. Because it is a special, one-time event, there are no current donors. Near the end of the drive, a letter is sent to prospects not solicited in other ways. This is followed by an additional request or two to those who didn't respond. The hope is that the magnitude of the building effort will influence prospects to give at reasonably high levels. In year-by-year funding programs, don't expect that a few mailings will produce all the income an organization is potentially able to generate.

National figures show that in a properly functioning annual mail campaign, about 60 percent of the people who make initial donations repeat the gift three more times in a year. So assuming a first response of $30, you can end up with $120 over a 12-month period from the same person. The second year's aim is to upgrade that contributor.

Donors are solicited at key times during a year's time. Following are the months commonly used:

    1st Mailing—September
    2d Mailing—December
    3d Mailing—March
    4th Mailing—May

Many organizations send fundraising requests in December; maximum results are often obtained during the holiday season. Skip the summer. In most locations, it's a terrible time for raising money.

The optimist looks at four solicitations in a 12-month period as not taking away the opportunity for a person to make additional gifts; the pessimist sees this practice as overkill. There are experts in direct mail who believe that three mailings will bring as much or more income as four. As you study each year's response to mailings a pattern will emerge. Through experience you will find the most productive times of year and how many mailings to schedule during that time period for your organization.

To work up useful projections you'll need to know:

- The number of current donors
- The category (e.g., visitors, patients, suppliers) and number of prospects
- Estimated costs of each mailing and the cost per package (unit) for current donors and prospects
- The percentage of return you figure on getting from current donors and prospect categories
- Dollar goals for current donors in each prospect category

To illustrate how a long-term mail program can be effective in reaching or exceeding its dollar and donor goal, let's assume that an organization:

1. Has 1000 current small gift contributors

2. Sets a mail dollar goal of $82,000

3. Desires 3100 gifts from current donors and prospects over a 12-month period (multiple donations from the same person each count as a single gift)

4. Figures a unit cost of $.40 per mailing for current donors or $1.60 for four mailings

5. Projects an average gift of $30 from present contributors

A Sample 12-Month Program

Using the above information, we can fill in a worksheet to show expectations from present supporters over a year:

Category	Pieces Mailed	Total Cost	Projected Donor Return	Number of Gifts	Projected Income
Four Mailings to:					
Current Donors	4000	$1600	60%	2400	$72,000

Even if the example organization meets its projections, it will not reach its $82,000 goal from the gifts of current contributors. A priority category of prospects is added to the next donor mailing called "Special Events," made up of people who attended a series of unique programs that the organization sponsored in the past. The unit cost for the special event mailing will be $1.10, considerably higher than $.40 per current donor cost. The example suggests that more money must be invested to get new givers than to obtain repeat donations from current contributors. High-priority prospects receive the most dynamic package you can afford.

Let's set the average gift at $25, project a 30 percent return, and look at possible results for the special events category.

Category	Pieces Mailed	Total Cost	Projected Donor Return	Number of Gifts	Projected Income
Four Mailings to:					
Current Donors	4000	$1600	60%	2400	$72,000
Special Events	1000	$1100	30%	300	7500
Total	5000	$2700		2700	$79,500

For a total investment of $2700 our example organization expects to pick up $79,500 in gifts from donors, a net of $76,800. Yet it is still short of the dollar goal by $5200 and still needs 800 more gifts to reach expectations. The group adds another category called "Visitors," people who have signed the organization's guest book when they came to tour the facility. Because these prospects are somewhat familiar with the organization, a 7 percent return is projected with an average gift of $25. The organization designs a package with a unit cost of $.63, an amount higher than for donors, but less than was spent on higher-priority special events prospects.

Category	Pieces Mailed	Total Cost	Projected Donor Return	Number of Gifts	Projected Income
Four Mailings to:					
Current Donors	4000	$1600	60%	2400	$72,000
Special Events	1000	$1100	30%	300	$7500
Visitors	5000	$3150	7%	350	$8750
Total	10,000	$5850		3050	$88,250

After three mailings, this group expects to raise $88,250 against expenses of $5850, a net profit of $400. But it is still short 50 gifts. The organization has two options: to take the small profit or to invest in a list rental and possibly lose money, but get donors for the future. Let's assume it chooses the latter option. For the fourth mailing it adds a rental list of 5000 persons. The unit cost is $.25, the return projected at 1 percent, the average gift expected to be $25.

Category	Pieces Mailed	Total Cost	Projected Donor Return	Number of Gifts	Projected Income
Four Mailings to:					
Current Donors	4000	$1600	60%	2400	$72000
Special Events	1000	$1100	30%	300	7500
Visitors	5000	$3150	7%	350	8750
Rental List	5000	$1250	1%	50	1250
Total	15,000	$7100		3100	$89,500

12-Month Results

Income		Donors	
Total Donations:	$89,500	Donor Goal:	3,100
Total Cost:	$ 7,100	Donors:	3,100
Net Income:	$82,400	New Donors:	700
Dollar Goal:	$82,000		
Gain:	$400		

The illustration points out:

1. Successful long-term mail programs concentrate on getting both gift income and new donors. The example organization picked up 700 new contributors. Many of them will continue to give in the next and succeeding drives, and organization expenses for their additional mailings will be less. Mail campaign strategies should be an integral part of long-range planning.

2. As with other forms of solicitation, the more involvement prospects have with an organization, the more they will fund its campaigns. In the example, the most supportive persons were current donors followed by special events participants and visitors. Having gambled on a rental list, prospects contributed as much

money as was spent on them. Reward for the investment was 50 new donors, nothing to sneeze at, especially when you're not out any money in acquiring them.

3. You must be prepared to make an investment of money, time, and patience to use mail solicitation successfully as part of your annual campaigns.

Upgrading Donors

What separates winning annual mail programs from failures is an organization's ability to continually elevate the contributions of current donors. A group that receives the same donations from supporters, year after year, has something wrong with the thrust and originality of its mail package, the capability of its campaign staff and leadership, or all of the above.

Rank donors by the size of their contributions so you can plan different approaches to upgrade them, as in the following example:

Gift Amount	No. of Gifts	Total Income
$100 +	35	$6125
$ 50–$99.99	75	5625
$ 25–$49.99	140	4900
$ 15–$24.99	220	3960
$ 10–$14.99	270	3240
$ 5–$9.99	350	2100
$ .01–$4.99	500	1250
	1590	$27,200

Although it's not news to you anymore, traditionally, the greatest amount of money comes from a small number of contributors, no matter the giving level. The example shows that 16 percent of the example givers donating $25 or more accounted for 61 percent of gift income. As always, concentrate on first upgrading the gifts of people in the highest giving categories. Following are some proven ways to attract all donors:

1. Earlier, you learned that asking a potential prospect to participate in share plans or to join a club, association, or society is the most convincing way in which to solicit small gift prospects in person or by phone. "I would like you to donate $100 to become a member of the President's Association," instead of, "I would like you to donate $100." These same methods also aid in motivating mail donors to raise their gifts.

2. Giving away such items as books, records, luggage, and other premiums to stimulate a contribution is an extremely feasible way to capture the interest of current supporters. Many national public radio and television stations do an outstanding job using premiums. Study their appeals carefully.

3. People like challenges. Have a supporter agree to match the amount of gift increases made by mail donors. Make the matching grant the strong point of your letter request.

4. Contributors often react favorably to a letter mentioning what they previously gave and suggesting a reasonable increase. Around 20 percent is a workable starting figure. For instance, "Your gift last year of $35 helped us provide needed equipment for the handicapped. I ask that you consider a new contribution of $45 to help continue this service."

5. When a specific donation is mentioned in the body of a letter, supporters will contribute that amount. Saying, for example, "a gift of $45 will allow us to . . ." often brings in many $45 contributions.

Ways to Say Thank-You and Get a Return

Structure acknowledgment letters to continue cultivating donors as well as thank them for contributions. Remember, your campaign case inspired them to give. Now make them aware you are beginning to make headway with the project they helped fund. It will prompt contributors to make larger gifts the next time around.

A return business reply envelope sent with an acknowledgment letter can often stimulate a bonus gift from donors. You can send a blank envelope, but you'll have better luck if you print "Enclosed is my special gift to (name of your organization or campaign)" on the envelope flap. One line of text is plenty. You don't want donors to think the note is a formal solicitation letter.

Don't forget to mail acknowledgment letters shortly after gifts are received. It helps contributors realize their gifts, no matter the amount, are valued by your organization.

What to Do with Nondonors

How long should you continue to invest in a prospect who never responds to your letters? My mother-in-law began her college career by attending a small university before moving on to a larger institution and receiving her degree. Although she never made a donation to the smaller school, yearly, without fail, the fundraising department sends her gift requests. Recently, the woman received a new association membership, an expensively produced, printed parchment certificate, sent by first-class mail. The last course my mother-in-law took at that small university was in 1932. Fantastic! That's stretching the idea of "never take away an opportunity for a prospect to give" beyond all common sense.

Unless a prospective donor notifies you that he or she doesn't want to be solicited, consider that person a prospect for two, perhaps three years. If after that amount of time you have not received a gift, retire the name to an inactive prospect file.

Creating a Direct-Mail Package

A mail solicitation is a sales device. Whatever personality it takes on—assertive, folksy, formal—don't lose sight of its purpose. Use your talent and that of others familiar with direct-mail marketing, design, and copywriting, to create an envelope, letter, and perhaps an enclosure that sells your audience. Only use a brochure or other publication if it greatly strengthens your case and you're pretty certain the piece will increase response. Otherwise, an enclosure will not be worth the expenditure.

It's not necessary for the signer of a letter to be its writer. Writing is a skill that many people such as corporate executives, politicians, and celebrities, don't possess. Ghostwriting is an accepted practice.

Carefully study commercial and nonprofit solicitation mail you receive. See which ideas and styles appeal to you most. If the letter is from a large enterprise or organization, be certain that much thought, research, and many dollars went into learning what motivates prospects to spend or donate money when solicited by mail. You don't need to agree with everyone's taste, but you will get a handle on the latest trends.

Creating successful mailing pieces is more a mystery than a science. No single type format or wording is always successful. But whether writing to members and constituents or sending letters to people you don't know, there are several factors that profitable mailings have in common.

Begin with the Envelope

You won't raise a nickel if nobody reads the letter. Prospects must be intrigued enough by the envelope to open it. If not, the whole package gets tossed in the wastebasket.

1. Have your letter signed by a person well known and respected so readers are impressed when they see the signer's name on the envelope's return address. This could be the campaign's general chair, your chief executive, an admired member of the community, or a national figure. Even if prospects don't know the individual personally, chances are they will open the envelope and begin reading the letter.

2. Use envelopes containing creative graphics, photography, a slogan, or a message.

3. Use handwritten envelopes instead of labels and indicias for high-priority prospects.

4. Use bulk rate stamps; although more expensive, stamps are preferable to indicias.

Writing Letters That Bring Donations

Personal Salutations.   Dear friend, member, supporter, or neighbor are impersonal ways to begin letters. If possible, address people by their names, "Dear Jane and Harry," or, "Dear Mr. and Mrs. Longtail." If you must use impersonal salutations, promise you won't send fundraising letters to "Dear Resident."

A Short Lead Line or Paragraph That Grabs the Reader's Attention. If it doesn't, the prospect may not be moved to read the rest of the letter. For example, instead of saying, "I am writing to describe the problem we have with air pollution, a growing concern . . . ," you might ask the reader, "Would you and your family rather live a full and healthy life or take a chance of contacting deadly illnesses because of air pollution? If we all pitch in, we can remedy this growing concern before the situation becomes desperate."

Central Themes. A fundraising letter is not a catalog. Don't try to justify every facet of your organization and drive.

Descriptions of the People Who Will Be Supported If the Drive Is Successful. Donors are moved by the plight of people, not organizations.

Mention of How the Prospect Will Benefit. "Supporting our religious values will bring you inner peace and harmony," or, "Your gift will help raise awareness that parapalegics can be self-sufficient and independent," or, "For a gift of $100 you will receive a hardcover volume of Shakespeare's sonnets."

Conversational, Intimate Styles Directed to the Reader. Make the reader feel your letter has been especially written to that person. Instead of saying, "Research is needed in the area of heart disease, and here is what we plan to do," tell your prospect, "I'm sure you realize that we need more heart disease research, and here is how you can help."

Personal Stories or Examples. Just as with solicitation methods, prospects respond positively to human interest reports illustrating why a project must be funded.

Easily Read Layouts. Make it simple for the reader to concentrate on your message. Use short paragraphs, lots of space to separate paragraphs, and underlines, italics, or boldface to highlight significant details.

Brevity. Don't write a tome. Several pages of text should be all that's needed. A single page is often enough.

Economy. If you require a second page, print it on the backside of the first page.

Positive Attitudes. Assume the reader is on your side. "I know you'll be interested in our project," instead of, "I hope you'll be interested in our project."

Specific Gift Requests for Specific Reasons. "Won't you donate $25 to help provide recordings of books for the visually impaired?" Or, "The enclosed gift card offers a year's membership in our Chapel Association."

Repetition of the Request. Ask for a contribution at least twice in each letter.

A Statement That Gifts Are Tax Deductible.   A must, especially for new or fairly unknown organizations!

Handwritten Signatures.   If unwieldy, have them printed in blue ink.

Postscripts.   Use them to personalize the letter, emphasize a point, or repeat a gift request.

Gift Reply Cards.   These cards give the prospect an opportunity to select from among several donations.

Enclosed Return Envelopes.   Make it easy for the prospect to respond.

Although not all successful fundraising letters use them, consider placing a (top-flight) candid, action photograph of the recipients of your services in the letter's layout. It will strongly bring home the point of the request.

Fundraising letters are sent to the three groups of people mentioned earlier:

1. Current donors

2. Past donor prospects

3. Other prospects

You could create the same solicitation letter for each category, but that makes little sense. *You wouldn't solicit a supporter or former supporter in person or by phone the same way you would a stranger. Neither should you by mail.* Approach each group on a different level.

Following is a sample fundraising letter upgrading current donors:

The Historical Society

Dear Bill and Betty,

Our interest may be in history, but our programs and facilities are totally up-to-date . . . and you deserve the credit.

Your $250 gift to the society's annual fund drive last year helped make possible:

- A completely rejuvenated exhibition hall
- A new demonstration showing what it was like to live in this region 100 years ago, praised by historians and the public alike
- The most visitors ever to see our exhibitions in the last decade

I'm sure you'll agree that we have a right to be proud of these achievements. I don't have to spell them out in detail, because I know you've witnessed many of our events first hand.

Since retiring last fall, I've devoted much more time to our society. As a volunteer tour guide, I've seen mild curiosity turn to sheer joy and enlightenment as visitors look into the past . . .

. . . people of every background, from our city, the region, and overseas. It's been fascinating to answer their questions and participate in discussions that contrast earlier trends with today's lifestyles.

<u>What an exciting and demanding time it is for our historical society.</u>

Although we are grateful for our success, we cannot afford to relax. Each year brings new challenges, and with them, new opportunities. We must serve a larger audience by maintaining present programs and starting new ones. The forthcoming Education Series described in the accompanying booklet is a perfect example.

<u>Your support will again make a difference!</u>

A $300 tax-deductible contribution to our society will help bring several of the finest lecturers in the country to conduct summer sessions of the Education Series.

This year we must raise the largest amount of money in our history. Everything points toward that happening, but to reach this goal we count on committed people like yourselves.

A gift reply card and return envelope is enclosed for your convenience. Our Board of Governors and I look forward to counting you again among our firmest supporters.

Sincerely,
K. L. Handle
General Campaign Chair

P.S. I know you'll find this exciting new educational series especially worthwhile and consider $300 as a worthy investment.

The gift reply card for the above letter could look like this:

The Historical Society Annual Campaign

Mr. & Mrs. Wm. Helper
123 Garden Lane
Kenux, MM 12121

I (We) would like to support this year's drive. Enclosed is my contribution to become a sponsor of the:

( ) Education Series $300
( ) Series I Association $200
( ) Jennifer Club $100
( ) Other Contribution $____

Please make your tax-deductible donation payable to: The Historical Society Annual Campaign, 100 Philanthropy Way, Kenux, MM, 11111.

The information on the gift reply card could also have been printed on the inside flap of a preaddressed, return envelope. Keep the reply card or envelope simple, mention gift options, and repeat that the gift will be tax-deductible.

The weakest part of a fundraising letter is the dollar request. Although a specific donation is solicited, you must suggest—as the above reply card does—that prospects give a lesser amount if the gift sought is too much. Given the choice, many people respond by sending in smaller contributions.

Do all possible to personalize letters to current contributors. In the sample letter, "Bill and Betty" were mentioned in the salutation, and the couple's last gift of $250 was noted. Then the donors were told the campaign chair knew they were attending various events held by the organization. Although printed, the postscript was hand-written. Personalizing letters can mean lots of research and extra work for staff or volunteers. Is the extra time worth the effort? It is if you want more than token gifts to your campaign. It definitely is if you are trying to upgrade current donors. Remember, *personalized letters bring larger contributions.*

Now here's a sample letter for past donor prospects.

Family Service Center
3565 Platt Way
Cannburgh, JK 28763

Dear Mr. and Mrs. Nedding,

For incoming organization representatives from across the nation, it was an otherwise typical beginning of our annual national conference. But somehow the mood was different . . .

. . . not depressive exactly, but you could tell by the talk in the lobby, without its usual banter, that long standing-rumors about cutbacks in funding from our parent organization and the city were taking a toll on many of those attending.

Little did I know what our agency was in for!

During the conference we were told to expect that 25 percent of next year's requested budget would not be funded. The choices were clear: reduce services drastically, or add the amount to the annual drive.

At first we felt sorry for ourselves. We were already short on space and staff. Layoffs, continual price increases, bills long overdue, in locales where it could least be endured, strained many family relationships to the point of bursting. Our caseload had been upped tremendously. This was no time for cutbacks.

Then we felt embarrassed.

Why? Because in feeling sorry for ourselves we neglected to put our faith in a community that has supported the work of this agency for almost three decades. People who care that each year hundreds upon hundreds of our fellow citizens, of all descriptions, ages, and lifestyles, are given the chance to again be productive . . . confident . . . able to positively contribute to their families and neighborhoods.

That's when we knew that somehow everything would turn out all right. Despite the economy our supporters would not let us down. Nothing would be cut from the increased need for our services. <u>We would not be forced to turn people away.</u> Our confidence returned.

Mr. and Mrs. Nedding, with all the recession has done to make times difficult, our organization does not have the option of living in the financial past. To reach this year's expanded goal we must rely on former friends as well as those currently funding our programs.

Asking that you consider a gift of $100 to help offset our recent funding reduction is not as pertinent as requesting that you make this contribution to permit troubled community members to become whole once again.

Gratefully,

Robin Cott
General Campaign Chair

P.S. A gift reply card and return envelope is enclosed for your convenience. Promote a bright future for those needing our assistance by making a $100 gift to this year's annual fund drive.

The third letter written for "other" prospects, is suitable for a capital campaign. But whatever the subject or readership, the fundraising recipe is the same—writing to people about people.

The Regional Hospital

Office of the Administrator

Dear Mr. & Mrs. Jones,

The spring night that started so peacefully turned into a series of sights and sounds that I will never forget.

You will remember it was shortly after sundown when the gas main explosion destroyed most of the First Street area last May. I had just left a meeting at the hospital and could hear ambulances responding from all over the area.

Our hospital's bed space was at capacity. Soon the well-equipped but small emergency facilities were overflowing with people injured in the explosion.

The community had outgrown us too rapidly. Many of those who had been treated were lying on stretchers all over the hallways because we didn't have rooms for them. It was an incredibly horrible time for the patients and a frustrating time for the staff who did brilliantly under the most adverse conditions.

<u>With your support, the same scenario will not be repeated.</u>

That unfortunate accident tragically pointed out the intense need to complete our capital drive to build additional emergency room facilities and a South Wing to add another 200 beds. The inability to respond effectively to such a tragedy as happened last spring cannot be allowed to happen again.

<u>We must be in a position to serve you, your family, and all those in the community should they need our care and facilities.</u>

Because of the contributions of many supporters, we have raised a substantial sum of money toward our goal. As we strive to obtain the remaining funds, <u>your generosity is essential to the campaign's total success.</u> The hospital has set up a special donor's fund in memory of those who were lost in the accident.

<u>Won't you please make a tax-deductible contribution of $450, payable over a three-year period,</u> to help endow this fund and help assure that groundbreaking takes place on schedule.

Take time to study the enclosed brochure which furnishes details about the entire building program. I know you will carefully consider our request and have enclosed a return envelope showing giving guidelines for your convenience.

Gratefully,

J. M. Brown
Administrator

P.S. I have often wondered how many more lives we could have saved during the night of the explosion if we could have provided the extended services that a successful building campaign guarantees. <u>Contribute $450 to life.</u>

Although relating to different causes and written to three different types of potential donors, the letters have much in common:

- The first paragraph is designed to capture the reader's attention.
- A central theme. The historical society focuses on the need to support new programs for an expanded constituency. The family service correspondence centers on funding an unexpected budget increase. The hospital letter revolves around the dangers of inadequate facilities.
- Who the funds will benefit. The historical society letter features an education series; the family service piece centers on the increased number of needy families from poor areas of the city; and the last concentrates on facilities to provide up-to-date medical services for an entire community.
- The text is written in a conversational style emphasizing people.
- Each letter tells personal stories related to the campaign case.
- Paragraphs are brief and to the point.
- The layout uses white space to make text easily readable and underlines to accentuate important information.
- Contributions are requested at least twice.
- Postscripts are used to reemphasize needs and repeat gift requests.

Testing Your Package

After the letter, envelope, and enclosures are written and designed, have the package looked at by people whose opinions you value before it goes to press. You don't have to accept every criticism, but you'll likely end up with a tighter presentation resulting from their input. Once the package is produced, try out the mailing on a sample group of prospects. See how much money it brings before sending the letter to other potential donors.

Contact some prospects you wrote, givers and nongivers alike, and get a sampling of what they thought of each part of your package. You will learn a great deal, just as manufacturers do when they test products on consumers. If this research tells you that 20 out of 25 people thought your envelope slogan didn't affect them one iota, you best think about a rewrite. It doesn't matter if you and your family loved it— your customers didn't.

Such things as writing style, theme, and layout make enormous differences in prospect's reactions to fundraising letters. If you are not satisfied with results over a reasonable period—not uncommon for both beginners and experienced professionals—you may want revamp the package. But how do you know what to change? What if your research shows no specific objections to the mailing? Your prospects are just not responding well. With all the possible variables, the only way to find a weakness is to test the ingredients one at a time. It may be agonizing, but *testing and retesting is part of the mail campaign experience*. For subsequent mailings to the same prospects, revise only one element of your package and analyze results. Take heart. Eventually you'll hit upon the right formula. Then you're on the way to showing a profit.

Much of the success of your mail program depends on outdoing the competition. Enlist the best volunteer thinkers and creative people around to help create your package. If these people aren't available, get advice from a consultant.

Additional Ideas to Stir Your Imagination

1. Enticing People to Open the Envelope
   a. Use colored envelopes instead of white.
   b. Use an off-sized envelope so it stands out.
   c. Consider specially designed envelopes. See your printer and look at samples.
   d. Use handwritten notes on envelopes.
2. Getting Prospects to Read the Letter
   a. Use a question or quotation as a lead paragraph.
   b. Use creative and provoking enclosures: a mahogany wood chip symbolizing a new church alter; a packet of seeds suggesting forthcoming growth. Novelty items don't suit everybody, but they will spur many donors and prospects to respond to your letter.

c. Use creative layouts to call attention to your cause:

> If we don't quickly do more about stamping
> out AIDS and stop turning our backs
> on the problem, making believe
> it will go away, there
> will be a lot less
> good people
> alive to
> help!

d. Use a second color along with italics and boldface to highlight important aspects of the letter.

3. Asking for the Gift
   a. Begin the letter with a gift request. "A donation from you will help us receive a matching grant of $75,000."
   b. Request an odd amount of money. Let's say you're holding a capital campaign for new facilities. The cost of your lecture hall seats is $34,900. Ask your prospects for a $34.90 donation, $\frac{1}{1000}$ of the cost of the seats.

4. Use Testimonials
   a. Have a letter signed by one or more recipients of your services, relating their experiences and strong viewpoints about the need for funding.

A Case Study

Remember the international sailboat race competitor used as an illustration of how sticking to fundraising principles can make even an obscure appeal successful? For his capital campaign, we created a new organization. The budget and prospect base were limited. Letters used to wrap up the $215,000 effort brought in a little over 2 percent of the goal, $4400. Five hundred letters were sent to interested prospects, about a third of which were contributors to a former appeal run by the sailor. The return was 22 percent, the average gift $40 from 110 people. Contributors weren't solicited personally or by phone because the start of the race was almost at hand and volunteers were depleted.

The letterhead and letter were printed by the sailor and his wife by computer. Expenses—paper, envelopes, and postage—amounted to $165. The letter was personally signed by two prominent businessmen and yachting enthusiasts known to most prospects. A handwritten note below the postscript was written to key recipients.

Following is the letter and comments:

Dear Mr. & Mrs. Mariner,
    We believe you know the sailor, adventurer, and author Hal Roth. His seven books have penetrated the mysteries of small boat sailing and portrayed life in the great and small ports of the world.

[Even if prospects didn't know Roth personally, the first paragraph would intrigue them enough to continue reading the letter. Most serious recreational sailors daydream about one day sailing the ocean in a yacht to foreign destinations. Here was a man who had done just that.]

Hal lives in Somesville, on Mt. Desert Island, and has entered the fiercely competitive 1990–91 BOC Singlehanded Round-The-World Race. <u>He has logged over 147,000 offshore miles in small sailing vessels,</u> and placed fourth in class in the last BOC race where he competed against the world's best sailors in the 27,000 mile marathon.

[If an organization is new or comparatively unknown, immediately establish the credibility of its leader. The letter notes the project head is from the same general area as his prospects are, a hometown boy, and that he has a solid record of experience. None of this background had to be described in detail. Supportive information was included in enclosures and reprints of articles about the competition and Roth.]

Our local sailor intends to be first across the finish line in the new BOC Challenge that starts this September 15th. "With experience gained from the last race, and new strategies and equipment, I believe I can win this race for the United States," Hal told me recently. We know that by starting time, he will have put two years of hard and useful work into the project.

[The paragraph begins with an optimistic statement and carries the positive atmosphere to the end. Instead of saying, "I would like to win," or, "I hope I can win," the reader sees that the sailor's intention is to win. That he has prepared himself properly for the journey. Only one thing can hold him back which is addressed in the next paragraph.]

All the determination in the world will do little good, however, if Hal doesn't find the money to outfit his 50-foot cutter, *American Flag,* to winning standards. He has taken on—along with scores of jobs to ready his sleek racer—the task of raising $215,000. Through the generosity of many individuals and a national corporation, Captain Roth has received approximately $211,000 so far. <u>This is a solid indication of great faith in his skills and competitiveness by many people throughout the nation.</u>

[Now that prospects have a sense of the project and a feeling for the participant's resolution, the middle part of the letter introduces the campaign, suggests the goal is attainable, and states that many others across the United States have supported the sailor. The prospects know they are being asked to help conclude what is bordering on a successful campaign.]

To start the race and successfully compete, Hal must continue to receive solid financial backing. We ask that you <u>join us in making a tax-deductible contribution of $150 to this great adventure.</u> Enclosed you will find a gift card that shows additional giving options.

[Notice that the gentlemen who signed the letter asked the reader to "join us in making a tax-deductible gift . . ." thus assuring prospects of their support. (For the record, these men were both major gift donors during the early part of the drive.) The paragraph ends with a specific gift request, and the letter continues by offering prospects an incentive.]

> Hal obviously cannot take a crew with him on this solo voyage. But he will carry a very special book with the names of donors on board his cutter as she hurries across the vastness of the Atlantic, the Pacific, and the 12,000 miles of the Southern Ocean. Please let us know your name will be among our supporters.
>
> Welcome aboard!
>
> Sincerely,
>
> Cochairs
American Flag Fund Committee

> P.S. To many of us Hal has already joined a select group of men whose great voyages began in their fifties and sixties, such as the famed Joshua Slocum and Sir Francis Chichester. <u>I know you will give the most serious consideration to our $150 request.</u>

The postscript reemphasizes Roth's credentials and again requests a specific contribution. The gift reply card looked like this:

> Please enter my name in Hal Roth's American Flag Donor Book. I enclose my contribution for $_____.
> $150   First Officer
> $100   Second Officer
> $75   Bosun
> $50   Able Seaman
> Make checks payable to . . . etc.

A successful effort. But, at this point, if you are wondering how much more money would have been contributed had those prospects been personally solicited by peers, then you truly understand where letter solicitations stand in the order of fundraising priorities.

After another break, let's move on to what needs doing following a campaign's closing date.

PART 5

Putting the Drive to Bed

14

Postcampaign Follow-up

As Yogi Berra, one of baseball's great philosophers said, "It ain't over till it's over." It would be pleasant to think that campaign completion dates, often the end of the fiscal year for annual appeals, signal a well-deserved rest for volunteers and staff. It usually isn't so. Loose ends have to be tied up, results analyzed, and thought given to future planning. Look at the checklist below:

For All Campaigns

( ) Complete solicitations.

( ) Update master prospect files.

( ) Prepare fundraising summaries.

( ) Evaluate the drive.

( ) Collect unpaid pledges.

( ) Hold a special worker's event.

For Annual Campaigns

( ) Enlist next year's leadership.

( ) Enlist campaign workers for the next drive.

( ) Initiate or rework a long-range plan.

Complete Solicitations

There are several reasons why prospects must be seen after a closing date has come and gone:

- Some were never assigned.
- Assignments were made but the workers never bothered to solicit one or more of their prospects.

- Some prospects haven't yet made a decision about their gifts.
- Others were unable to be contacted.
- Some asked to be solicited following the closing date.

The great enemy of the postcampaign period is lethargy: most workers let down considerably and don't want to involve themselves with further campaign chores. But since gift income cannot afford to be lost, a cleanup force of trusted volunteers must be recruited and remaining prospects assigned to them. Here are the steps to be taken:

1. List prospects that must be visited, phoned, or written, using the following form as a model.

Postcampaign Solicitation Follow-up						
Name	Address	Category or Division	Evaluation	Assigned to	New Worker	Comments
The Brown Corp.	6 Business Ln.	Industry	$1800	D. Johnson		First visited 5/28. Revisit after 6/30.
C. Cronin	26 Thorpe	Special	$1000	Samuels		Awaiting change in economy. Decade long supporter.
D. Davis	34 Town Square	Advance	$5000	Jonas		Visited 4/19. Consulting family members for joint gift.

2. Hold assignment meetings and distribute prospects just as you did during the campaign. When reassigning prospects, tell the original workers you have done so. Make sure each follow-up worker has an assignment sheet listing his or her new prospects, such as this one:

```
Worker Assignment Sheet

Worker's Name: A. Jones          Chair: Lopez

Category or Division: Business   Phone: 123-8473

Phone: 123-5694
```

Name	Address	Phone	Evaluation	Gift	Named Facility	Remarks
Brown Corp.	Business Ln.	345-9875	$1800			Revisit after 6/30.

3. Hold report meetings weekly. If impossible, make sure to phone workers for their reports.

Update Master Prospect Files

Make certain that gifts, pledges, reassignments, and other information are entered to keep records in order.

```
Prospect File Form

LAST NAME: Brown Corp.            CATEGORY/DIVISION: Business
FIRST NAME (MR.): Art Brown       EVALUATION:
FIRST NAME (MRS.):                GIFT AMOUNT:
ADDRESS: Business Lane            PLEDGE CARD SIGNED (Y/N):
CITY/STATE: Local                 TERMS:
ZIP CODE: 11111                   WORKER'S NAME: A. Jones
HOME PHONE:                       NAMED FACILITY:
BUS. PHONE (MR.):                 *:
BUS. PHONE (MRS.):                *:
MEMBER:                           *:
TYPE OF                           DATE ENTERED:
  MEMBERSHIP:
```

(*Continued*)

Annual Giving Record (10 Yrs.)		Comments
82-	87-	Seen 5/28 by R. Smith.
	88-	Asked to be visited after
84-	89- $500	6/30. Reassigned to A.
85-	90- $750	Jones on 7/6.
86-	91- $1,500	

*Spares for additional information.

Prepare Fundraising Summary Sheets

To evaluate a drive, statistics need to be on hand. Complete the following:

Comparison of Expected and Actual Gift Income

Projected				Actual		
Number of Gifts	In the Range of	% of Goal	Totaling	Number of Gifts	% of Goal	Totaling
( )	( )	( )	( )	( )	( )	( )
( )	( )	( )	( )	( )	( )	( )
( )	( )	( )	( )	( )	( )	( )

Next, furnish the figures for a category and division summation sheet.

Gift Income by Category or Division

Category or Division	Projected Income	Number of Prospects	Gifts	Totaling
( )	( )	( )	( )	( )
( )	( )	( )	( )	( )
( )	( )	( )	( )	( )
( )	( )	( )	( )	( )
( )	( )	( )	( )	( )

Your phonathon leader will provide you with a final phonathon report.

FINAL PHONATHON REPORT

Date: _____   Chair: _____

Volunteers needed _____   Phonathon prospects _____
Volunteers enlisted _____

Calls attempted _____   Average per volunteer _____
Calls completed _____   Average per volunteer _____
Pledges _____   Totaling $_____
Unspecified _____   Totaling $_____
Refusals _____
Unable to reach _____

There are two forms to use for mail campaign final reports, depending on whether your program was for a capital or annual campaign:

1. Capital Campaign—Direct-Mail Results

	Number of Prospects	Cost per Unit	Total Cost	% Response	Net Profit or (− loss)
1st Mailing					
2nd Mailing					

Total % of Response: _____
Total Expenses: $_____
Total Profit or Loss: $_____

2. Annual Campaign—Direct-Mail Results

Category	Pieces Mailed	Total Cost	Projected Donor Return	Number of Donors	Projected Income	% Dollar Goal	% Donor Goal
Current Donors (	) (	) (	) (	) (	) (	) (	)
( ) (	) (	) (	) (	) (	) (	) (	)
( ) (	) (	) (	) (	) (	) (	) (	)
	------ ------			------ ------		------ ------	
( ) (	)			( ) (	) (	) (	)

Income		Donors	
Total Donation: (	)	Donor Goal: (	)
Total Cost: (	)	Projected Donors: (	)
Net Income: (	)	New Donors: (	)
Dollar Goal: (	)		
Gain (or – loss): (	)		

Evaluating the Drive

Examining the statistics from a completed campaign reveals much about its planning and execution. Leadership discussions should focus on answering such questions as:

- Did the campaign live up to expectations?
- How closely was the operating plan followed?
- Was the correct goal set?
- How did prospect evaluations compare with donations?
- Was adequate worker training furnished?
- How did the workers perform? Did they use their training to the best advantage?
- What was donor reaction to named gift opportunities?
- What can be done to dispense with weaknesses?

The evaluation session will enable you to think up new strategies and approaches to benefit the next undertaking.

Let's look in on a portion of a campaign committee evaluation meeting: a half-million dollar drive that didn't meet its goal. The members have just finished studying the final category and division summation sheet, following.

Category or Division		Projected Income	Prospects	Gifts	Totaling
Challenge	(50K+)	$50,000	6	1	$65,000
	(25k–50k)	$55,000	15	4	$65,000
Leadership	(12.5K–25k)	$75,000	20	6	$80,000
Advance	(5k–12.5k)	$100,000	40	15	$95,000
Special	(1k–5k)	$95,000	210	90	$80,000
Associates	($500–$1000)	$50,000	250	130	$45,000
Sponsor	($100–$500)	$20,000	320	240	$10,000
General	(below $100)	$15,000	635	400	$7,500
Corporations		$40,000	25	10	$35,000
Foundations		$5,000	8	1	$5,000
		$500,000	1529	897	$487,500

CHAIR: We surpassed expectations in the $12,500-and-up giving ranges.

MEMBER 1: Yes, but then we took a nosedive and fell short of our projection for gifts between $1000 and $5000. We wanted 210 gifts and received only 90 that averaged less than $900.

CHAIR: Jim, you were in charge of that group. What accounts for these figures?

JIM: Too much guesswork. We completely misread the capabilities of many new prospects.

CHAIR: Seems like we need to restructure the evaluation committee. In any case, we know a lot more now than we did before about these people. That will be useful next year.

MEMBER 2: Our small gift canvassing wasn't as effective as it should have been. I don't think we put enough emphasis on training.

CHAIR: That shows its value. You can't expect people to know how to solicit inherently. Next campaign, let's put together a stronger training program.

MEMBER 3: The phonathons went well, but the direct-mail campaign was mediocre.

CHAIR: Let's get more coverage by phone. Surely there's a way to enlist more phone solicitors. Also, we should freshen up the entire mail package. Although we've come up short this year, a good many individual and corporate supporters have become friends of the organization. I'm sure our next campaign will go over the top.

Pledge Collection

Few volunteers want to be members of a collection committee, but you must try and get prospects who have promised a donation to come up with the money. It's a sensitive business. Threatening people with nasty letters or lawsuits isn't usually reasonable for nonprofits. You don't want to lose future support, and it's rotten public relations for nonprofits. There are two major reasons why people don't pay contributions.

1. A prospect makes a pledge because he or she is momentarily swept away by the emotion of a drive or a solicitor's presentation. Following the solicitation, other priorities occupy the person's time, and the pledge payment becomes secondary or forgotten. This happens most often in nonmembership campaigns. With proper follow-up these promised contributions are often collectible.

2. A prospect's financial picture changes for the worse. These gifts or pledges are most often uncollectible.

After several billings, collection should not be the responsibility of the book-keeping department. Enlist a committee of peers to visit or phone nonpaying donors and see if they can offer assistance. Some contributors may need more time before paying their donations. Create or revise payments schedules when necessary. Remind them you are depending on their payments to provide seriously needed programs, services, or facilities.

Enlisting Next Year's Campaigners

At the least, get commitments from those you want to chair your drive, categories, and divisions before someone else captures them. Waiting until just before the next funding effort often means settling on last-moment, second, third, or even fourth choices. That practice, as you know, invites fundraising catastrophe.

It will be far easier to retain campaigners you already have if:

- The recently completed campaign was successful

- Volunteers are pleased with their performance in the just-completed drive

- Workers know leaders and their peers were impressed by their efforts

Long-Range Planning

Project your funding requirements for the next several years by using information obtained from the recently completed drive, results of past appeals, and future needs. Projections are guidelines for planning, and subject to change as time passes.

Long-Range Projections				
Category or Division	Actual 1991–92	1992–93	Projected 1993–94	1994–95
( )	( )	( )	( )	( )
( )	( )	( )	( )	( )
( )	( )	( )	( )	( )
etc... Totals	_____	_____	_____	_____

Organize a Special Event
for Campaigners

Host a get-together to celebrate the end of a campaign, and say "thank you" to workers for giving time and effort to support your organization. Volunteers deserve to be formally recognized, and an upbeat event will do wonders for worker retention. Depending on the size of the workforce, many organizations hold separate functions for various categories and division campaigners. Usually spouses are welcome. Whether formal or casual, be sure your professional and top campaign leadership attend each function, make the occasion festive, and keep speeches to a minimum.

PART 6

Getting Your Messages Across: Communications

15

Publicity: How to Get It Used

The demand for news is never-ending. Editors must fill pages and minutes of air-time each day of the year. Stories about your organization and campaign can help satisfy that demand. Any marketing pro knows the value of publicity, as do promotion-minded fundraisers: it gives an organization and campaign visibility and credibility at no cost. But publicity is free only *if* you convince editors to print or air the releases you submit, and *if* you get reporters to write favorable stories about your organization and drives.

Press releases that only describe plans are not as interesting to readers or listeners as those in which people are part of the story. Compare the following examples:

(1)

The Long Acres Civic Group plans to mount a $5 million capital campaign to fund a new Community Center located on a 20-acre tract of land on Pinetree Road in East Warren.

Scheduled to be kicked off September 15th, the drive is being held in response to studies that determined the Civic Group's need for new facilities, essential to keep up with population growth in the region.

(2)

The Long Acres Civic Group plans to mount a $5 million capital campaign to fund a new Community Center located on a 20-acre tract of land on Pinetree Road in East Warren, according to Chairman of the Board James Pierce.

The drive, scheduled to begin September 15th, will be chaired by Rose Watson. Mrs. Watson, owner of Argo Industries, has served in many key civic group positions during the past decade.

Following a year of studies conducted by the firm of Polster & Polster, with offices in West Hill, it was determined that new facilities are needed if the organization expects to keep up with population growth in the area.

"I can't tell you how excited we all are," said Mrs. Watson. "For many years we have been looking forward to a center that will serve the entire population. Now we're finally prepared to ask the community for its full support."

Relating people to facts and figures does two positive things: it makes the campaign story come alive—therefore likely to get printed and aired—and it puts the names of leadership in front of a large audience, a reward for their volunteerism.

The aim of fundraising publicists is to have their present and future supporters see and hear the organization's name often during a campaign, especially during the small gifts phase. The second civic group story might be a feature on chairwoman Watson and the study findings, followed by an article about the architects with pictures of facility renderings. For each release, find an angle, a slant that is fresh and exciting. Rehashing what's been published or broadcast will assure that the material will not be used again.

Remember that businesses as well as nonprofit groups vie for free space and airtime. Chances of getting a release used increases when you hand it to the right person. Becoming friendly with editors is often a challenge, but that separates dynamic publicists from the wallflower variety. Although many of them would like you to be, don't be intimidated by newspeople. Be persistent and aggressive. Those are attitudes they understand. Phone them, take them to lunch, get them to respect the job you're doing for your organization.

If you can't see an editor personally, mail the release with a personal note.

Which newspaper editor should receive your publicity release depends on the subject of the story. If a special dinner is coming up, send it to the society editor. If it's a sports banquet, obviously the material goes to the sports department. Other departments might include business, entertainment, religion, and features. Local radio and television station submissions go to the news director. Editor's names can be found either in the publication or by phoning the media involved.

Write publicity in the style of the medium for which it will be used. Because of time constraints, unless it's a feature, broadcasters are concerned only with the main points of your story. The style should be more informal and sentences should be shorter since it's difficult for listeners to absorb long strings of words and newspeople to read them aloud. Let's look at a portion of the civic group story rewritten for radio or television:

> A new community center is in the offing. Long Acre Civic Association Board Chairman James Pierce announced today that a $5 million communitywide fundraising campaign will kick off in mid-September. It will be chaired by long-time philanthropist Rose Watson of Fall Hills. If all goes as planned, the new center will be located on a 20-acre tract on Pinetree Road in East Warren . . .

Compare hard news stories in newspapers with radio or television versions and you'll quickly learn the differences between the two.

Following is the general format for a press release:

- Type your release, double-spaced, on 8½″ × 11″ paper. Leave margins of at least an inch. Include the date you mail the piece and the person who should be contacted for additional information.

- Write the words "FOR IMMEDIATE RELEASE" under the contact name or, if you want the story held, specify a date, e.g., "FOR RELEASE AFTER JUNE 1."

■ Supply a headline. It may not be the one used, but it easily identifies the reason for your submission.

■ Stick to facts, not editorial comments.

■ Keep technical wording to a minimum: avoid "bureaucratese."

■ At the outset, be sure to mention *who* the release is about, *what* it is, *when* it is, *where* it is, *why* it is, and *how* it came to happen. See how the working press handles these basic journalistic tenants by studying various newspaper and magazine hard news stories. You'll find the five "W's" in the first paragraph of the story.

■ After the story, type in "#" or "30," the traditional end-of-article symbols.

Here's a brief example:

The Community Service Organization
1234 Roger Road
Philipton, MM 12345

Contact: George Spelvin   June 1, 1991

(123) 123-4567

FOR IMMEDIATE RELEASE:

YOUTH GROUP TO SPONSOR WALKATHON

A walkathon [*what*] to benefit handicapped young people [*why*] sponsored by the Jolly Roger Organization [*who*] will be held on June 15th, beginning at 7:30 A.M. [*when*]. Starting at the organization's headquarters on Ninth Street, the course will lead participants through Irving Park and conclude at the North end of Symons Avenue [*where*].

Jane Doer, President of the community service organization, said that the walkathon was suggested by a group of children who wanted to participate in the event by wheelchair [*how*].

Always submit photographs, drawings, or artwork to enhance your article. In the above example, a picture of President Doer and the children who thought up the event, along with a drawing of the walkathon route, would be appropriate.

Getting reporters to cover an event or write feature stories about your project expands visibility. But there's no guarantee how the story will turn out. I once invited members of the press to interview a foreign statesman before he made a fundraising dinner speech. The toughest and most talented reporter in the area asked if he could put the first question to the statesman during the news conference. That would be okay, I told him, but the statesman wanted questions limited to why he was in town. "Be nice," I told the print journalist. He nodded, looking as if I had defiled his integrity.

Just before the event, with television news cameras rolling, this reporter began the press conference by asking the statesman about a financial scandal he had been involved in at home. And whether the man thought the scandal damaged his credibility and continued professional usefulness. The red-faced diplomat's embarrassed answer was the lead story on the 11 o'clock news that night and made the front page of every morning newspaper. He and his press secretary were livid. I was upset for another reason: the coverage of my fundraising dinner became an afterthought.

I did my job by inviting the reporter to the news conference; the journalist did his by getting the most newsworthy story possible.

Another time, I found myself in trouble as a college vice president for development and public relations because of a newspaper story. I spoke at a local chapter of a professional organization for fundraising executives at which a reporter covered the speech. Here's how the headline and first two paragraphs appeared in his paper the next day:

FUNDRAISER TELLS HOW TO GO AFTER BIG BUCKS

How do you motivate professional fundraisers to think about motivating big givers to give bigger?
Tell them the story about "Naming The Men's Room."

Years before I gave that speech, I came across a small named gift plaque on the men's room door of a prominent law school. I told the story, which took about half a minute, to add humor to an otherwise serious address of one-half hour. Although the rest of the article faithfully reported the importance of raising major gifts, for some time I was reminded how upset the trustees and president of the college were when they read the first two paragraphs.

Remember, no matter what material you'd like printed or aired, reporters seek the juiciest angles to get their stories published. That's what they get paid to do. When you ask a member of the press to cover one of your events, there is no assurance that you'll be pleased with the result. But if you are, you couldn't pay for better organization or campaign marketing.

16

Graphic Design for Nondesigners

An organization can have the most imaginative marketing committee, the best thought-out creative plan, and still fall flat on its face if publications are visually dreadful. Don't confuse inexpensively produced with poor-quality publications. Save money by learning how to create your own stationery, brochures, newsletters, and other campaign pieces.

Go with the Flow

Study high-quality graphic design in magazines, newspapers, brochures, and advertisements to learn ideas and executions. Notice the juxtaposition of shapes, placement of material, use of black-and-white versus color, and size and thickness of type. These uses and arrangements were not chosen randomly. Each part of a publication's layout is meant to capture the attention of a specific audience. That's why the *Wall Street Journal, USA Today,* and *The National Enquirer* look totally different; each appeals to the tastes of different readerships.

Tailor campaign literature to *your* donors, prospects, and workers. If, for instance, you represent a conservative, established institution of higher learning, printed materials should visually reflect tradition and appear subdued. It doesn't matter if the students have purple hair sticking straight in the air and wear sleeveless blue blazers and striped running shoes. They are not your fundraising constituency (for the time being). Current and past supporters, potential contributors, and volunteers are the people you are trying to reach. Think in their terms; reflect their feelings.

Getting a Feel for Composition

Although some have more innate talent than others, many people don't need a design course to arrange a series of items that please the eye. An obvious example is the placement of furniture and wall hangings in a room. By eyeballing, each piece is set in an attractive way to create the impression the owner desires. In publications, the outcome should be the same, but the tools are different. Eyeballing is not enough. Laying out one-dimensional, empty pages requires some technical know-how—a basic understanding of composition, typography, and layout.

A completed design is the sum of many elements, all of them intertwined. These components are hard to place in niches, like letters in post office boxes. But to obtain a basic understanding of what's available, let's try and separate them.

1. Balance: Symmetry and Asymmetry

The balance used exclusively in the architecture of the early Greeks was symmetry. The word is derived from that culture. Symmetry is visual information in which equal arrangements of shapes are placed on each side of a real or imaginary horizontal or vertical center line. Withstanding a few peculiarities, the human body is symmetrical. If you draw a center line from head to feet, equal parts are found on both sides. Look at the symmetrical letters and shapes below.

$$--- H --- \quad [[\,\vdots\,]] \quad /// \text{ I } \backslash\backslash\backslash \quad \text{OOO OOO}$$

Symmetry is perfectly ordered, formal, regal, and symbolic of great strength in the classic manner. If you want to show an organization as powerful, staid, and observing old-fashioned values, symmetry is for you.

A more modern and less formal way of balancing information is by using asymmetry, which occurs when visual information is not identical on each side of a center line, as in the next series of shapes:

$$- H \ --- \quad [\,\vdots\,]] \quad // \text{I } \backslash\backslash\backslash \quad \text{O OO OOO}$$

Following are two of many ways to set up a symmetrically balanced letterhead:

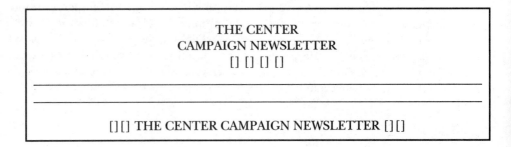

While the next two are asymmetrically balanced:

[][][]   THE CENTER CAMPAIGN NEWSLETTER

THE CENTER CAMPAIGN

[] NEWSLETTER []

All four illustrations are pleasing to the eye—each is balanced. The first two, typical of symmetry, are more formal than the last two. Consider the symmetrical balance used in structures such as courthouses, churches, and synagogues. If you look at the Lincoln Memorial in Washington, D.C., past the reflecting pool to the Washington Monument, you see pure symmetry, simplistic in design but majestic, powerful, and awesome.

Symmetry has its attributes, but it appears archaic, old-fashioned, ponderous, repetitious. That accounts for the predominance of various forms of asymmetry in much of today's design.

2. Proportion

This is a comparative relationship between visual masses. It has to do with size, color, and shape, and is closely tied to balance. Picture a tiger. Now imagine you've exchanged its head for that of a pussycat. The head would be completely out of proportion to the rest of the tiger's body.

Consider this use of shapes:

```
    (( ))))))              (( ))))))
    (((((((((              (((((((((
    )))))                 )))))



                                          ]]]
              ]                          ]]]]]
                [              [[[       [[[[[
```

The top three lines of parentheses in the left illustration appear to outweigh, therefore overcome, the bottom brackets. In the right hand picture, additional bottom brackets were added to get standard proportion. We end up with an asymmetrically balanced, proportionally acceptable, traditional design. That's not to say that the layout of the left-hand picture is incorrect or unusable. For instance, picture each shape as a person. Then visualize the two bottom figures separated from the crowd. With a little imagination they could represent starving children, the homeless, or discrimination. Again, use design elements to express your campaign case.

Let's look at how proportion works with words:

The Suburban Council Annual Campaign Gala
Y'all Come

The relationship between the size of the first and second lines is an obvious example of totally unsuitable proportion. It doesn't appear as if the council cared whether the reader came or not. Study how designers use proportion to promote their messages in your favorite publications.

3. Line

As in all elements of composition, different lines provoke definite reactions in people:

- Vertical lines are sturdy and classic, as well as static.
- Horizontal lines remind us of rest and repose—we sleep that way.
- Diagonal lines are dynamic. They give the illusion of moving from one place to another. Lightning is represented as a series of diagonal lines.
- Curved lines are quiet, romantic, and not particularly active.

Study full-page, sophisticated advertisements that appeal to you; analyze balance, proportion, and line. Discover how the use of these elements brings home the point of the message offered. Think of how you could use these components to best illustrate your case statement.

4. Rhythm

If you visualize proportion being tied to balance, you will see rhythm related to line. It is a recurring regular or irregular pattern used with lines or shapes to get a sense of movement or dimension. Here are some common rhythms that appear both active and inactive.

Repetition:

----- ///// TTTTTT C C C C

This sequence appears solid and strong, like an army marching. And, like soldiers, there is total uniformity.

Echo: skim a rock across the water and you'll get the sense of an echo, symbolic of arriving, departing, growing, and shrinking.

The Need for Funds is Now!
The Need for Funds is Now!
The Need for Funds is Now!

Alternation can show indecisiveness, perhaps the search for an alternative.

$$> < > < \text{ or } () () ()$$

Take time to identify and understand how and why rhythm is used in the ads and other publications you've been studying.

5. Color

Color represents various moods and qualities. Earth colors are sunny and warm. Cool colors, the many shades of blues and greens, are soothing and relaxing.

Unless you're fundraising for an outfit like a circus, don't overuse color. Campaign materials, like business brochures, usually need to be low-key.

The Basics of Typography

Typefaces—the way a set of printed characters look—are available in many styles, sizes, shapes, lengths, and widths, and are known by numerous names. Each uses balance, proportion, line, and rhythm to create a visual effect. Some are strong, others flamboyant, archaic, or ultra-modern. The trick is to pick the face that most reflects your organization and printed piece. Examples of typefaces are readily available from your printer or graphic art supply store. Here are several that are commonly used:

Century: A sample of Century ... AaBbCcDdEeFfGgHhIiJjKkLlMmNnOoPpQqRr
Times: A sample of Times ... AaBbCcDdEeFfGgHhIiJjKkLlMmNnOoPpQqRrSsTtUu
Caslon: A sample of Caslon ... AaBbCcDdEeFfGgHhIiJjKkLlMmNnOoPp

Notice that the above faces have been created with serifs, small curved designs attached to the top and bottom of each letter. Now compare these with another group of typefaces that don't have these distinctive designs, called sans serif:

Avant-Garde: A sample of Avant-Garde ... AaBbCcDdEeFfGgHhIiJjKkLlMm
Futura: A sample of Futura ... AaBbCcDdEeFfGgHhIiJjKkLlMmNnOoPpQqRrSsTtUu
Helvetica: A sample of Helvetica ... AaBbCcDdEeFfGgHhIiJjKkLlMmNnOoPpQ

Generally, serif characters are easier to read because the serifs lead the eye to the next letter. Sans serif letters are most often used for larger letters than those required for text—headlines, signs, or banners.

Most typefaces allow you to emphasize words, phrases, sentences, and the like by giving a choice of italic and boldface letters along with standard counterparts, like this:

It is *your support* that has helped make this campaign a success.
Early Campaign Results Show A Reachable Goal.

Look at a newspaper. Note that the typeface of the paper's news sections is always the same. The publication has chosen a type style that it feels is effective for its image and readability. You see that some letters are larger than others—headlines and somewhat smaller subheads. Type is measured in "points." The more points, the taller the letters and words appear. Seventy-two points is about one inch. Text is usually from 9 to 12 points. Anything smaller is difficult to read; anything larger is distracting. Here are some illustrations:

The text in this book is set in 10 point type.

This is 12 point type.

The following is a 36 point headline:

Campaign Goal Reached.

This is a 22 point sub-head:

Ground-Breaking to Take Place May 1.

Type can be compressed or expanded horizontally, making the letters closer together or farther apart in relation to each other, like this:

Worker enlistments are coming along better than expected.
Worker enlistments are coming along better than expected.

Typesetters or computer operators can also compress or expand words to create an even margin in the right-hand column as well as the left, as this book does. The technique is called justification. Having each margin justified lends formality to a publication because of its symmetrical balance.

The amount of space between lines can also be controlled. On typewriters or word processors, it's called single or double spacing. Typesetters and operators of desktop publishing programs, who have tighter control over the space between lines of text, call the same effect "leading" (led'-ing), which is also measured in points. This book is set in 12 point leading. Here are 2 more examples.

This is an example of 9 point leading:

You can produce better looking publications by learning the fundamentals of typography because it is an important tool of the graphic designer. As well, proper communication can be had with your printing company representative because you will both speak the same language.

This is an example of 15 point leading:

You can produce better looking publications by learning the fundamentals of

typography because it is an important tool of the graphic designer. As well, proper communication can be had with your printing company representative because you will both speak the same language.

See how the style of type, its size, and the use of space affects the readability and tone of different publications. Figure out why that face represents the publication.

Again, don't choose a typeface for your campaign materials because it looks pretty. Or because another organization you admire uses that face. Select one that is in harmony with your project and the piece you are designing.

Layout Considerations

Plan each document by asking yourself what the publication is going to say visually. For example, an annual report is an account of what has already happened. A casebook is mainly a document that projects what an organization hopes will happen if necessary funds are raised. What are the most powerful ways in which to make each document effective? What will be your general format? How will composition and typography point out the major theme of the piece?

Where you place items on a page depends on the importance of each. When first picking up a publication, people mostly focus on the top third of a page. If there is a large headline or picture in that area, it will be looked at first. Since English is read from left to right, we usually glance at a page from upper left to lower right. Newspapers often start the most important story on the far-right column of the first page, or across the top third. Use these principles when selecting the placement and flow of text and the positioning of graphics and photographs.

Don't overextend columns horizontally. Lines of text running over four and a half inches are difficult for the eye to follow.

Except for special-effects documents, stay away from many typefaces and fonts, and don't use an assortment of sizes in the same piece. Use the same face for all headlines and don't use that face for anything else.

Continue to study the publications you admire, and discover how the placement and sizing of elements make them appealing.

Here are some additional printing and design terms you should know:

1. Art or artwork. Anything drawn (including electronically) or photographed. The term has nothing to do with artistry. If a five-year-old draws a stick figure for a publication, it's called artwork.

2. Line drawing or line art. Anything drawn in black on white without any shades of gray or color.

3. Halftone. A drawing, illustration, or photograph in black, white, and shades of gray. For reproduction, printers place a screen over the art, then photograph it. The result is a series of dots that, when printed, reproduce the original values of the photo or drawing. The more dots, the better the reproduction. Look at a newspaper photograph with a magnifying glass and you'll see the dots clearly.

4. Reversal. Text or line art printed in white on a black background. Display advertisers often use this technique to make their ads stand out among the more common black-on-white ads of competitors. Conservatively used, reversals can point up an important headline or piece of art.

5. Color separations. The process of overlaying art with pieces of colored transparent material which, when placed one on top of the other, show the full range of colors that the artwork contains.

6. Dummy. A layout of a page or pages, roughly showing the placement of text and artwork. It can include instructions for typeface, size, ink colors, and so forth. No matter how primitive, always sketch several layouts before committing yourself to a final document.

7. Pasteup. The technique of attaching typeset text and photostats of line art to a layout sheet scaled to each page of a publication. (Have line drawings photostated instead of taking a chance on someone accidentally ruining the originals.)

8. Camera-ready layout or mechanical. Pasted-up typeset or computer-printed text and line art on a rigid white cardboard or similar surface with blank space left for halftones and color artwork. (Always show the size of the art, or anything else you don't want printed, in nonreproducible blue pencil, available at office supply stores.)

9. Proof sheet. A photocopy of typeset text to be examined for mistakes before it goes to press. It's the customer's responsibility to assure that errors are corrected on proof sheets, despite who made them. If you find a mistake in text or layout after the piece is printed and want it corrected, charges will be made for reruns.

17

The Frugal Way
to Smashing Layouts

Slashing Your
Publications Budget

Saving money means being self-sufficient. The cost to print a publication, even in large quantities, is relatively inexpensive. Typesetting, layouts, and associated services provided by print shops are not. Computer desktop publishing (DTP) and graphics programs are the greatest boon so far invented for nonprofessional designers. These advancements allow talented amateurs familiar with composition and typography (and determined to learn computer operation) the ability to create striking, camera-ready layouts. Such desktop publishing programs as Ventura Publisher, Pagemaker, and Express Publisher allow you to choose from an enormous number of design and typographical options. Generally, the more expensive the program is, the more advanced selections are, and the more difficult the software is to learn. Prices seem to change every week, but count on the first two of the above programs being about three times as expensive as the third. Pick the program that most fits your future, not your immediate, needs. You may not require color separations or the ability to interface a DTP document with a typesetting machine for the moment, but perhaps later you might.

Examine several programs, get in-depth demonstrations, and then make comparisons. Inexpensive doesn't necessarily mean severely limited. A program like Express Publisher has the capability of producing sophisticated letterheads, brochures, newsletters, invitations, and can be presently bought for under $100. Find out what software other organizations (nonprofit or commercial) are using, what successes they had, and what problems their users encountered.

Powerful word processing programs also have desktop publishing features, but are limited and clumsy to control. Everything you can do to keep the frustration level down and the output up will be rewarded. Assume you have been given text and artwork and asked to produce a campaign brochure. Here are some options:

- Take the copy and artwork to a graphic designer who will create the piece and return a completed, pasted-up layout ready for the printer. This is the most expensive choice.
- Bring text and artwork to a print shop and let its personnel design, paste up, and print the brochure.
- Design a dummy layout in-house. Then, using computer software, create a camera-ready piece and deliver it to your print shop. This is by far the least expensive option.

Let's say that after receiving copy, figures for a graph, a line drawing, and black-and-white photographs, you create a layout on paper showing how you want the finished brochure to appear. If a printing company is engaged at that point, you will pay for typesetting and a person to create the graph and paste up the typeset copy, your line art, and all else necessary for a camera-ready layout. And what if you are not entirely visually satisfied with the completed layout? This can lead to additional charges and time delays.

Now imagine you're working the same assignment with a computer and DTP software. First, using the dummy, you indicate the size and number of pages and columns you will use for the brochure. Then the text, typed on a word processor, and the graph, created within a graphics program, are imported (transferred) into the desktop publishing software. The font (typeface), its size, and other formatting options are chosen for the text. The same is done for headlines and subheads. With the aid of a scanner, you trace the line drawing and it appears on your screen where you size it to fit the layout. As the pieces come together, using a simple command, you refer to an electronic layout composed on your monitor of each full brochure page as it will appear in the finished product. You leave the correct amount of blank space for halftones. (You'll see how to calculate that space shortly.) In some cases you make the text flow around a photo for easy readability. Using various commands, you can view the arrangement of multipages or zoom in on specific parts of a page for a close-up to check the exact placement of art. If a headline doesn't quite fit, it's easily adjusted. If you have more text than you bargained for, you could specify a slightly smaller typeface, change the column widths, or reduce the leading.

It's easy to experiment. Using various effects, you might want to place a border around a portion of copy, show a reversal for a subhead, bend a headline in an arc, or try your hand at other graphic arrangements the program offers. When the placement of elements is finally suitable, each camera-ready page is reproduced on a high-quality, laser printer. No money is spent for design, typesetting, pasteup, or revisions. You will pay for halftones and printing, the most reasonable of the services a print shop furnishes.

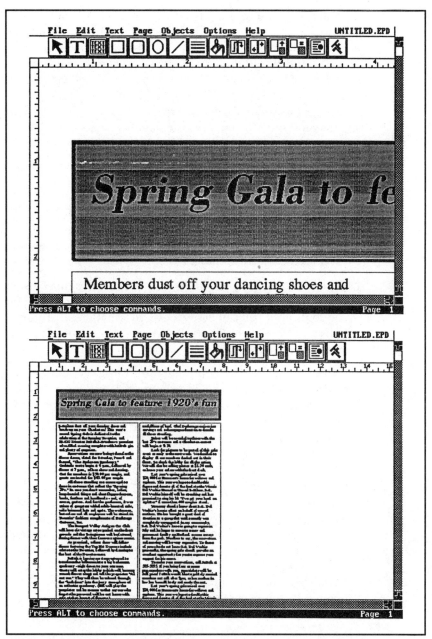

The workscreen from Express Publisher showing two views of a two-column layout. (*Courtesy of Power Up Software Corporation.*)

I don't want you to think commanding DTP software is simple. Quite the opposite. It takes time and a tremendous amount of patience to learn how to take full advantage of these programs. To compound the problem, many manuals are not at all easy to follow. Often, these texts are written by people who may understand the esoterics of programming, but don't approach their subjects as do lay people. Even with all of this, it's well worth the effort it takes to get involved. Let me point out several things that will make getting acquainted with DTP easier and will aid you in getting the most out of computer-originated layouts.

1. Have a solid understanding of layout and typography *before* you learn desktop publishing.

2. Learn to command word processing software for entering text before using a desktop publishing program.

3. Sketch a basic design first. Creating layouts from scratch using a computer can be excessively time-consuming.

4. Begin learning the program by giving yourself simple assignments using a basic layout and a few paragraphs of text. Experiment with the appropriate commands and tools until you can easily move information all around a page. Try different fonts and sizes. If you don't like what you've done, it's easy to erase the material and start again.

5. Choose the speediest computer possible. DTP software operates much more slowly than word processing programs. For instance, each time you enter text, artwork, or other commands the computer screen often completely redraws itself. So, on a slower machine like an XT, if you correct a letter in a word, choose a printer, change from a text cursor to one that makes lines, and so on, you often must wait half a minute or more before being able to issue the next command. Quicker processors like a 386 or 486 handle the same tasks in almost the blink of an eye. Similarly, slower processing means slower document printing: one page of text and several graphics can take 30 to 45 minutes to print. Since typos are common and it's rare to line everything up perfectly on a screen the first time around, documents usually have to be printed several times before everything is satisfactory. So, if you are truly a laid-back, ultrapatient sort with a small workload, and don't have to work under constant deadlines, the older Apple, IBM, or compatibles will fill the bill. But if you're like most of us, a computer with the fastest processer is a must for keeping sanity intact and blood pressure normal.

6. Large type, say 36 points or more, may print out with ragged edges. Look at it through a magnifying glass. You might be better off having it typeset.

7. Images from scanners of 400 dots per inch do not give first-class results. For sophisticated pieces use them for indicating size and placement on a mechanical

(make sure to print "For position only" on each one) and let the printing company handle the reproduction from an original or photostat.

8. Don't use every graphic device your software offers in a single publication. A common fault of beginners is to use too many visual effects because a program has amazing versatility.

From complex brochures to simple newsletters, investing in a computer and publications software will allow your organization amazing in-house potential and the ultimate in flexibility and speed, while keeping the publication budget to a minimum. Following are basic features that you'll want in DTP programs:

- Templates for letters, newsletters, and book pages, as well as the ability to design custom-sized pages.

- The ability to import text and pictures from most word processing, graphics, and drawing programs.

- The ability to size and crop imported pictures and drawings.

- Access to fonts of many sizes appropriate to the computer printer used.

- The capability to draw lines, rectangles, squares, ellipses, and circles.

- The ability to couple and uncouple columns of text. Let's say you have designed a three-column newsletter. You want a story to begin on column one of the first page and conclude on column three of the following page. You can command the program to uncouple columns two and three of the first page and couple column three of the second page to accept the remainder of the story.

- The capability to electronically cut and paste, which means to move text from one place to another.

- The choice of using footers and headers.

- A screen which shows the layout of several full pages. Just as in word processing, one normally works with a portion of a page at a time.

- Viewing options that allow you to zoom in or out on sections of a page.

- The ability to flow text around a photo or graphic so the continuity of a story is not interrupted.

- Formatting features like justification, hyphenation, leading, and line and paragraph spacing.

- Special effects such as shadowing or curved headlines, or text that gets larger or smaller character by character or that can be rotated to various angles.

- The ability to print pages in portrait (vertical) or landscape (horizontal) formats.

- The capability to print a document to disk as well as a printer. If you don't own a laser printer, take the final version on a floppy disk to someone who does.

A Sample Newsletter Template

I purposely chose an inexpensive (under $100) piece of software to design the newsletter title page template shown on p. 273. Included with the program are many line drawings (clip art) ready to be imported into a layout. Two were chosen. Here's how each appeared:

For the layout, each picture was scaled down, then moved into place using a mouse. As well, the chain on top the anchor was removed electronically since it was extraneous, and the sun's mouth was filled in so the smile would be more pronounced in the smaller picture.

The newsletter, a self-mailer, is designed to fit an 8½″ × 11″ page with one-half inch margins. Following are the specifications I gave the software:

- Sans serif headlines and subheads.
- "Save the Reefs Foundation," 12-point, bold, italic, small caps.
- "Research Diver's Notebook," 44-point, bold, small caps. Additionally, the normal spacing between the letters of each word was reduced to give the line added visual strength.
- "Quarterly Report on Preserving the Ocean's Reefs," and "Summer 1992," 10-point, bold, italic.
- The top and bottom line patterns were selected from among the many available.
- Headline text boxes were drawn using a rectangle tool.

To compare computer processing speeds, the template printed by an IBM-compatible XT at 180 dots per inch (DPI) took 35 minutes, 28 seconds, as compared to 7 minutes, 5 seconds by an IBM-compatible 386 using the same DPI and printer.

Save the Reefs Foundation

⚓ Research Diver's Notebook ☼

Quarterly Report on Preserving the Ocean's Reefs   *Summer 1992*

(1st Story Headline)

(Feature Story Headline)

(1st Story Text)

(Feature Story Text)

If You Don't Have a Desktop
Publishing System, Then What?

Upon turning in copy for a short brochure recently, the head of the organization was asked who was going to produce his piece. "I found a woman in the yellow pages who specializes in desktop publishing," he said. "I'm going to give her a try."

The organization's 8-page pamphlet was designed to fit a standard business envelope. The computer-generated, camera-ready layout cost $60. A printer quoted $115 for typesetting and pasting up the same material. Another plus: When the layout was completed, a printout was shown to the organization head. He made several changes that enhanced the text and layout. These revisions were entered on the spot and within a few minutes of his arrival, the organization leader was on the way to the print shop with a camera-ready brochure.

Often, printing firms use computer-generated text and layouts. Check the cost. Because of overhead, they usually get paid far more for their services than do free-lancers.

Getting Artwork to Fit Your Design

Publications usually require drawings or photographs placed between sections of text. Artwork rarely measures the same as the space in which it needs to fit. So you must calculate how much art must be enlarged or, more commonly, reduced to adapt to your design.

Enlargements and reductions are spoken of in percentages, with 100 percent being a reproduction equal to the original size of a piece of artwork. Therefore, a 3″ × 5″ drawing to be placed in a 3″ × 5″ space would have a notation on it of "100%." Anything less is a reduction, anything more an enlargement.

You might be thinking, "My job is to show where the artwork belongs. Let the printer figure out the percentage of reduction or enlargement." That could be done, but how are you going to know that you've left the correct amount of space for the artwork in your layout? For instance, if you are squeezing a photograph or drawing into a few columns of text, as in a campaign newsletter, the space you leave must be correct; otherwise, text or white space will have to be eliminated.

There are two simple tools to help you find out the new size required: an enlargement-reduction wheel found in graphic arts supply stores or a calculator. The enlargement-reduction wheel has two scales numbered in inches. The inner wheel shows the original size of a piece of art; the outer wheel the desired new size. Lining up the numbers shows the size of reduction or enlargement in inches. The percentage appears in a window cut out of the inner wheel. Take my word: the wheel is even simpler to use than to describe.

Here's an example: Assume you have an 8″ × 10″ photo that needs to fit a 2″ wide column. You must find out the reduction needed to fit the 8″ width of the picture into 2″. That would take care of fitting the picture horizontally. Then you'd want to know what the height of the reduced photo would be to make sure you leave enough vertical room on the layout. Line up 8″ on the inner wheel, 2″ on the (desired new size) outer wheel. Then find 10″ on the inner wheel. By reading the number on the outer wheel (2½″) you have found the vertical size of the reduced photo. The percentage of the original size shows in the window as 25 percent. As you can see from the illustration, the 8″ × 10″ photo reduced for a 2″ column measures 2″ × 2½″, a 25 percent reduction.

Look at the same example using a calculator.

Step A: Divide the desired size by the original size and press the percentage button. The answer is the percentage of enlargement or reduction. Example: Enter 2, press the division sign, enter 8, press % = 25, which becomes a 25 percent reduction.

Step B: Multiply the answer in Step A by the second original size and press the percentage button to find the new vertical size. Example: Enter 25, press ×, press 10, press % = 2.5 or 2½ inches.

By accurately measuring the horizontal size, the vertical size can easily be found. If you're concerned about fitting a vertical space, reverse the process and work to solve the vertical size first.

Once you've found the new size of a piece of artwork, write down either that figure or the enlargement or reduction percentage on a piece of paper. Place a strip of tape across the top of the paper and attach it to the bottom of the art on the reverse side so the figure can be seen by print shop personnel.

Editing Artwork

What happens when a vertical length is too long to fit a layout? Or there is more background than subject in a photograph? You alter the composition of the artwork by "cropping." Though cropping sounds like a term better used on a farm, it means recomposing artwork to fit space requirements or optimize composition.

Show crop lines on photographs with a red crayon sold at stationery stores—pens and pencils dig into the photo's emulsion. When pictures are returned from the printer, these indicators are easily erased by rubbing them off with a tissue, keeping the photo intact.

18

Logos, Papers, and a Few Other Hints

Logos are symbols that graphically represent a country, a business, product, or organization. The logo of the United States is the American eagle. General Motors is recognizable by its treatment of the letters, GM. The graphic trademark of the Red Cross—a red cross. Logos immediately identify the groups that created them. So should yours. It will appear on everything you send out. Logos are to graphic design what poetry is to prose. These symbols must express the essence of your organization in the most succinct way possible. There is no room for any visual waste. Make them first-class. You might want to get help from a graphic designer.

What You Need to Know About Paper

In the printing business, paper is called "stock." How well text and artwork reproduce on stock depends on the paper's makeup, thickness, and texture. Obviously, the better the paper, the more expensive. The least costly is newsprint. That's why words and photographs in newspapers often appear fuzzy, and the ink comes off on your hands. Inexpensive papers tend to allow print from one side of a page show up on the other side.

Offset paper is a step up from newsprint. Many organizations order large quantities of offset stationery for mass mailings and use letterheads and envelopes printed on a better grade of stock to communicate with board members, large gift prospects, corporations, foundations, and suppliers.

There are several grades of rag bond paper used mainly for formal stationery. The finer the paper, the more bits of rag it contains. Compare various grades of rag bond with offset paper. You'll see and feel a discernible difference.

Stock is referred to by weight, based on 1000 sheets of a particular size of paper. A thousand sheets of 8½" × 11" paper weighing 60 pounds is called 60-pound stock. The heavier the paper, the more elegant it will feel and the better it will reproduce text and artwork.

For publications, there are two types of stock to be concerned about, one used for pages of text and a heavier one used for covers. Text stock less than 25 pounds is flimsy and the print quality will not be sharp and crisp. A 70-pound cover stock does nicely for most publications. If you want finer reproduction, look at a coated stock. The coating is made up of clay and adhesive and gives the paper body. The more coating the stock has, the sharper the text and pictures will be reproduced. Cover stock used for finer reproduction requires a coated, opaque sheet of paper not under 100 pounds.

Suit the selection of paper to your publication. You wouldn't print a major gift function invitation on newsprint or an organization newspaper on rag bond. Get a quick and worthwhile education in various grades of paper by visiting a print shop and examining samples.

Strike a balance between appearance and cost. Consider the reaction of your members or constituents. You don't want them to say, "How come we don't have renovations, but we can afford that slick looking brochure?" If you have a meager budget, you might want to say what you have to say in few words and use a medium or high-quality paper.

Use Plenty of White Space

Blank space is a powerful design tool. Except for an organization newspaper, don't cram every page full of text and artwork. Use white space to separate text, feature photos, and graphics. Imagine a moving statement of just several words in a striking typeface on an otherwise blank page. Often, nothing more needs to be added. Advertisements use this technique all the time.

Proofing

Everyone makes mistakes. Even using a computer spell-check program doesn't guarantee a lack of errors. For instance, software cannot discern that you meant "fundraising" when you wrote "fun-raising," or "no" when you meant "know." Proofread slowly and carefully. Some proofreaders look for mistakes by reading from the bottom of page upward so context doesn't get in the way of looking at each word. When you get the least bit tired, take a break.

You may or may not choose to use standard proofreaders' correction symbols, but however you show changes, do them neatly so revisions are unmistakable.

Coordinate Your Graphic Look

I used to ride a commuter train with a successful advertising creative director. The trouble was that outside his agency no one thought he was successful because of the way in which he dressed. A typical outfit consisted of a medium-green jacket, a purple shirt, red tie, brown pants, white socks, and dark green loafers. It's the same with graphics. The visual image of an organization is directly related to a constituent's perception of its ability to accept a challenge and reach a goal. To show unification, use one graphic theme, a single dominant color scheme, and the same typeface for all publications.

19

The Still Camera in Action

A good photograph should set a mood or tell a story having to do with your case. If not, it doesn't belong in a campaign publication. Look at the following picture of the Western Wall in Jerusalem.

The Western Wall, site of the biblical first temple, is highly symbolic and compelling to the Jewish people. My aim was to make the wall stand out from its surroundings and give it a sense of antiquity. To do so, I employed several darkroom techniques to heighten contrast by darkening the sky and foreground. The photo was used for a brochure that asked for support for Israel's humanitarian projects.

In the reproduction on the left, I followed John the accordionist around town for a long while to get the photograph that expressed the plight of many older home-less men. In contrast, David, the boy on the right, was used in a publication to stim-ulate funding of children's programs and services for a social service agency.

I like the picture of the Western Wall. It's been requested for publication many times. But unless the subject matter is as meaningful to your audience as the wall picture, you will get more support using pictures of your beneficiaries than land-scapes. Here are some clues about obtaining candid pictures to help support the case statement:

1. Before taking photos, know what you want them to express. If you hang around waiting for inspiration, the drive may be over before a revelation arrives.

2. Capture the inherent drama, mood, and emotions of your subjects.

3. Photograph people, not backgrounds. Compose pictures so the subject takes up most of your viewfinder. Crop out nonessential elements and perhaps throw the background out of focus by using a telephoto lens or a large aperture. And don't be afraid to shoot extreme closeups to show character and expression.

4. Be certain that nothing in the background interferes with the composition. For instance, a tree limb that appears to be stuck in the ear of a subject can ruin an otherwise superb picture. Before pushing the shutter release button learn to carefully study everything appearing in the viewfinder—from edge to edge.

5. Let subjects become familiar with you and your equipment. When a camera is first pointed at people, they usually become self-conscious. After a time they'll forget you're around. That's when the best shots can be had.

6. Capture subjects doing something. Don't ask people to pose; they look artificial. That's why pictures of people shaking hands at a banquet and smiling into the lens—pros call them "grin and grip shots"—are generally dull. To get exciting photographs, have your subjects in action or concentrating on something other than you taking their picture.

6. Use lighting to your advantage. Flat photos without contrast are usually undramatic. Study the effect of early morning or late afternoon light on people.

7. Understand lenses. You don't need a bagful of them to be a great photographer. Henri Cartier-Bresson, one of history's foremost photojournalists, used a 35mm camera and one lens. For small and large groups you'll need 28mm and 35mm wide-angle lenses. An 85mm or 108mm and a 135mm telephoto will give all the telephoto coverage you need. Or more simply, use a pair of zoom lenses that will allow you to cover both wide-angle and telephoto ranges. Make sure to get quality lenses, no matter what style or size you prefer. Understand how wide-angle lenses distort a composition by expanding it, and how telephoto lenses compress the view. Telephoto lenses, especially larger millimeter versions, allow you to focus on a subject while throwing the remaining part of the composition out of focus—often a useful way to concentrate a viewer's attention. The earlier picture of David was photographed with a 200mm lens. He was just ahead of a group of children who appear as blurs.

8. Stick with a few films you know. Understand the film's characteristics, discover what each will do under various conditions. Don't be swept away by advertising. While you go mad experimenting to find subtleties claimed by film manufacturers, you'll be missing great pictures. Use a fast film for dully lit days and interiors, and a slower film for sunny weather.

9. Show the action when shooting movement. Suppose you are photographing a fundraising marathon and want to give the illusion of speed. One way is to position yourself so the walkers or runners pass you in profile. As they approach, pan the camera to follow the runners. As they pass, without stopping the pan, press the shutter button. If you did that while shooting at a slow speed, say $\frac{1}{60}$, $\frac{1}{4}$, or $\frac{1}{8}$ of a second, the result would show the runners in focus and the background out of focus. The viewer gets a sense of speed and excitement, making the marathon come alive. Practice this technique before covering an event.

10. Use angles as means of expression. For instance, shooting a person or group of people from a low angle makes them appear powerful. Photographing from above does the opposite.

11. Study news and other forms of editorial photography. See which compositions and techniques appeal to you the most and why.

12. Photograph, photograph, photograph. Don't scrimp on film. Unless you're prepared to take many pictures of the same subject, you may never get the shot that creates a desired mood. Remember, with each click of the shutter, one instant of time is captured. In that slim moment, you want subjects to be totally revealing. When only several shots are taken, chances are that the picture you thought you saw wasn't recorded—the subject's eyes were closed, the body distorted, or a similar unnatural image was captured instead. It is nothing for pros to shoot many rolls of the same subject, attempting to get a couple of publishable photos.

Remember, it's not the number of pictures placed in a publication that helps move people to fund projects. It's what a particular shot says to them and how it affects their emotions. One superb photograph will do more to support your case and inspire your constituents than 10 so-so pictures or 100 snapshots.

20
Wrap-up

Before asking people for contributions, make certain you have met the six fund-raising requirements first mentioned on p. 8. Then eliminate the 10 prime reasons why campaigns fail by completing the precampaign activities relevant to your funding effort.

Thinking it was time to retain a consultant, one chief executive happily told me his organization had begun a capital campaign for new facilities. He and a few volunteers had already solicited and been verbally promised several gifts of $500,000, $200,000, and $100,000—12 in all.

"What's your goal?" I asked him.

"Twenty million," he answered.

"Are the gifts you mentioned from your best potential contributors?"

"Absolutely," he said.

"Has anyone done a feasibility study?"

"We're already committed," said the administrator. "We don't need a study."

"What's your time frame?"

"Well, we don't have one for the moment. As long as it takes," the administrator told me.

By not properly preparing for his campaign, the chief executive and his board had made some terrible mistakes:

1. Promises of future gifts mean little; signed pledge cards are commitments you can count on.

2. Had the organization leadership worked up a "Table of Gift Expectations" they would not have been so pleased with the 12 pledges from their most affluent prospects. It would have been obvious that a gift in the neighborhood of 10 percent or $2 million *and* several million dollar donations were needed up front. The lesser amounts promised only served to set a substandard giving pattern for the remaining group of major gift prospects.

3. Ignoring a feasibility study to carefully measure potential community support for a campaign of this magnitude is sheer lunacy.

283

4. An open-ended timetable gives no sense of urgency for volunteers or prospects to immediately support the project.

You can guess the rest of the story.

Don't become lethargic about identifying new prospects. While in San Francisco one year, I visited a restored liberty ship, a relic of the Second World War. It was owned by a nonprofit organization who employed a director of development. Deep in the engine room a man who had seen service on similar vessels showed me around the ancient but gleaming machinery. I was terribly impressed with the historical value of the project, the quality of the restoration, and the day-to-day upkeep taken care of by loving volunteers. Knowing that ticket sales to tour the ship couldn't have totally supported its maintenance, I asked the former merchant mariner how the fundraising program was going. "It's tough," he told me, "as the years go by people forget about these old ships that were so important during World War II." Upon leaving, I signed the ship's guest book and remarked how fascinating the visit had been in the comments section. My assumption was that those out-of-towners who did would be entered into a database for direct-mail programs. The liberty ship organization never contacted me. In not doing so, it lost a donor.

Remember who prospects are—people you *hope* will be motivated to contribute to your drives. Having identified a potential giver, don't count on the person to make an immediate contribution. The next step is to cultivate the prospect, raising his or her awareness, by fostering involvement with your organization. That takes time and patience. You know that a cultivation program has achieved its goal when prospects think of your organization almost on a day-to-day basis.

It's easy to spot an involved prospect. Let's say you attend a business luncheon. Towards the end of the meal, the person seated across from you mentions that he is looking forward to attending a campaign organization meeting that evening. There, he and other volunteers will look at plans for a new project that needs funding during the coming year. As he describes the undertaking, it is obvious that the man is very excited about the organization's future . . . he is a highly cultivated potential contributor.

Plan donor recognition programs early on. Recall that in the literal sense philanthropy and fundraising are not synonymous. Reward givers for their support. Allow them to name part of a facility, offer memberships in clubs and associations, furnish premiums, send them acknowledgment letters.

Don't let solicitor training take a back seat to other facets of a drive. Not everyone you enlist will be totally dedicated to your mission. The orientation session should not only teach and rehearse sales techniques, but also inspire volunteers to consider your campaign an immediate priority.

Continual worker follow-up is an absolute necessity. Most volunteers have so much to do that it's easy for them to relegate campaign assignments to the bottom of the pile. A drive that loses momentum because appointments aren't made and solicitations don't take place soon finds itself in big trouble. And if this slowdown takes place in the early stages, those enlisted to become active later on often become disenchanted—their interest in the funding effort quickly diminishes.

Having examined the various methods of solicitation, please remember that fundraising is a volunteer business. It's not a prospect's *obligation* to live up to a solicitor's expectation. The campaigner's job is to combine enthusiasm with the ways discussed in this book to persuade prospects to become totally committed to a project and make generous contributions because of that commitment. Too often, volunteers, men and women from all walks of life and all means, become outraged at fellow citizens whom they believe short-changed a campaign by refusing to say "yes" to their gift request. In moments, word gets around—from the chairman of the board to the campaign office secretary—about the terrible cheapskate who is sabotaging the drive. Usually it turns out that prospects who receive this abuse are not cheap or insensitive, they just don't have a passion for the project. If vindictiveness is the release that some solicitors get from the frustrations of raising money, I feel sorry for their organizations. That type behavior eats away at the very nature of what charitable funding efforts are all about. Instead, they should be using their total energy to strive for quality. If you can motivate those around you to achieve a degree of excellence in every bit of work they do for your organization, you will help fulfill the hopes and dreams of many others, and your personal satisfaction will be priceless.

Again, I wish you great success.

Recommended Reading

AAFRC Trust for Philanthropy, Inc. *Giving USA*. 25 West 43d Street, New York, NY 10036. A yearly publication.

Arthur Anderson & Company. *Charitable Giving: Tax Guide for Individual Doners*. 11th ed. 1991. Information on such subjects as bequests, annuities, and trust funds.

Arthur Anderson & Company. *Tax Economics of Charitable Giving*. 11th ed. 1991. Information on such subjects as bequests, annuities, and trust funds.

Chronicle of Philanthropy. P.O. 1989, Marion, OH 43306-4089. Published biweekly.

The Davis Information Group, Inc. *The NonProfit Times*. 190 Tamarack Circle, Skillman, NJ 08558. A monthly tabloid.

Dove, Kent E. *Conducting a Successful Capital Campaign: A Comprehensive Guide for Non-Profit Organizations*. Jossey-Bass, 1988.

Fisher, James L., and Gary H. Quehl, eds. *The President and Fund Raising*. MacMillan, 1989.

Hauman, David J. *The Capital Campaign Handbook*. Taft Group, 1987.

Hoke Communications, Inc. *Fund Raising Management*. 224 Seventh Street, Garden City, Long Island, NY 11530-5771. A monthly magazine.

Huntsinger, Jerry. *Fund Raising Letters*. P.O. Box 15274, Richmond, VA 23227: Emerson Publishers.

Seymour, Harold J. *Designs for Fund-Raising: Principles, Patterns, Techniques*. McGraw-Hill: The Fund-Raising Institute, 1988.

Warner, Irving R. *The Art of Fund Raising*. Bantam, 1984.

Index